The Gardens of English Heritage

The Gardens of English Heritage

Gillian Mawrey and Linden Groves

F

FRANCES LINCOLN LIMITED
PUBLISHERS

Frances Lincoln Limited
4 Torriano Mews
Torriano Avenue
London NW5 2RZ
www.franceslincoln.com

PAGE 1 A glimpse of the Winter Garden at
Belsay, Northumberland.
PAGE 2 A snowy view of the orangery at Wrest
Park, Bedfordshire, seen from the terrace.
PAGE 3 Andromeda, now restored and
resplendent, at Witley Court, Worcestershire.
THIS PAGE Spring comes to two English
Heritage gardens with bulbs against the old
walls of the moat at Eltham Palace, London
(right), and cherry blossom at Charles Darwin's
home, Down House, Kent (opposite).

Contents

Introduction

WE ARE ACCUSTOMED in England to living against a glorious backdrop of buildings, monuments, landscapes and, of course, gardens, a heritage accumulated over many hundreds of years. As Man has always had a tendency to crave the new and the convenient, that these treasures have survived is quite remarkable. This is not, however, a happy accident, but rather due to national pride, and the hard work of owners and organizations dedicated to looking after England's historic environment.

English Heritage – officially The Historic Buildings and Monuments Commission for England – came into being through Act of Parliament in 1983, having evolved over several decades from being first a part of the Ministry of Works, then of the Ministry of Public Buildings and Works, and finally of the Department of the Environment. In the following year, 1984, it began to manage the hundreds of state-owned properties that had been in the care of these bodies.

Although a few places, such as Osborne House, were important tourist attractions which contained valuable collections and were surrounded by significant gardens, far more representative of English Heritage's inheritance were the Scheduled Monuments: archaeological sites from the distant past (of which Stonehenge is the best known and arguably the most problematic) and the assorted medieval ruins of both religious buildings which had been pillaged, for their stone as well as their contents, after Henry VIII dissolved the monasteries from 1536 to 1541, and of the castles which were 'slighted' or demolished during the Civil War just over a century later. These two events were catastrophic for many of England's historic buildings, but they are not the reason why so few gardens survive from before 1700. It was the eighteenth-century fashion for informal picturesque landscapes which swept away almost all our earlier formal layouts, with the landscape designer Lancelot 'Capability' Brown being the best known but certainly not the only villain.

Even when English Heritage was set up in the 1980s, historic gardens were not widely recognized as being the important cultural assets that they are, and the fledgling English Heritage had no garden specialists on its staff – a far cry from today, when it employs landscape architects, landscape managers and specialist gardeners, in order to preserve the nation's historic designed landscapes effectively.

English Heritage also instituted the *Register of Parks and Gardens of Special Historic Interest in England*. This record of the history and current state of the most important designed green spaces in the country was started in the 1980s and, initially, was the work of a single person, Dr Christopher Thacker, who carried out almost all the research and visits unaided. Today, the list contains just over 1,600 sites – not just parks and gardens but other ornamental or recreational landscapes, such as cemeteries, hospital grounds and town squares – all deemed to be of national or even international significance. They are ranked Grade II, Grade II* or Grade I – with fewer than 10 per cent being worthy of the latter highest status.

Most of us would recognize English Heritage's insignia, a red portcullis design, but what does English Heritage do? If we are looking for an easy description, then it is probably best to say that English Heritage busies itself with three kinds of activity: it encourages the research and understanding of our historic environment; it is actively involved in conservation to enable this to survive the demands of the modern world; and it owns and manages historic properties for the benefit of the nation. The parks and gardens around these houses, castles and monasteries are the subject of this book.

As part of its research-oriented role, English Heritage is responsible for the National Monuments Record, an archive, open to all, of over 10 million photographs, plans, architectural and archaeological reports and other items, many of them related to historic parks or gardens. In 1998, for instance, the gardener and garden writer Christopher Lloyd sold to the NMR a collection of the photographs and files belonging to his father, Nathaniel Lloyd, who had commissioned Edwin Lutyens to work on the family house and the now well-known garden at Great Dixter in Sussex.

Another facet of English Heritage's remit is to educate the public about the past, often through collaboration with schools and community groups. Middlegate Gardens in Great Yarmouth are just one illustration of such a project. Here English Heritage worked with the Seachange Trust, an arts development organization, to involve young offenders and local residents in creating a new garden area in the previously derelict public open space between two English Heritage-owned merchants' homes dating from the seventeenth century, the Row Houses.

Understanding our cultural legacy is only the first step towards successful conservation, and English Heritage is also actively engaged in protecting our heritage. Its influential voice is one of the chief tools that can be used to bring the dangers facing that heritage to the attention of the public and politicians. (It is ironic that while gardens such as Wrest Park were once designed as coded statements signifying loyalty to king or party, the hierarchy of the planning system now means that their survival is essentially at the mercy of whichever government is in power.) Useful warning bells are rung through Heritage at Risk, an annual record of all nationally important designated heritage assets, including many buildings, monuments, shipwrecks, battlefields, conservation areas and, of course, parks and gardens, that are suffering severe decay. This can be the direct fault of neglectful owners or sometimes the result of delays caused by England's complex planning procedures.

Although garden and landscape structures, such as follies, lodges and bridges, have always been included on the At Risk list, in 2009 registered parks and gardens were added in their own right – ninety-six of them. A few examples with a connection to places in this book include the unique William Barron layout at Elvaston Castle in Derbyshire, Boreham House in Essex, which has work by landscape designer Richard Woods as well as an earlier formal canal, Brocklesby Park in Lincolnshire, and several parks designed by 'Capability' Brown and Humphry Repton.

English Heritage also plays a statutory role at the heart of the planning system because local authorities are legally obliged to seek the opinion of both English Heritage and the specialist amenity group the Garden History Society on applications that may affect sites that are registered Grade I or Grade II*. So being on the register does offer some protection to a park or garden threatened with neglect or development, but this has nothing like the legal force of the safeguards that protect buildings of equivalent value. And appropriately outside English Heritage's sphere of control altogether is the planting within a historic park or garden. Except where trees are subject to a Tree Preservation Order, changing the contents of avenues, borders or parterres does not require permission. Indeed, the owners of a precious Victorian formal parterre or a Gertrude Jekyll herbaceous

RIGHT Middlegate Gardens, created for public use outside English Heritage's Row Houses in Great Yarmouth.

border are at liberty to dig it all up and replace it with a plain grass lawn, if they choose.

English Heritage not only gives an opinion when the planning system demands it. Its experts are also on hand – as are publications, workshops and the English Heritage website – to offer owners and managers detailed and pragmatic advice, ranging from how graffiti can be removed from statues in public parks to how disabled access to historic properties can be facilitated.

This considered approach can be seen in its own garden management. For instance, English Heritage gardeners have not adopted organic gardening wholesale but might use hoeing and mulching to get rid of weeds in some places, while turning to chemicals elsewhere if it seems a more appropriate solution. In many cases, English Heritage is itself 'test-driving' new conservation techniques. It has recently been working with the Royal Horticultural Society and the

Forestry Commission to track diseases like the bleeding canker that afflicts horse chestnut trees, causing their bark to ooze a sticky fluid. This project has included awareness-raising but also the trialling of a garlic-based material that is pumped into the tree with the potential of protecting against the canker. It is hoped that the treatment will also deter the leaf miner moth that is currently damaging horse chestnuts across England by causing their leaves to turn brown and fall off prematurely.

Another natural event which English Heritage helped historic parks and gardens to manage was the 'Great Storm' that battered the south of England in October 1987, and was responsible for the loss of millions of historic trees and for much damage to gardens and garden structures when they fell. Appalling as the aftermath looked, the storm proved to have the proverbial silver lining. Many of the fallen trees turned out to be surprisingly rotten, and so needed to be removed. And, with new short-term government funding, English Heritage was able to offer 75 per cent of the cost of a restoration plan based on thorough research, through which many owners found out the historic significance of their gardens for the first time.

There are other instances, too, of how English Heritage occasionally has to become directly involved with a site belonging to someone else, offering either specialist advice or, very rarely, a monetary grant. At Kensal Green Cemetery in London, one of the earliest planned garden cemeteries in the country, the Dissenters' Chapel was restored thanks to English Heritage offering both money and advice to the other groups involved.

Another example is Danson House, an eighteenth-century villa in Bexley, on the borders of London and Kent, where English Heritage spent ten years applying its expertise to a restoration before handing the property over to a community group, the Bexley Heritage Trust, for management. The trust was then able to restore its grounds, which were possibly designed by 'Capability' Brown, and are separately owned and run as a public urban park by the local council.

At several sites, English Heritage needs to work closely with other bodies because of complex divided ownership issues. For instance, English Heritage owns the High Victorian St Mary's Church which lies within the National Trust's Yorkshire estate of Fountains Abbey and Studley Royal, a World Heritage Site and one of the most important landscape gardens anywhere. So English Heritage works

OPPOSITE Kensal Green
Cemetery, an early garden
cemetery in an urban setting.
RIGHT An aerial view of
Danson Park.
BELOW The Picturesque view
over the ruins of Rievaulx
Abbey.

closely there with the National Trust, as it does at Rievaulx Abbey, also in Yorkshire, where the ruins of the twelfth-century Cistercian abbey belong to English Heritage, while the National Trust owns the eighteenth-century Rievaulx Terrace above, which was designed as a viewing platform from which devotees of the Picturesque could look down on the ruins and admire them. This sharing of the Rievaulx landscape is not new: the curving grass terrace, with a classical temple at each end, was, in turn, once part of Duncombe Park, a property that remains in private ownership.

English Heritage does not actively seek to acquire sites simply in order to build a portfolio of properties, but sometimes ownership by English Heritage is the only way to save and protect vulnerable sites that are of too great a national importance to let rot or crumble. Usually, this comes about through an amicable arrangement with the previous owners, as at Belsay and Brodsworth (see pages 124 and 144) (though rarely does English Heritage also receive the endowment that the National Trust insists on before it takes over a property); but in other instances English Heritage has to intervene more forcefully. In the case of Apethorpe Hall in Northamptonshire, for instance, a compulsory purchase order had to be used to rescue from the owner's neglect an important fifteenth-century Grade I listed building and its Grade II landscape, which includes gardens by the early twentieth-century architect and garden designer Reginald Blomfield.

As the goal is always to set a property back on its feet, in some instances there must be a pragmatic approach to conservation; and so at Apethorpe English Heritage carried out essential rescue works before looking for a new owner willing to take responsibility for further restoration. Similarly, Hill Hall in Essex, an important Edwardian house also with a garden by Blomfield, was bought by English Heritage, whose experts worked closely with developers to convert it into desirable apartments, which were then sold on. (The gardens are still open to the public on an occasional basis during the summer – see pages 208–9.)

But the vast majority of sites that come into English Heritage's hands will be held by it for ever – and regularly opened to the public who, after all, are the ultimate owners of our national heritage. Here the organization has a difficult balancing act to perform. Its first loyalty must be to the properties themselves, to make sure that they are respected and preserved with their historic integrity intact; but as a largely publicly funded body it must also always have an eye to visitor involvement, enjoyment and education. Indeed,

winning the public's interest and enthusiasm is not only fundamental to fulfilling English Heritage's educational role but also crucial if it is to earn invaluable revenue from entry tickets – and then from teas, souvenirs and plant sales.

And conservation today does not, of course, mean preserving the historic environment in aspic, but rather maintaining the best of the past while enabling potential treasures of the future to be created. With both these factors in mind, several new gardens have been made over the past decade and these are proving extremely attractive to visitors. Of the three opened in 2009, those at Kenilworth and Carisbrooke Castles (see pages 12 and 194) involved large-scale interventions at historic sites, while at Kenwood there was a smaller project, designed by Arabella Lennox-Boyd, to enhance the area around the café.

Many 'dry' attractions, such as ruined abbeys, are increasingly being brought alive with the addition of new gardens where there was little or no garden before. The monastic-style herb border by the striking modern visitor centre at Castle Acre Priory in Norfolk is an example of a scheme which complements the medieval spirit of the place, while at St Mawes Castle in Cornwall exotic plants were added around a sixteenth-century defensive castle on the coast to take advantage of the mild Cornish climate. An even bolder initiative was English Heritage's Contemporary Heritage Garden Scheme (see page 200), through which today's leading garden designers have added a new chapter to the history of a variety of heritage sites.

In parallel with these creations, English Heritage continues to carry out exemplary restoration works. Extensive documentary and archaeological research is facilitating a restoration of the walks and vistas at Wrest Park (see page 56), while at Witley Court (see page 134) dramatic archaeology has informed the restoration of Nesfield's East Parterre.

For the future, there is still much research to be done – at Framlingham Castle (Suffolk), for instance, where English Heritage hopes that documentary evidence for two Tudor gardens will be confirmed by archaeology, and similarly at Tintagel Castle (Cornwall), where an enclosure on a 1530 drawing is tantalizingly labelled 'the garden' and needs investigation on the ground.

LEFT Exotic planting at St Mawes Castle.
RIGHT A reconstruction drawing of Framlingham Castle, showing two possible Tudor gardens.

And finally we come to the real subject of this book: the parks and gardens which English Heritage owns or manages. Some are spectacular and important, while others are tiny or new. They form a hugely varied collection, but English Heritage does not claim that its array is representative of the entire spectrum of garden history. You will not find a design by Gertrude Jekyll in these pages!

Whatever their attraction, be it an important role in history, a stunning landscape, atmospheric surroundings or simply a pretty floral show and a good tea, we hope that you will visit them, that you will enjoy them and that as a result of these pages you will understand them a little better.

As opening times are subject to change, please look at www.english-heritage.org.uk, where up-to-date visiting details of the parks and gardens described here are listed. These can also be found in the annual English Heritage handbook, given free to members and available to others from English Heritage shops and the website.

Kenilworth Castle

WARWICKSHIRE

ENILWORTH was a royal castle which from time to time passed to a nobleman who was currently enjoying the monarch's favour, only to revert to royal ownership when he or his descendants fell from grace. It was set on a slight hill and protected by a small lake created in Norman times by the damming of two streams. Early in the thirteenth century, King John added a curtain wall and flooded more land to create what became known as the Great Mere. As a result the castle became easier to defend, and the family also had the aesthetic benefit of a view from their private apartments over a beautiful expanse of water extending from the foot of the castle towards the horizon.

The wooded land surrounding the castle was regarded as one of the finest hunting parks in the entire country. Women as well as men would pass whole days on horseback here, chasing deer and wild boar. At what point a garden was made inside the castle walls is not recorded, but there was certainly one in the late fourteenth century when Kenilworth was held by John of Gaunt, Duke of Lancaster, who was regent during his nephew Richard II's minority. The most powerful man in the kingdom, he added a large

new wing in the most up-to-date style, containing the magnificent Great Hall, and it is highly likely that he would have included a garden in the specification for his builders and decorators.

But the first outdoor area at Kenilworth we know was used purely for pleasure was the 'Pleasance in the Marsh' Henry V created in 1414–17 on the far side of the mere. A substantial wooden building, intended as a rustic retreat which the king and his privileged guests could visit by boat and where they could stay for a meal, the Pleasance was surrounded by a garden of about 2½ acres (1ha), set within a park of 9 or 10 acres (3.5 or 4ha) which had alleys for strolling in. It was still being maintained in 1463, and the accounts for that year also mention a garden within the castle walls that was being dug up to make a jousting place. The implication is that it had been there for a while, but there are no clues about what it was like.

Luckily there is evidence for the glamorous garden that Queen Elizabeth I's favourite, Robert Dudley, Earl of Leicester, laid out in the sixteenth century. The queen had given the castle to Dudley in 1563 and visited him there several times. By 1571, building in the local red sandstone as had previous owners, he had added a sumptuous new wing with apartments for the queen; and by 1575, in anticipation of a further visit by Elizabeth that July, he had created a wonderful garden. Designed both to be enjoyed at ground level and to be viewed from above, it was a rectangular garden in the latest Renaissance style laid out to the north of the oldest part of the castle, but inside the curtain wall. In addition to offering horticultural, sensory and intellectual delights, it would also act as a theatrical backdrop to some of the entertainments with which

LEFT The first 'Tudor-style' garden, made in the 1970s.
RIGHT English Heritage's recreation of the Elizabethan garden lies below the ruins of the medieval castle.

Leicester proposed to divert Elizabeth and her court over a three-week stay. These included bear-baiting, pageants and nautical displays on the Great Mere, and one of the guests was Sir Thomas Tresham (see page 211), whom the queen knighted during her visit.

Elizabeth would have caught her first glimpse of the garden from a small Italianate courtyard which Leicester fitted alongside the Norman keep. Then she would have moved down a flight of steps within the wall, emerging between pedestals surmounted with the bears of Leicester's crest on to a high terrace. Such terraces had become common on the Continent but this was among the first in England actually to be described as a terrace. On the steep garden side was a balustrade featuring obelisks and spheres on 'curious bases', all painted to look as though they were carved in red sandstone. The garden below was divided into four rectangular beds by two broad paths, and where they crossed stood a magnificent white marble fountain. Its octagonal base was ornamented with raunchy scenes from Ovid's *Metamorphoses* and fish swam in the basin, while above two great Atlantes supported a sphere from which water was sprinkled from 'sundry pipes'. The sphere was topped by a ragged staff, another element of Leicester's crest.

Obelisks gave height to the centre of each bed; these appeared to be of porphyry, but were probably made of skilfully painted wood. Like many parts of the garden, they had a symbolic as well as aesthetic purpose. Since Egyptian times, obelisks had represented eternity – a reference that the aristocratic audience for this garden would have appreciated. There were arbours, too, and the fact that they were covered with the eglantine rose – a symbol of virginity and so a reference to the Virgin Queen – would also have

during the queen's visit, there is evidence that it survived to be updated in the early 1600s. A Parliamentary survey shows that the fountain was still there seventy-five years after its creation, but when the castle's main buildings were ordered to be slighted and made uninhabitable after the Civil War, Kenilworth's garden and the fountain were destroyed in the process. The Parliamentarians also drained the Great Mere, and the fertile acres left behind have been used for agriculture ever since.

Yet, even without being dramatically reflected in its waters, by the late eighteenth century the castle's impressive ruins had become one of the most famous Picturesque sights in the country. Sir Walter Scott capitalized on their Romantic qualities by using the castle as a setting in his novel *Kenilworth* (1821), which tells a version of the Elizabeth and Dudley story. His picture of Leicester's unfortunate wife, Amy Robsart, falling to her death in the middle of the queen's visit is one that many readers found highly convincing, but Scott had been quite cavalier with the historical facts. Amy's unexplained death had actually taken place fifteen years earlier and (as Scott does make plain) many miles away, but the castle came to be associated more with this infamous episode than with any real events that took place there.

Leicester's garden eventually became a kitchen garden and orchard, while his gatehouse, which was spared when the castle was slighted and turned into a house by the Parliamentary commander, remained inhabited until well into the last century. In 1937 the castle was bought by the motor manufacturer John Davenport Siddeley, who that year was made the 1st Baron Kenilworth. He created very liveable apartments for his family in the gatehouse and in front of this a small garden, which has recently been renovated in a way that retains its 1940s flavour. (Surprisingly, it never became a 'dig for victory' vegetable garden.) After his son gave the castle to the town of Kenilworth in 1958, its management became the responsibility of the Ministry of Works, from whom English Heritage took over in 1984.

In 2003 the decision was taken to research the garden Robert Dudley had made outside the keep and create an

been comprehended by the audience, as would the link between the spheres and wisdom. Elizabeth was one of the cleverest women in Europe and she would have easily 'read' such symbolism in all its multilayered and sometimes ambiguous complexity – biblical, mythological, chivalric.

Descending to ground level, Elizabeth could approach the aviary, a 30-foot (9m) long structure in classical style, which contained exotic birds, imported from mainland Europe and as far away as Africa – a continent then scarcely explored. Their warbling and fluttering were as much an aspect of a garden's aesthetic pleasure in the late sixteenth century as sweet scents and bright colours.

After 1575, Elizabeth paid no more visits to Kenilworth. Leicester died in 1588 and, although some scholars have suggested that his prodigious garden was no more than a flimsy and temporary backdrop to the pageants presented

'A garden then so appointed, as wherein aloft upon sweet shadowed walk of terrace, in heat of summer, to feel the pleasant whisking wind above, or delectable coolness of the fountain-spring beneath, to taste of delicious strawberries, cherries, and other fruits, . . . to smell such fragrancy of sweet odours, breathing from the plants, herbs, and flowers, to hear such natural melodious music and tunes of birds, . . . the fruit-trees, the plants, the herbs, the flowers, the change in colours, the birds flittering, the fountain streaming, the fish swimming, all in such delectable variety, order, and dignity; whereby, at one moment, in one place, at hand, . . . to have so full fruition of so many of God's blessings, by entire delight unto all senses . . . at once.'

evocation of it – something which would delight modern visitors as his had delighted the first Queen Elizabeth. A 'Tudor-style' garden had in fact been made in this area in the 1970s, but this was not as authentic as it could have been. Designed by Harry Gordon Slade, one of the ministry's inspectors, it had yew trees and box hedges around beds filled with lavender. His plan was based partly on a plate in *The Antiquities of Warwickshire*, published by antiquarian Sir William Dugdale in 1656, and partly on wishful thinking, since the archaeology carried out in preparation had yielded little solid information and certainly not the layout of paths pictured by Dugdale. Unfortunately, thirty years on, as the yews matured, their roots began to grow deep into the soil and it was feared they might cause damage to anything buried beneath. And, of course, a fresh generation of archaeologists was itching to use new techniques, such as geophysics, on this potentially rich site.

To guide where they dug, and indicate what they might hope to find, they were aided by a long letter describing the queen's 1575 visit, written by Robert Langham, a former London mercer who held a post as gentleman-usher to Leicester. Although ostensibly addressed to a friend,

Humfrey Martyn, the letter was almost certainly intended for publication – or at least for circulation amongst the gentry in London – and Leicester himself was most likely aware of its contents, so flattering is it to his person, his garden and his ambition.

Langham (the name is sometimes written Laneham) recounts how his 'good friend Adrian' (Leicester's gardener) let him in through a door in the enclosed garden while the queen was out hunting. Although there were at first many reservations about the extent to which Langham may have exaggerated the garden's splendour in order to increase his master's glory – and his own in being there to see it – he seems to have been a reliable witness. He was correct, for instance, about describing the fountain centrepiece of the garden as 'of rich and hard white marble'. This was corroborated when the archaeologists found several chips of white marble attached to the fountain foundations which, when analysed, could be traced to the famous quarries at Carrara in Italy. The new fountain was therefore specially made of marble from Carrara, and the erotic scenes from Ovid's *Metamorphoses* on its base were carved by hand as they would have been in the Renaissance. The archaeologists also located the foundations of the fountain, proving that it was indeed octagonal as Langham described, and it has been replaced exactly where they proved it had been originally.

Among other discoveries were a culvert to bring water in (possibly from a spring on Camp Farm a few miles away, where an Elizabethan conduit head is said to have been found in the nineteenth century), an outlet pipe and a cavity near by which may have been used as a cistern to catch surplus water that could be used for watering the garden. Sadly, no trace was found of the water jokes Langham mentioned but something of the kind has been reinstated. Such jets, a popular feature of aristocratic gardens for several centuries, could be switched on to shower unwary guests with water and amuse those who stayed dry.

Nothing of the aviary had survived above or below ground, a lack of evidence suggesting that, like the terrace balustrade and the obelisks, it was made of painted wood, and so Langham's description was used in its re-creation. The holes in the back wall for the birds to roost in have been included in the reconstruction but, as modern minds are more sensitive to animal cruelty than those of the Elizabethans, English Heritage took advice from a specialist on the best way to care for the birds.

Another crucial element of the garden would have been the pleasure of picking and eating fresh fruit. Langham mentions that the beds of Leicester's garden were planted with strawberries (which would not at all have resembled modern varieties but been more like alpine strawberries). He also mentions eating cherries from the trees, along with apples and pears – though these would not have been ripe when the queen was there in July. So apples, pears, cherries and strawberries have all been planted in the new garden.

Much effort has gone into tracing what else Leicester's gardeners might have grown. Langham mentions the diversity of the flowers and how sweetly they smelled, but nothing by name, not even the gillyflower, one of the most popular plants in the period. Today the word is taken to mean carnation (*Dianthus*), but in the sixteenth century it also referred to other flowers with a strong scent, including stocks, wallflowers, sweet Williams and the lesser-known sweet Johns – all of which have been included in the beds. Apart from fruit, the only trees Langham refers to specifically are hollies in the aviary. Topiary was an important element of gardens in this period, because it gave height to the beds, and therefore *Ilex* spp. and *Laurus nobilis* have been planted, together with *Crataegus* and *Cornus mas*.

The new garden cost £2.1 million (including research); some of this was raised locally but the Wolfson Foundation was also a major contributor. The aviary, loggias, staircases and posts are all in English oak, and the trellis is in chestnut. Some of this wood is painted, as it would have been originally, for the Tudors liked their gardens to be extremely colourful, with red and green paint as well as bright flowers and birds.

In addition to reproducing the structure and planting of Leicester's garden as closely as possible, English Heritage had to incorporate features that would make it compatible with modern legal requirements. For instance, in Elizabethan times, after the garden had been well considered from above, those who wished to wander in it, and perhaps taste its fruit or feed the birds, probably had to descend an extremely steep staircase. For today's visitors a second, less steep staircase has been built – outside the perimeter of the original garden so as not to compromise its integrity – and equipped with a chairlift for the disabled.

With some of the most spectacular ruins in England, and so many links to great men and women, the castle at Kenilworth has always been one of English Heritage's most popular properties. Following the formal opening of the new 'Renaissance' garden in April 2009, the most important phase of its long life became brilliantly illuminated.

BELOW The beds are filled with plants that grew in Elizabethan times, including carnations, small strawberries and sweet Williams.

Kirby Hall

NORTHAMPTONSHIRE

THE HISTORY of the evocative ruined house we see at Kirby today dates back only to the 1570s. Sir Humphrey Stafford inherited his family property in 1548 but waited twenty-two years before building himself a larger, more modern home. Although Northamptonshire contained no royal palaces, the county was no backwater in terms of sixteenth-century political or social life. On the contrary, many of the most influential men of the time were building houses there, attracted by its central situation geographically and perhaps by the famous deer hunting. One was Sir Walter Mildmay, Queen Elizabeth's Chancellor of the Exchequer, who built Apethorpe (see page 9), and another Sir Thomas Tresham, responsible for Rushton and Lyveden (see page 211). Even the Secretary of State, Sir William Cecil, built his great mansion Burghley House in the county, though boundary changes have since moved it elsewhere.

A plan of Stafford's house survives, drawn by a surveyor named John Thorpe and dated 1570. Unfortunately, although Thorpe gives the ground plan in great detail, he makes no mention of whether a garden was laid out. Stafford died in 1575, his house unfinished, and the estate was sold to Sir Christopher Hatton, another of Elizabeth's favourite courtiers, who had an estate at Holdenby, only 25

LEFT A view of the restored Great Garden before the statues were put in place.
BELOW The house and garden, seen from the mound.

miles (40km) away. By the time he became her Lord Chancellor in 1587, he had finished Stafford's plan and completed the clearing of the medieval village and the demolition of its church.

Two surveys made by Ralph Treswell in 1584 and 1586 show the house and a rectangular area to the west labelled 'Garden' in the first and 'the garden and orchard' in the later one. This area may have had a terrace overlooking a sunken area and was enclosed on the north, west and south sides. By the corner of the house it connected to an unlabelled smaller space, which may have been, in practical terms, part of the garden-orchard. A small blue spot in this second area of Treswell's map possibly marks a well or pool.

But Kirby was still less grand than Hatton's other house and garden at Holdenby, so he added some impressive rooms to the south-west corner of the house and created a grand entrance forecourt, which had two monumental gateways on opposite sides. (Visitors today still arrive at the one to the west, but they find its great gates closed and are shunted

round the outside of the courtyard to enter by the north gateway, which was placed there later.)

Hatton hoped Queen Elizabeth would visit Kirby, but she never did, and after he died in 1591 his much-encumbered properties eventually passed to a distant relation, another Christopher Hatton. Christopher II sold Holdenby to pay off the debts and then had enough money to be able to make further changes to Kirby. He filled in Stafford's sunken garden and raised the overall soil level outside the west façade of the house – and for some way to the south of it. On this platform he laid out a formal garden, called the Great Garden, and made a door (later turned into a window) in the west façade of the house, on which the axis of his new garden was aligned. On its northern and western sides, the garden was bounded by terraces, which may have been ornamented by statues, and the entire garden was surrounded by brick and stone walls.

Christopher II did succeed in welcoming royalty to the house: James I visited several times, and his wife, Anne of Denmark, who was very knowledgeable about gardens, stayed for three nights in 1605. By the time of the king's final visit in 1624 Kirby was owned by the third Christopher Hatton, who inherited from his father in 1619 and made yet more improvements. Christopher III brought in Nicholas Stone, the royal master mason, who had worked with Inigo Jones, the most innovative architect of the age, and was famous for an elaborate entrance to the Oxford Botanic Garden. Stone was at Kirby from 1638 to 1640 and, as well as embellishments to the house, was almost certainly responsible for two new gateways. One, a blind gateway decorated on only one side, was placed on the western side of the Great Garden to provide a focal point at the end of the axis from the west façade. The other, which has two different faces, one rusticated, the other vermiculated, seems to have been placed at the garden's southern end, providing a connection to and from the area beyond, which may have been a flower garden. Both were subsequently moved.

Despite supporting the Royalist cause, Christopher III kept his estate during the Commonwealth, though he went into exile in France. The diarist and tree expert John Evelyn, visiting Kirby in 1654 during Hatton's absence, complained that, although the garden was 'agreeable', the avenue was

'ungraceful and the seate naked'. While Christopher III was in France, he became passionately interested in plants, and in Paris he probably met John Rose, who became gardener to Charles II after the Restoration, but how much of his new interest was reflected in changes at Kirby is not clear.

When Christopher III died in 1670, his son, yet another Christopher (called Kitt by his friends), succeeded to Kirby. He inherited his father's interest in horticulture too, as did his younger brother, Captain Charles Hatton, and a series of letters between the brothers survives in which, in the middle of political news, they discuss plants, trees, grafts and seeds.

As early as 1659 Charles seems to have been sending plants from both London and Paris and the plant collections at Kirby became famous. Fruit was as important to him as ornamental trees or flowers, and pears were a particular interest. In 1676 Charles writes that he was sending 'pear seed, hopps, plumtree stocks, chestnut stocks', and the following year grapes and almonds, mentioning that a gardener had been found skilled in growing the aforementioned hops. In 1679 grafts of 'Mr Beauvoir's peare' were dispatched (Richard Beauvoir was a Guernsey connection, and more came from him the next year). Charles was more than just a legman for his brother: he was an acknowledged expert in his own right, and two major naturalists, John Ray and Paolo Boccone, dedicated books to him.

On 6 March 1689/90, addressing his brother formally as always, Charles writes about a visit to the antiquarian Elias Ashmole:

Mr Ashmole hath, my Ld, ye best baking pear I ever saw, both for largeness, firmeness, and good tast. Many eate it raw, but it is then harsh. It keepes ye year round. It is in his garden grafted on a dwarfe stocke, and an excellent bearer. It is in shape and colour very like ye Spanish Bon Christien. He calles it ye Ashmole peare. I sent 4 grafts to Mr Knight this morning, desiring him to take care to convey them carefully to yr Lordship; which he promised me he wou'd.

(Ashmole had inherited the Lambeth property of the great plantsman John Tradescant, so it is presumably grafts of Tradescant's pears that Charles is being given.)

Professional gardeners were also involved. In 1679 George Ricketts supplied apricot trees, two rowans and two orange trees from his nursery in London's Hoxton; two pots of passion flowers arrived in 1690 from the Chelsea Physic

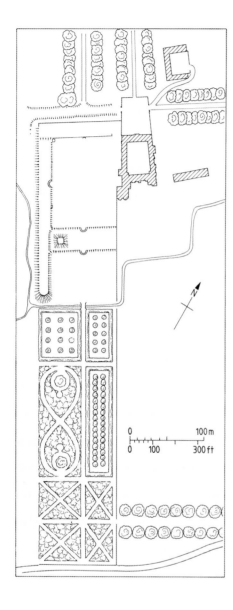

ABOVE The probable layout of the Wilderness, based on a map found in a nearby house.

OPPOSITE ABOVE This blind gateway was moved from the west to the north wall of the Great Garden.

OPPOSITE BELOW A 1920s photograph showing how Kirby Hall's fine stonework had deteriorated.

Garden – to be increased to twenty, Charles hoped, by layering – and plants and seeds often went back in exchange.

Letters also survive between Christopher IV and his second wife, Frances, and some refer to the trouble she had with a gardener called Harry Pincard, who was eventually sacked and in 1678 replaced by John Simpson. A contract drawn up later between Hatton and Simpson sheds light on the way a head gardener was employed at that time. Although food would have been provided for him – and for one other man, as well – out of £72 a year he had to pay all the garden staff, including specialist weeders (usually women), and also buy 'tooles and seedes and nailes'. The document refers to 'several gardens' at Kirby and there was probably a kitchen garden to the east of the house near the service wing, allowing Simpson to add to his income by selling surplus produce from the garden. He stayed until his death in 1689 and papers in his handwriting detail how much he had to pay out for certain items: 'leveling . . . digging borders, bringing of moulde and dung', for instance, cost £59 7s. 4d. in 1686.

Until 1680 Christopher IV spent much of his time in Guernsey, where he was governor, but he took enough interest in Kirby to make small alterations to his estate and tidy and stock the garden with plants, with his brother's help. Then, in 1689, and by now Viscount Hatton, he began a long, continuous project of garden improvements. First, diverting the little Kirby brook which ran across the property, he prolonged the gardened area way beyond the southern wall of the Great Garden and up the hill to a new site called the Wilderness. This word did not then have its modern connotation of being overgrown or untended: it was related to 'bewilder' and implied being lost in a series of maze-like bosquets, which were quite formally laid out and planted with shrubs and trees.

Few gardens of this late formal type survive and nothing of Kirby's Wilderness can be seen now, though Wrest Park (see page 56) has similar bosquets. But a sketch map found in Deene Hall (a nearby house, whose owners, the Brudenells, did several land swaps with the Hattons) gives some impression of it and of the complexity of the bosquets where the Hattons and their friends could wander and amuse themselves by getting a bit lost.

Charles Hatton sent his brother both fruit and ornamental trees for the Wilderness (his own favourite was beech) and within a year John Morton, a naturalist who lived in the county, remarked that 'almost the whole variety of our English trees is to be met with on the pleasant wilderness'.

Finally, in 1693, Christopher IV undertook what can only be described as a makeover of the Great Garden, keeping its area as it had been since Christopher II laid it out in the early years of the century but integrating it much more with the extension to the south. The designer and nurseryman George London was working at nearby Burley-on-the-Hill in 1693, and he came to Kirby to advise on the 'upper gardens'. The resulting layout could well be his design.

The retaining walls of the terraces were removed to make grassed slopes and the main axis was changed so that, instead of leading east to west, it ran north–south towards the Wilderness. Because the Nicholas Stone gateway on the west side was no longer needed to provide a stop at the end of the east–west axis from the house, it was moved in 1694 to the north wall, where it performed the same function on the new north–south axis, with fruit and flowers grown in borders to either side of it. As George London suggested, the south wall was demolished, and the Nicholas Stone gateway, which allowed access through to the Wilderness, was relocated on the north wall of the forecourt (visitors now enter the property through it).

The ground in the Great Garden was raised again and a fashionable *gazon coupé* parterre made on top of Christopher II's garden. The plain lawns with curving cut-out shapes of *gazon coupé* patterns depended for their impact on crisp edges, so it was a high-maintenance style, but Christopher IV economically achieved the same effect by using a series of wooden frames; these were probably filled with turves for an instant result and helped keep the grass inside them in shape. Height and horticultural interest were introduced by evergreen shrubs in oak tubs, which were moved or replaced when they deteriorated. The other ornaments were four statues, one in each of the four quadrants.

It was probably at this time that the remains of the village church, just beyond the Great Garden's southern boundary, were covered with soil and turfed over to make a viewing mound from which the Hattons and their friends could look down and admire the cutwork pattern.

As with the Wilderness, all this was laid out and planted incredibly quickly. By 1694 Charles was congratulating his brother on 'ye finest garden in England', and from the top of Wilderness Hill, Christopher IV could look back across the Kirby brook and along the axis of the Great Garden to the relocated Nicholas Stone gateway. Beyond that, a double avenue of trees prolonged the view to the horizon – though Charles was probably exaggerating when he claimed they led the eye into the next county of Rutland.

Fruit trees and seeds continued to occupy the brothers almost until Christopher IV died in 1706. His estate eventually descended to the Earls of Winchilsea and Nottingham, a family who had other properties they were more interested in. So, although a little landscaping was carried out later in the eighteenth century (the damming of the stream to make a small lake and the building of a sham bridge) and there may have been some new planting in the Great Garden, Kirby was virtually ignored and gradually fell into decline. On the plus side, though, there was no wholesale sweeping away of the formal layout as at so many other estates. A sale of Kirby Hall's contents took place in the 1770s and the catalogue lists one lot as a Hercules and a Mercury in stone (not lead), while another consisted of two other garden statues which were broken. These must have been the four statues from the 1690s Great Garden.

During the nineteenth century, Kirby was unmaintained and the Wilderness became grazing land. A picnic for nearly two thousand children was held in the grounds in 1894, but by then the house was already partly ruined. The architect John Alfred Gotch described how only 'variations in the levels of the grass fields suggest terraces and parterres', while the terrace was 'broken in places, but still presenting the remains of a large fountain'. He was mistaken about the fountain, but 'the distant fruit trees clustered together in the corner of another field' may well have been the remnants of the Wilderness.

In 1930 the Office of Works took over management and began to consolidate the crumbling house. There was never any hope of a complete restoration, such as

In 1990 the soil level across the area was raised by 4–6 inches (10–15cm), which returned it to its height in the 1690s and had the advantage of preserving the 1930s design underneath for the interest of future generations. The following year the paths were relaid on the correct lines and in 1992 it was decided to make a new Great Garden which would be as close as possible to how Christopher IV's looked. A plan George London had drawn for a lost *gazon coupé* parterre at Longleat in Wiltshire was chosen as a model and rescaled for the slightly differently shaped panels at Kirby. The four main beds were laid out in grass patterns with fine crushed stone between the lawns, and late seventeenth-century practice was followed in ornamenting the parterres with oak tubs containing evergreens – bays clipped into pyramids and balls, *Viburnum tinus* and even cedar of Lebanon. At the same time the north border was replanted with period plants, particularly those mentioned in the Hatton letters. Espaliered fruit trees were trained against the mellow brick wall and the flowers and shrubs include scarlet lychnis, lavatera, Moses-in-the-bullrushes, day lilies, sweet peas, sea holly and physalis grown over wicker obelisks. (An excellent exhibition inside the house explains the background to what can be seen in the gardens.)

Fragments of what were almost certainly the original urns were preserved in the garden of a nearby house which had belonged to Kirby's land agent, and their pattern has been copied to make a series of new urns and four large vases which have been filled with box balls and other plants, and placed where the archaeology indicated. The original statuary could not be traced and so some contemporary statues of Neptune, Mercury, Apollo and Hercules at Wrest Park (see page 56) were copied. When they were put in place in 2008, the Great Garden looked as close as possible to the one the fourth Christopher Hatton had created in the 1690s. English Heritage had brought to fruition one of its most serious re-creations and put Kirby Hall firmly on the garden-visiting map.

putting back fallen roofs or lost fireplaces, but attention was paid to the garden at this time. In a supportive local gesture, in 1935, to celebrate the Silver Jubilee of George V, Northamptonshire Girl Guides planted the avenue of chestnuts that now lines the approach; and at some point in the 1930s (perhaps inappropriately if the Guides were around) an eighteenth-century statue of the Rape of the Sabine Women was installed in the Great Garden, where its truncated vestiges can still be seen near the house.

More importantly for the history of gardens in general, in the early 1930s it was in the Great Garden that George Chettle conducted the first trial of garden archaeology in England. Chettle's papers have been lost and although he is believed to have identified the form of Christopher IV's garden correctly, unfortunately his archaeological work destroyed most of its remains because he scraped them off in order to find Christopher II's garden, which lay beneath. His re-creation of the earlier garden was also far from correct. The paths were not in their right places and in the new beds he planted 4,000 totally anachronistic modern roses.

By the 1980s these rose beds were suffering from replant disease; garden archaeology and attitudes to recreating period gardens had also both moved on. So further archaeology was undertaken, and it was lucky that Northamptonshire's own County Archaeology Unit was the leading specialist in investigating gardens. Bases of arbours, seats, statues and urns were found, but less than had been hoped in the areas where Chettle had already dug – although enough survived to indicate that there had definitely been some sort of cut-out pattern.

OPPOSITE Hercules was one of four statues installed in 2008 to complete the restoration.
ABOVE The 1930s recreation of Christopher II's garden remained as another phase of archaeology was started in the 1980s.

Ashby de la Zouch

LEICESTERSHIRE

*A*T FIRST GLANCE, Ashby de la Zouch looks almost like a stereotype of the properties English Heritage took over from the Ministry of Works: a romantic series of dilapidated castle walls overlooking some grass-covered earthworks. But in the last few years it has emerged as potentially one of the most exciting garden sites in the country. Prompted by the enigmatic nature of some earthworks in front of the ruins, English Heritage decided to try to find out when they were made and what they had originally been.

Exactly when gardens were created at Ashby and what they looked like is still far from clear. Perhaps three – or even four – gardens were made at different points. A reference in 1467 to 'great gardens near the manor house' indicates that before the castle was built there were gardens at Ashby worth mentioning, but whether these were ornamental or for growing medicinal plants or vegetables is not known and, like all gardens of that time, they have disappeared. Then there may be an unexplored one from the cusp of the period when the Plantagenet

RIGHT Thundery skies dramatize Ashby's ruined towers.
BELOW Strange indentations in the earthworks have puzzled historians.

kings, who had ruled England throughout the Middle Ages, were being supplanted by that tough, modern dynasty the Tudors. As political power changed hands, so cultural life was moving on dramatically, with the Renaissance sweeping away unfashionable medieval styles in art and architecture – and in gardening. A third garden might date from about 1530, the time of Henry VIII, when Tudor power had been consolidated; and a fourth appears to have been made around the time of the next change of dynasty, when the Stuarts took over the throne and the change of régime again coincided with new cultural tastes.

The French-sounding name of Ashby de la Zouch comes from the family of Alan la Zouch, originally from Brittany. They owned the estate from 1160 to 1399, taking over the previous fortified manor house and then building a castle. Around this, by the early fourteenth century, were a 60-acre (24.3ha) deer park (the Old Park), a rabbit warren, fishponds, orchards and a dovecot; and, as the original manor house was set on the edge of a marshy area, there may have been a deliberately flooded 'landscape', such as those at Framlingham, in Suffolk, which we know Alan la Zouch saw, and Kenilworth, which would have provided an aesthetic setting as well as improved security.

In 1464 Edward IV gave Ashby to his Lord Chamberlain, William, Baron Hastings, a rising grandee from a local Leicestershire family and owner of nearby Kirby Muxloe Castle. In 1474 Hastings was granted licences to crenellate Ashby and to impark 3,000 acres (1,215ha): these were the trappings of nobility at the time and a sign of considerable royal favour. Such licences were often granted retrospectively, and he may have begun adding to the Zouch family's castle ten years earlier, as soon as he took on ownership. The work included a kitchen block, a magnificent more-or-less freestanding building (now called Hastings Tower) and a chapel, which was remarkably large for a private dwelling.

Hastings may not have imparked all the acres his licence permitted, but certainly at one point the Ashby estate had three parks, the Little Park, the Great Park and Prestrop Park. The Little Park was adjacent to the area of enclosed gardens and an avenue of trees extended into it, indicating

LEFT The remains of one of the banqueting houses.
RIGHT A reconstruction drawing showing how the gardens may have been in their heyday.

that it may have been the principal entrance to the property. And even allowing for the 'great gardens' near the old manor house, more must surely have been made to enhance his splendid new residence. Hastings had been on diplomatic missions, and so would have seen gardens on the Continent, perhaps including the Duke of Burgundy's extraordinary park at Hesdin in northern France.

Having fallen foul of the future Richard III, Hastings was beheaded in 1483, but the family managed to retain their land through all the upheavals of the following centuries and still technically own Ashby today.

It may have been William's grandson, George, created Earl of Huntingdon in 1529 by Henry VIII, who made the next garden. Or it could have been his grandson, Henry, the 3rd Earl, who succeeded in 1560. George had travelled abroad, and both he and Henry had connections with the court and with other great houses, so they would have been in a position to see all the best new gardens of their time. Unfortunately, the material so far obtained by archaeological excavation does not get us any closer to dating the enigmatic earthworks.

Archaeological work has so far taken place only in the area to the south of the castle, which is covered by grass. This part was once entirely walled in red brick, although only the wall on the eastern side survives intact, as does an interesting stretch to the north which has niches in it, intended to hold beehives. Such walls were not for defence but for privacy, and indicate that this was a privileged place

for the lord, his family and their friends. On the southern corners stood two brick towers, one octagonal in plan and a slightly larger one that was clover-leaved – both now dilapidated. Again, these were not for defence: they were banqueting houses, built for pleasure. Such small pavilions, where the noble family and their guests could eat dessert (not a whole meal) while admiring the garden or countryside through large windows, were fashionable in aristocratic sixteenth-century gardens.

Inside the walled area, strips of higher land act as wide terraces or walkways for promenading on and looking down on an indented sunken area. This lower area covers about 2 acres (0.8ha) – a remodelling of the previous landscape that would have involved a huge amount of earth-moving. It is divided into almost equal halves, separated by a higher strip of grassed land forming another walkway, running north–south. While the western part is an almost perfect square, with mostly straight edges, the rather deeper eastern half is further divided into two by an east–west walkway, which has several turf buttresses jutting out from it to make a scalloped pattern. Although walkways were a common feature in gardens from the Middle Ages onwards, such spurs jutting out from them are not known elsewhere.

For many years, it was believed that the sunken areas were medieval fishponds, which had been grassed over, or even a water garden; but the archaeologists found no evidence of standing water and suggested instead that they could be the remains of a sophisticated pleasure garden, designed to be enjoyed at ground level and also viewed from the walkways or the top of Hastings Tower.

One of the most interesting archaeological finds within the western compartment was an assortment of different coloured stones – orange, pink, purple and yellow – which seem to have been edged with some white material, as though in a frame. Although these were obviously sourced from the local sandstone, which varies according to the amount of iron pigment various seams contain, there is a difference of opinion concerning whether they occurred naturally in the trench or as part of a pattern. Were they part of a heraldic device, perhaps a temporary ornament designed to be seen from the tower in the course of a feast or pageant? Or was this a tiny part of the design of an emblematic garden, known from descriptions to be popular in the early Tudor period but surviving on the ground nowhere else? Were the indented edges of the walks a further heraldic reference? There are no definite answers at present, though further archaeology might yield more detail.

Another exciting discovery was a tower – a third banqueting house or the remains of it – in the middle of the causeway running across the eastern area. This one was round and had a spiral staircase leading down to the sunken level, indicating that the family and their friends could gain access to the lower level – to walk, or dine, or perhaps to play games?

Other archaeological indications came from studying the burnt plant remains found on the site. One sample, mainly ash, oak, birch and hazel, seems to be what was cleared away when the sunken garden was made, and it is interesting that the accounts for Hastings's other castle at Kirby Muxloe mention that 'Thomas the gardener' was to clear oak, elm and ash trees from the garden. A second sample, including ferns and a single violet seed, may represent what was growing at Ashby when the area was altered later, probably during the Civil War.

In its heyday the property was considerably larger than that now managed by English Heritage and the sunken gardens were part of a larger garden area, in total 14 or so acres (5.67ha), which continued further south and eventually to the Little Park. This was probably accessed through the larger of the two corner towers, the clover-leaf-shaped one, which had stairs leading down to a basement with a door leading outdoors. Both the sunken gardens near the castle and the larger gardens became known as the Wilderness (a term which did not imply criticism but meant a garden to be wandered in, as at Wrest Park and Kirby Hall).

In parallel with the archaeology, documentary research was carried out both in local archives and as far afield as the Huntington Library in California, where the Hastings family papers are deposited. The results show that many kings and queens stayed at Ashby: Mary, Queen of Scots, was twice imprisoned there; James I came three times; and his wife, Anne of Denmark, visited in 1603 with their son Henry, Prince of Wales (both were seriously interested in gardens). How they were entertained is not recorded, but a garden building is said to have been put up for one of James's visits and turned into the laundry room after he left. Charles I and Queen Henrietta Maria came together, and the king alone, during the Civil War. More relevant to the gardens may be the account of a masque held at Ashby in 1606/7 to celebrate the 5th Earl of Huntingdon's coming of age and in honour of his mother-in-law, the Dowager Countess of Derby. She is described as entering through a temporary 'antique gate' on the edge of the Little Park, built and painted for the occasion, and as leaving by a fountain or spring.

Other work may have been done on the Ashby gardens at this time, and accounts from the next decade mention a gate being made in the Wilderness: it cost a good deal of money, was 'coloured' and had a lock. There are also records of fruit trees and other plants.

During the Civil War, for the first time ever Ashby was seen to have some strategic value and became a headquarters for the Royalist army; and as, strangely, it had never had a moat, ditches were made outside the garden walls. It may have been during these preparations that the garden was turfed over. Certainly, the 8-inch (20cm) deep layer of soil that was at some point deliberately placed there has been the fortunate means of preserving whatever lies underneath. Ashby was besieged and held out for fifteen months, but finally had to surrender in the spring of 1646. Parts of the castle were later slighted – deliberately wrecked by gunpowder – but it was not completely destroyed.

Documentary evidence gradually becomes more frequent, including a mention in 1677 by the antiquarian William Dugdale, and in 1730 we get the first surviving views of Ashby, two engravings by Nathaniel and Samuel Buck. In one, showing the castle from the south across the garden, the sunken areas and some of the spurs on the banks show up clearly, as do the two banqueting houses at the corners, already in ruins.

A survey of the estate carried out in 1735 shows the outlines of the Wilderness and T-shaped avenues of trees, one leg of which stretched down into the Little Park, which by now had shrunk from 70 acres to 42 (17ha). There seems to have been no move towards creating a Brownian-style landscape park in the later eighteenth century, though by then there may have been efforts to make something of the garden once more, as the archaeologists discovered flower beds of that period at the base of the spurs in the eastern sunken area, while the western one was used as a bowling green.

Like Kenilworth, Ashby was popularized by Sir Walter Scott, who set the jousting scene in his novel *Ivanhoe* (1819) here, and the castle ruins certainly appealed to tourists attracted by the new fashion for the picturesque. The first guidebook was published in 1824 and the castle was painted by J.M.W. Turner in 1830. Today the ruins look more like a watercolour by John Piper: the walls, in the beige, dark red and ochre local sandstone, are tinted with lichens – yellow, rust, acid green, grey-blue, dark blue – delighting visitors with myriad subtle colours. In 1932 the Commissioners of Works took over guardianship of the ruins and the Wilderness, and later transferred the site to English Heritage.

A great deal more research remains possible into the early gardens at Ashby. Manuscript sources might help with dating, while further archaeology could yield evidence of the statues and fountains Tudor gardens usually contain. What was there in the late medieval period and the early seventeenth century is also worth pursuing; and perhaps eventually time and resources will permit the investigation of other areas of this fascinating landscape. The complex water feature known as the Moats near the old manor house; the courtyards of the Zouch castle; the brick wall to the north with niches in it; the Mount to the east and the remains of the triangular tower that still stands there; a house known as Ashby Place which was made within the ruins and pulled down in 1830; the flower beds by the nineteenth-century front entrance – all offer fascinating possibilities.

Although, except for a row of shrub roses planted along one boundary fence, no obvious signs of horticulture can be seen today, there is good evidence from historical documents and archaeology for a garden in the late sixteenth or early seventeenth century, with the buildings hinting that there may be elements so far undiscovered of a Tudor design, and perhaps too of the garden mentioned in the late fifteenth century. Ashby is certainly an important example of a rare earthwork garden; it could also be a garden of unique national and perhaps international importance, but for the moment we have to exercise a certain amount of imagination.

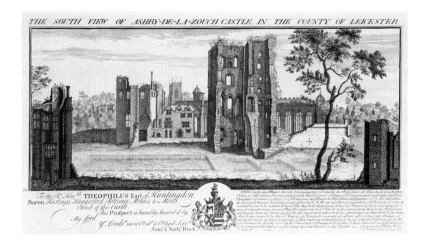

RIGHT FROM TOP Three views of Ashby de la Zouch: a Buck brothers engraving showing the garden and ruins in 1730; J.M.W. Turner's thoroughly Picturesque portrayal of the castle in 1830; and a photograph taken later in the nineteenth century showing Victorian flowerbeds and ivy-covered walls.

Bolsover Castle

DERBYSHIRE

ERHAPS THE MOST FRIVOLOUS of all English Heritage's properties is the Little Castle at Bolsover. Although built high on a ridge where there was once a medieval stronghold, it is a castle in name only – more a place for parties and dalliance than for defence or day-to-day living. Begun by Charles Cavendish in 1612, and finished by his son William, it was within easy riding distance of their main property, Welbeck Abbey, in Nottinghamshire, and its purpose was to provide a place where they could take their guests for a pleasurable day out. There were hunting parks beyond the castle walls, but it was inside them that more varied entertainment was proposed.

Charles Cavendish was the son of Bess of Hardwick and it seems probable that the architect of the Little Castle was Robert Smythson, who had designed for her the revolutionary Hardwick Hall ('more glass than wall'). By the time Smythson died in 1614 and Charles three years later, the building was structurally complete, and it was decorated and embellished inside and out by their sons, John Smythson and William Cavendish, who then added a separate range of more sober and formal buildings, now known as the Terrace Range. Finally, Robert Smythson's grandson, Huntingdon, probably designed the Riding House – the finest surviving *manège* in Britain, where William Cavendish, a famous horseman as well as a courtier, soldier and poet, practised dressage with his precious horses.

Born plain Mr Cavendish in 1592/3, William, through royal favour, ended his life as 1st Duke of Newcastle. He would have approached the Little Castle along the escarpment and then entered through a small forecourt and up a grand flight of steps. Today, visitors walk through a gateway with magnificent rusticated piers, into the Great Court, where the Riding House can be admired and the roofless but splendid Terrace Range of buildings begins. Passing a fine copper beech tree, and under a baroque gateway into another courtyard, they are faced with what at first glance seems to be a small battlemented medieval castle. The give-aways that place it in the seventeenth century are the large window with its classical pediment in the middle of the façade, the shape of the four towers that crown the building's corners and the two domes on the summit.

Set into the lawn in front of the castle is an extraordinary fountain, commissioned by William after 1628, which has also clearly come a certain way stylistically and symbolically from the fountains of the Middle Ages. At its top, a life-sized

LEFT The Venus fountain in front of the Little Castle.

RIGHT Privileged guests could admire Venus from the Little Castle's balcony.

Venus, made in a shining white local stone, presents her callipygous rear and loosely dressed hair for admiration. Described as 'lumpy' by the architectural historian Nikolaus Pevsner, she was carved at a time when Rubens-esque ladies were fashionable (and William counted the painter amongst his many artistic and literary friends). Indeed, she could be the sister of the Venus Spinaria at Wilton in Wiltshire of about the same date. The statue stands on a white plinth, placed on a larger plinth in sandstone, on each side of which is a lion's mask spouting water into a circular basin. This in turn is set on another plinth, which at each corner has a small urinating cherub (not unlike the famous Manekin Pis fountain in Brussels, which dates from 1619).

Bolsover's Venus was based on a drawing of a rather more etiolated Mannerist statue by Giambologna, and was once accompanied by several naked ladies, lurking in niches in the large basin and indulging in what would now be called inappropriate behaviour. By the late eighteenth century they had been replaced by more decorous busts of helmeted Roman emperors, and it is these that were reconstructed when the fountain was recently restored. About twenty items of the fountain's decoration had been damaged, destroyed or stolen – cherubs, Caesars, a series of mythological beasts and lion masks – and all were painstakingly researched and then either repaired or copies commissioned.

Like many fountains of the period, this one may never have worked properly, but in the restoration the waterworks also received attention and now, thanks to an electric pump, it plays away as merrily as Cavendish and his guests could have wished. The water, brought in through four conduit houses and a cistern house, flows into a larger basin, lying below ground level and decorated with vermiculated and rusticated niches and an unusual battlemented surround.

The Venus fountain forms the focal point of the inner courtyard, and into the thickness of the surrounding wall three deep embrasures were inserted – small rooms really (one actually a suite of three), where amatory couples could find privacy. Each had stone seats and niches, which may have held lights; two even had fireplaces. Running along the wall between these arbours were wide flower beds, once decorated by more statues. The beds are currently planted with period plants: bear's breeches (*Acanthus mollis*), euphorbia, honeysuckle, the guelder rose (*Viburnum opulus*), herbs such as lavender, rosemary and rue, and old roses, including 'Ferdinand Pichard', 'Reine Victoria' and 'Comte de Chambord'.

Both fountain and garden were designed as much to be seen from above as to be lingered in at ground level. The Elysium Room of the Little Castle had a balcony, its railings painted with rare and expensive green paint. Added by John

Smythson for William Cavendish, this was a space where the owner and one or two privileged guests could stand to look down on Venus and see into the deep basin with its statues. There was also a walkway, known as the Stone Walk, which ran at first-floor level from a door in the castle around the courtyard, offering a wide space where guests could promenade.

In July 1634 William invited Charles I and Queen Henrietta Maria to Bolsover and among the entertainments he put on for them was a masque by Ben Jonson, *Love's Welcome*, which was played partly indoors and partly outside in the garden. But such fun and splendour had to be put to one side once the Civil War began in 1642. William, with Prince Rupert, led the Royalist side in the disastrous battle of Marston Moor in 1644. He went into exile until Charles II was restored to the throne and returned to find Bolsover despoiled.

William made what repairs he could and lived until 1676. His Venus can just be glimpsed in Kip and Knyff's c.1698 birds'-eye view of Bolsover, but the courtyard seems bare of flower beds and of the walkway. The dukedom died out with his son, Henry, and Bolsover passed through the female line to the Dukes of Portland, who handed it over to the Ministry of Works in 1945. By then the castle was slipping off its heights into the valley because of the coal mines that ran underneath, and a long programme of consolidation and repair had to be undertaken. English Heritage took over in 1984 and the Little Castle and Venus fountain were restored from 1998 to 2001. In the future, it is hoped to restore the walkway, and then this rare survival of an early seventeenth-century garden will appear as splendid to modern visitors as it once did to the courtiers of that period.

OPPOSITE FROM LEFT TO RIGHT Cherubs, lion masks and mythological beasts spout water from their varied orifices.

RIGHT ABOVE Part of the walkway and a fine copper beech in front of the Terrace Range can be seen from the Little Castle.

RIGHT BELOW Two of the small private spaces made in the thickness of the medieval walls, where today the air is thick with the scent of lavender and roses.

Boscobel House

SHROPSHIRE

TUCKED AWAY in the well-farmed hills near Wolverhampton, Boscobel House is one of English Heritage's most peaceful properties. A timber-framed building surrounded by quaint barns and pretty gardens with fruit trees and walks, it is sure to entice even the most hardened of visitors into dreams of retiring to keep chickens and grow vegetables. In fact, though, not all at Boscobel is what it seems, its gardens having fostered four centuries of intrigues.

Boscobel's first intrigue is how it hid a king and the part it played in one of England's best known adventure stories. In 1651, Boscobel was a hunting lodge belonging to White Ladies, a large house nearby that had grown from a ruined

BELOW The oldest part of Boscobel is the timber-framed range to the left. On the right is a more recent addition, thought to have been built in about 1630.

RIGHT Boscobel's farmhouse, where a quiet scene belies an exciting past.

decided to go first to White Ladies, to throw any followers off the scent. So Charles and his gang left Worcester that evening and rode to White Ladies, where they arrived at four o'clock in the morning. George Penderel let them in and sent a boy to fetch his brothers Richard and William, the latter of whom was the caretaker at Boscobel.

Charles then sent away the rest of his party and stayed at White Ladies to disguise himself as a countryman in the Penderels' clothes. Now Charles could not decide whether to head for London or to a port in Wales. He spent the day hiding in a woodland near White Ladies and during the course of this decided to go to Wales, so that night he and Richard Penderel duly set off. They soon discovered, however, that the River Severn ferry crossings were being guarded, so they had to spend a day hiding in a barn, before deciding to head for London after all, via Boscobel.

By the time they arrived at Boscobel, again extremely early in the morning, it had already acquired a Royalist fugitive – Major William Careless. The men felt that it would be too dangerous to spend the day in the house and so Careless suggested hiding in the branches of an oak tree. Many years later, after he had successfully regained the throne, Charles dictated the story of this to Samuel Pepys, so we are able to read first hand in Pepys's diary of the suggestion that they

> get up into a great oak in a pretty plain place where we could see round about us for they would certainly search all the wood for people that had made their escape. Of which I approved and we . . . went and carried some victuals up with us (only bread and cheese and small beer) for the whole day and got up into a great oak that had been lopped some three or four years before and so was grown out very bushy and thick and could not be seen through.

By the time night came they were understandably pretty fed up with the tree so went back to the house. Charles must

nunnery. White Ladies was owned by Frances Cotton, who had inherited it from her father, John Giffard. Widowed Frances did not actually live at White Ladies, so both it and Boscobel were occupied by members of the large Penderel family, who worked as her servants and caretakers.

Meanwhile, the throne of England had been in dispute for some time, Charles I having been beheaded in 1649 and his son Charles II exiled. However, Charles II had no intention of staying away for long, and by 1651 he had a modest army and was busy fighting Oliver Cromwell in an attempt to win back the throne. In September, though, Charles suffered a major defeat to Cromwell at Worcester and had to flee for his life.

Charles desperately needed to separate himself from his conspicuous fleeing army and hide until he could discreetly make his way to a port and thus France. One of Charles's party, Lord Derby, had sheltered at Boscobel a few weeks earlier and suggested it as a useful place. As one of Frances Cotton's relatives, Charles Giffard, was with the royal party, it seemed like a good choice. As a precaution, the party

LEFT Pictures from a 1660 broadsheet narrating the story of Charles's flight from the Battle of Worcester.
RIGHT ABOVE The Replacement Royal Oak is a short walk from the house, now through open fields but probably in woodland when Charles was staying at Boscobel.
RIGHT BELOW The Royal Oak, showing signs of the lightning damage it suffered in 2000.

Old Wardour Castle

WILTSHIRE

ONE OF THE MOST romantic ruins in England, Old Wardour Castle was begun in 1393, quite late in the medieval period when serious fortifications were optimistically felt to be of decreasing importance. It was intended less as a stronghold than as a comfortable gentleman's residence with big windows and a richly decorated interior. The master mason was probably William Wynford, the then equivalent of a big-name architect. He had worked at Windsor Castle and Wells Cathedral and, in the 1390s, was working on Winchester Cathedral, just 40 or so miles (64km) from Wardour. For his client, John, the 5th Lord Lovell, Wynford created a two-storey hexagonal keep, extended on the north-eastern side by two towers and with a hexagonal courtyard at its heart – a daring design, probably based on French models.

By the 1570s a new owner, Sir Matthew Arundell, thought Wardour needed bringing up to date. He may have employed Robert Smythson, who was working at nearby

OPPOSITE Today, as in the eighteenth century, Wardour's ruins make the perfect Picturesque view.

LEFT This photograph, taken from a balloon, shows the Old Castle, the Banqueting House and the Great Pond. The late seventeenth-century house can be seen in the left foreground.

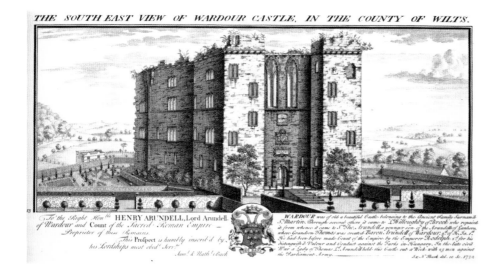

THE SOUTH EAST VIEW OF WARDOUR CASTLE, IN THE COUNTY OF WILTS.

Longleat at the time. If so, Wardour again had a major architect on site.

So far, the castle's history had indeed been as peaceable as the Lovells had hoped, but in the middle of the next century the Civil War impacted on it in a literal way. In May 1643 the Parliamentarians besieged Wardour and captured it. They caused relatively little damage, but in December Henry, 3rd Lord Arundell, set about retaking his family home for the Royalists. In the course of his assault, he laid gunpowder mines in a tunnel – a common siege tactic. When, probably accidentally, the gunpowder ignited, one side of his castle and most of the upper floor came crashing down. (Henry was also a poet, which may explain his military incompetence.)

This made Wardour uninhabitable and from about 1686 the family, on their rare visits, lived in a house to the south of the ruins, adapted from some outbuildings and then extended, perhaps by Vanbrugh. They planted an orchard and later turned it into a geometric garden, whose terraces, rectangular beds, clipped bushes and hedged compartments appear in an engraving of the castle published by the Buck brothers in 1732. A map of about the same period shows the castle surrounded by the Old Orchard, a new orchard and a series of elm walks. The Great Pond (often called the Swan Pond because of its shape) appears, as do several other ponds, and there was a grove, with straight paths radiating out from a central point, a bit like an irregular umbrella. Statues were placed in the Lady Grove at this time, and a row of yews planted behind the castle on the lowest terrace. The statues have long gone but most of the yews survive.

Although the great John Cheere supplied a statue of Diana and Apollo in 1742, by then Wardour's design was looking outmoded. But, luckily, very soon the ruined castle began to be seen with different eyes. It had become 'Picturesque', and so could serve perfectly as the focal point or eye-catcher of a landscape park, in the style fashionable at the time.

A survey commissioned by Henry, 7th Lord Arundell, from a 'WD' in 1753 showed the Grove as the most prominent element, with a chain of natural ponds fed by springs, the Great Pond near the ruined castle, a bowling green and woodlands on the higher ground. Wanting something more up to date, the next year Arundell consulted 'Capability' Brown (see page 89), who spent five days on site considering potential alterations. His plan has been lost, and how much of it was implemented is unclear: probably only a walled kitchen garden set behind the ruin. The problem may have been that Arundell died in 1756 before more could be done. Certainly, Brown had difficulty getting paid and only received his fee from the 7th Lord's widow in 1757.

The 8th Lord Arundell, another Henry, who was only sixteen when he inherited, did not push forward any existing projects; but in 1763, just two years after he came of age, he married an heiress and decided that they needed a proper family seat – a modern house and a park to complement it. In that year, Joseph Spence, the anecdotist and commentator on Picturesque landscapes, who was advising the young couple, referred to 'Mr. Brown's plan', so presumably it survived that long.

In 1764 Lord Arundell called in Richard Woods to draw up a plan for the park, a setting for a house that had not yet been designed, let alone built. The various layouts he suggested for Wardour had all the accoutrements of the aristocratic eighteenth-century park. The River Nadder would be dammed to create a lake in front of the old castle on its most ruinous side. This would be crossed by two bridges (one Palladian) and further damming would create cascades. The water level in the Swan Pond would be raised (and a boat supplied for use thereon) and a new pond would be dug next to it (this was named for John Creswell, who supervised the works). The area between the Swan Pond and the Old Castle on its mound would be a lawn, and groves of trees would be planted behind the ruin to set it off. The Lady Grove would be softened in plan and separated off by a ha-ha, and a 1-mile (1.6km) long walk called the Great Terrace constructed on the higher ground, offering picturesque views down over the Old Castle. Follies in a variety of styles – Chinese, Gothick, Ionic and Doric – would pepper the park, and there were also practical buildings, such as an ice house, and even that most up-to-date garden feature, a cold bath.

At first Arundell's idea was that his new house should be sited near the ruined castle, but by about 1769 he had decided, perhaps at Woods's suggestion, that it would be better to build the mansion on slightly higher ground about 1 mile (1.6km) to the north-west. James Paine was commissioned in 1770 to design it, and Woods was retained for the landscape. From now on, though, the landscape's centre of gravity moved away from the Old Castle to what, in spite of its Palladian style, became known as the New Castle.

By 1769, near where the house was going to be built, Woods had completed a new kitchen garden. Inside its walls, constructed with his signature curved corners, a magnificent greenhouse and pineries were erected, and near by (unusually for the period) was an orchard.

Although Arundell had sufficient confidence in Woods to employ him on his other estate, Irnham in Lincolnshire, he did not accept all his suggestions for Wardour, turning to James Paine for the bridges and deciding against the additional lake. Some of the follies were also never built: the Egyptian pyramid with stables underneath, for instance, which seems a pity.

There is a good archive for Wardour, which has been explored by Woods expert Fiona Cowell. She found

RICHARD WOODS

Richard Woods was born in Yorkshire in 1716, the same year as Lancelot 'Capability' Brown, and died in 1793, ten years after Brown. In their day he was almost as well known but later his fame was overshadowed by that of his contemporary. He generally worked for middle-class patrons and on smaller sites, while Brown tended to the aristocratic and extensive. His designs have horticultural as well as aesthetic interest, reflecting the late eighteenth-century vogue for shrubberies and for the exotic plants newly arriving from North America.

Woods was originally an architect and surveyor, and it was 1749 before he undertook his first landscaping commission, at Byfleet in Surrey; but as his client there was Joseph Spence, friend of Pope and commentator on art and gardening, it was a prestigious start. Most of his work, such as Belhus for Lord Dacre, was carried out in the south-east of England, particularly in Essex, where he lived, and, as a Roman Catholic, he often received commissions from fellow Catholics, including Lord Petre at Thorndon Hall (Essex) and the Arundells at Old Wardour Castle (Wiltshire).

Because of the trough in his reputation, much of what Woods created was lost and he is rarely mentioned in books on garden history, but his contribution to the English landscape movement is now being re-evaluated and some of his surviving parks and gardens have been restored. Those to be seen today include Hartwell House (Buckinghamshire), Brocket Hall (Hertfordshire), Cusworth Hall and Cannon Hall (both Yorkshire) and Wivenhoe Park (Essex), painted by Constable and now the campus of the University of Essex.

Richard Woods and English Heritage: Audley End (page 86) and Old Wardour Castle (page 42).

documents indicating that as early as 1764, when Woods had only just started work, he brought in four wagonloads of plants. It is not clear what these contained, but other papers show him suggesting a mixture of trees (including conifers and flowering trees), shrubs (including evergreens) and herbaceous plants. Some were purchased in large quantities – 300 campanulas, for instance, costing 6s. – and he bought seeds, as well, including rare items from America. There were also 60 orange trees for the walled garden, obtained from a Mr Sesarego, who had premises in Air Street, near what is now Piccadilly Circus.

Even with minor economies such as transplanting fruit trees from Brown's old kitchen garden to the new one, the expense must have been considerable, and by 1771 Lord Arundell had paid Woods almost £4,000. In 1773, possibly finding himself short of cash and worried that this design was proving too expensive, he asked a surveyor called George Ingman to draw up exactly what his estate now included after all Woods's work. How the Old Castle appeared may perhaps be seen in a frustratingly undated engraving by James Canter in the British Library, which shows it from the ruined side, with flower beds in front.

Then, believing that a fresh plan might save money, Arundell wrote to 'Capability' Brown. The great man did not reply: he may have been too busy or ill – or wary because of the difficulties he had encountered in obtaining payment for his work a decade before. But at the beginning of 1774, Arundell wrote to Brown again. This time he responded and in 1775, after a visit to the New Castle, designed a layout for the 600 acres (243ha) around it, including improvements on the now-important west side of the park. His plan included an enormous new lake – 150 acres (60ha)! – which gave the illusion of a serpentine river. But, yet again, nothing much was implemented.

Seen from the New Castle, the Old Castle made a spectacular eye-catcher, but the Arundells and their guests could also appreciate its romantic aspects from another viewpoint, that of the Banqueting House. This pretty building with fashionable Gothick windows, on the edge of the Swan Pond, was adapted by Paine from a former guardhouse set at the foot of the medieval mound. Here, in a manner reminiscent of sixteenth-century nobility, desserts or light refreshments could be nibbled and the romantic ruins, set amidst trees, admired or contemplated.

Should anyone wish to venture to the other side of the castle, they could enjoy the fun of being startled by the Grotto and taken aback by the Stone Circle, two follies made in 1792 by Josiah Lane. This noted maker of garden features lived in the next village of Tisbury, where there was a real neolithic stone circle, which he is said to have pillaged to make this pretend one. The Grotto, made of brick and volcanic lava sourced near Bath, had stone seats and a *claire voie* which framed a view of the ruins. Such fake relics of ancient times were admired in the Sublime parks fashionable in the late eighteenth century, and the gloom created by the yews on the terrace, by now grown far out of their earlier formal shapes, was considered to add an appropriate frisson. Woods's cedars around the castle had also matured enough to be described as 'This amphitheatre of agèd trees' in a

sonnet by the landscape poet William Lisle Bowles, probably written around the turn of the century.

The 8th Lord Arundell died in 1808 and by the time an 1822 guidebook was published his successors had added a flower garden and an American garden (which would have been planted with shrubs and trees from the New World) and at some point turned Woods's greenhouse into a camellia house. But by the end of the 1820s the family's financial position was deteriorating – and the estate with it. This had the advantage that they could not afford to make changes for fashion's sake, so the landscape park suffered no overlay of mid-nineteenth-century Italianate terraces or formal bedding. Indeed, it was never much changed and, with Brown's kitchen garden, survived into the early twentieth century.

In 1936 the Old Castle and a small amount of land around it were placed in the guardianship of the Ministry of Works. This signalled the beginning of the break-up of the

estate, which was accelerated after the 16th and last Lord Arundell died in 1944. Wardour New Castle and 800 acres (324ha) were sold to the Society of Jesus in 1946, but the Jesuits showed little respect for the historic landscape: the park was neglected and many trees sold for timber. In 1960 the New Castle and 50 acres (20ha) were bought by a school, and by the time this closed in 1990 most of the eighteenth-century landscape park, including the Lady Grove, had passed into various private hands. The mansion has now been divided into apartments and there are few indications of its once-splendid pleasure gardens. Although Woods's camellia house has been restored, his kitchen garden is in poor condition and its pineries have disappeared. The smaller ponds are silted up and Creswell's Pond is dry. The Gothick Summer House became derelict, but was rescued by Fiona Cowell and re-erected at Hatfield Peverel Priory in Essex, another Woods landscape.

But although visitors to Old Wardour cannot see much of the work by Brown or Woods, or the picturesque view from the New Castle to the romantic ruins of the old one, the 6 acres (2.5ha) owned by English Heritage still have much to offer. The Swan Pond, the Banqueting House, the Cold Bath, the Grotto, and vestiges of the Stone Circle, terraces and yew walk all survive, to be enjoyed with fine trees, a peaceful setting, birds and bluebells – and, above all, a profound sense of history.

RIGHT An ancient stone circle was pillaged to create a fake one, itself now mostly disappeared.
FAR RIGHT The dank grotto, which from inside offers framed views back to the Old Castle.

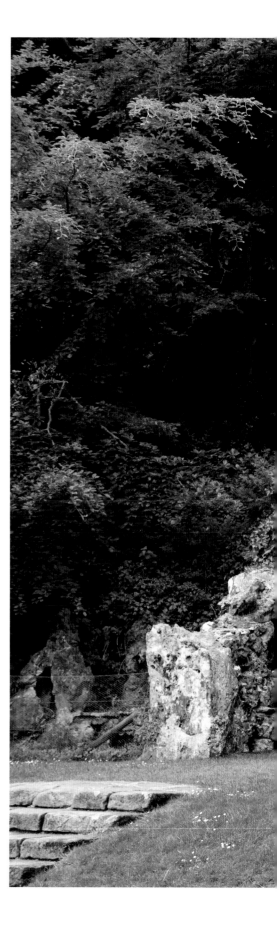

Appuldurcombe House

ISLE OF WIGHT

ENGLISH HERITAGE has the care of so many ruins from the Middle Ages that Appuldurcombe comes as a surprise, for here is the shell of an elegant country house from much later, the eighteenth century. Like Witley Court (see page 134), Appuldurcombe was damaged in the middle of the twentieth century – not, as there, by an accidental fire but by a German bomber which, while laying mines in the Channel, dropped its last mine before crashing.

In its heyday, and until Osborne House was built, this lost house was considered the finest on the Isle of Wight, as indeed had its predecessor, a substantial Tudor mansion with a walled garden and a bowling green. Appuldurcombe's architect, commissioned by Sir Robert Worsley in 1701, is not known for certain. The architectural historian Nikolaus Pevsner thought him probably 'a minor provincial architect, whose one great chance this was', but others believe the sophisticated style indicates someone practising in London, probably John James, usually known as James of Greenwich, whose best-known work is St George's

Church, Hanover Square, in London's Mayfair. Whoever it was, Appuldurcombe's main façade, in a toned-down baroque style, was considered good enough to figure in the third (1725) volume of Colen Campbell's *Vitruvius Britannicus*, where the best of current British architecture was illustrated to be admired and aped by landed gentry with aspirations. And if James was indeed the architect of the house, he may have been involved in designing its formal garden too, as he was interested enough in the subject to translate, and publish in 1712, the seminal French treatise *The Theory and Practice of Gardening*.

Sir Robert Worsley was a serious gardener, 'perpetually' in his garden according to his wife, Frances, in a 1702 letter to her father; but as she was the daughter of Lord Weymouth of Longleat, who had employed George London there to lay out a significant formal garden, her referring to the garden at Appuldurcombe as 'no bigger than your parlour' need not mean that it was at all unambitious. The accounts mention paying £183 18s. for the wall round it,

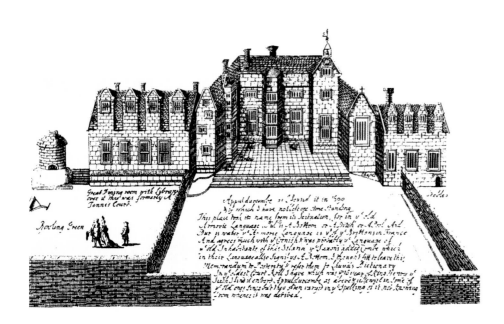

LEFT The Bowling Green was an important enough element of the gardens around the Tudor house to be labelled on this view published in 1781 in Sir Richard Worsley's *History of the Isle of Wight*.

RIGHT This is the approach to the house that 'Capability' Brown envisaged, although the stone basin was added later.

while a small-scale map drawn by Andrews later in the century in 1769 shows rectangular flower beds, which could have contained the rare plants sent by Robert's brother, Henry, a diplomat, who travelled to Spain, Portugal and Barbados. The garden was an on-going preoccupation for Sir Robert. He wrote to Henry in 1717: 'I have a great deal of planting to see done, which is at present my reigning folly'; and he went on to discuss varieties of melon and setting out

jasmine, but refuses the offer of orange and lemon trees, as they 'require fire in my Greenhouse'.

Little remains from this early eighteenth-century period (except a stone gateway, known as the Hampton Court Gate, now moved from its original place) and it is not clear where the hothouses and melon pits were, but there is evidence that beyond the formal garden was a 'new park', with walks and an oval basin.

Sir Robert was succeeded by his cousin, James Worsley, and it was James's grandson Richard who inherited, very young, in 1768 and, in the next decade, modernized the house and grounds. Again the architect who made changes to the house and designed the Freemantle Gate, a triumphal arch over what was then the main entrance drive, is not known for certain, but it was probably James Wyatt, the most fashionable architect of the day.

Sir Richard, a noted art collector and author of a history of the Isle of Wight, also expanded the park, probably working by himself at first. A survey and plan of the estate, prepared in 1773 by William Watts, show many changes from the 1769 map. The formal garden and the wall around the house have disappeared and everything has been opened up to a picturesque landscape with a serpentine drive, eye-catchers and clumps of trees to emphasize distant features of the terrain and a stream widened to give an expanse of water. All was designed to make the park appear larger than it really was – and more interesting. This work may have allowed for the retention of earlier landscaping carried out by Sir Robert Worsley, and one of the eye-catchers was a 70-foot (21.35m) obelisk erected in his memory in 1774. Also from this period is Cook's Castle, a Gothick 'ruin' set as an eye-catcher some way away on the downs; and, during this phase, Sir Richard built an ice house to the west of the house and planted fruit trees in a new walled garden to the east, out of sight of the house. But the Watts map was changed later, and it is not easy to tell what was there in 1773 and what was done soon after.

Although much of this work was Brownian in its aesthetic, Sir Richard did not actually bring in 'Capability' Brown (see page 89) until 1779. An unusual reverse ha-ha to the south-east is perhaps the most striking element that can definitely be attributed to Brown, and he also planted certain clumps of trees. Brown, who was later paid £52 10s. for travel expenses and his subsequent plan for 'alterations of the Place', was then coming to the end of his career and Appuldurcombe does not seem to have been one of his most inventive efforts, even though that great theorist of the picturesque William Gilpin wrote of it approvingly.

Scandal hit the Worsleys in 1782 when Sir Richard accused his wife of adultery. The resulting trial reflected credit on

neither party; they separated and Sir Richard went abroad for several years. After his return, one of Brown's collaborators, Samuel Lapidge, continued working at Appuldurcombe. As late as 1792 he was corresponding with Sir Richard, apparently about a plan for cultivating vines there. 'I am highly pleased with your vineyard business,' Lapidge wrote, '& you cannot do better than attend to the man that came from France to do it properly for you & then success will attend it.'

When Richard Worsley died in 1805, Appuldurcombe was inherited by his niece Henrietta, who married Charles Pelham. The house and park had begun to look unfashionable again and the Pelhams made changes to both. An inner park with walks was created around the house, separated from the Outer Park by a ha-ha on the south and west sides, and a wall or an iron fence running round the other sides. Shrubberies in the Reptonian manner (see page 117), including a rhododendron collection, were planted to the south, and exotic trees near the house. Later a stone basin with a small fountain was set into the lawn in front of the east façade, as were some rather bitty flower beds, which can be seen in nineteenth-century photographs. Inevitably, all these Regency-style introductions changed Brown's concept of a great house arising from green lawns.

After Charles Pelham inherited Brocklesby Park in Lincolnshire in 1823 and became Lord Yarborough, the family mainly lived there, coming to Appuldurcombe only in the summer. His death in 1846 marked the beginning of Appuldurcombe's decline. Within five years his son began to sell off the profitable parts of the estate, until only the house and Inner Park, dominated by its trees, remained. A failed hotel had been turned by 1867 into a school, which lasted until the 1890s (the tennis courts made on the lawns then were still visible in the 1980s). At some point in this period the poet Gerard Manley Hopkins visited Appuldurcombe and made some drawings there; he mentions it in his 1878 poem 'The Loss of the Eurydice'. In 1901 the house became a temporary home for the exiled monks of the great Benedictine abbey of Solesmes, expelled from France by anti-clerical laws, but after the monks moved to Quarr Abbey on the other side of the island in 1908 it was left empty.

In the 1930s Appuldurcombe was owned by a Mr Henry Bury, but, in spite of a campaign, encouraged by Queen Mary, to save it, the great house seems to have remained uninhabited and gently deteriorated until the German mine brought catastrophe on 7 February 1943. Although it did not fall on the house itself but near the ice house, it was close enough to make the already failing roof unsafe.

In 1952 the Historic Buildings and Monuments Commission for England accepted responsibility for Appuldurcombe House and park, and the decision was taken to consolidate rather than demolish the house. Then the Royal Parks seem to have become involved, as they did at Osborne, for in October 1962 the Superintendent of the Royal Parks sent a memo to the Royal Parks Bailiff referring to the trees around the house. 'Two large mature plus Austrian Pine grow on the South East side of the mansion, they are completely out of place and ugly, they spoil the amenity of the tree and shrub bank in the rear which is probably all that remains of the Capability Brown plan,' he wrote, adding forlornly that, 'everything of note is old and dying.'

More positive in his tone, he refers to the original early nineteenth-century line of rhododendrons, and recommends the famous garden at Exbury, just across the

Solent, as a source for replacements. On 9 December 1970 a single specimen *Rhododendron* 'Loderi King George' was ordered from William Carter in Marlborough at a cost of £26 5s. This great expense was presumably justified by its size: it was to be 7–8 feet high and 7–8 feet wide (over 2m square).

In 1980 Elizabeth Banks, then with landscape architects Land Use Consultants, was asked to prepare a restoration report. Her summary of the situation was bleak. 'All the design factors have disappeared and as a result the landscape is disturbing and unsatisfactory. The initial impression is one of gloom and despondency . . .'

After English Heritage took over in 1984, it was decided to restore the garden to its third phase, that of the Yarboroughs. They were the last people to live at Appuldurcombe as a family, and it was felt they had not

BELOW AND RIGHT By the late twentieth century, the house had become a shell, the Freemantle Gate was standing in the middle of fields and the obelisk had been truncated.

changed the eighteenth-century park too drastically when they created their Regency landscape.

Jobs scheduled for April 1991 included 'set up Croquet Court and Clock Golf', which scarcely looks as though serious restoration was under way (luckily perhaps, this instruction seems not to have been implemented). During the following winter, work was carried out on the Shrub Border. This involved pruning existing shrubs, cutting back herbaceous plants and re-edging the bed to its original shape with a half-moon tool. The gaps were then replanted with shrubs such as *Lavandula spica*, *Rosa rugosa* and *R. rubrifolia*, *Cytisus scoparius* and *C. purpureus*, *Lonicera tatarica*, *Viburnum opulus* and *V. acerifolium*, and *Mahonia aquifolium*.

At its apogee the estate had 100 acres (40.5ha) and four entrance lodges. Today, only 12 acres (4.8ha) are open to visitors, roughly corresponding to the Inner Park created by the Yarboroughs. Apart from this area, maintained by English Heritage, Appuldurcombe is in the hands of a distant relation of the Worsleys, who runs a falconry centre in the stables. The parkland is a mixture of fields and enclosed downland, in the middle of which are Wyatt's Freemantle Gate and the remains of the obelisk (which was struck by lightning in 1831 and then capped at about half its former height). There is no trace of Cook's Castle, which was demolished in the mid-twentieth century, although the ice house and walled garden are in good condition. Even the simple gate near one of the lodges, which until recent years allowed visitors to enter the nineteenth-century Inner Park and approach the magnificent east front of the house first, as Brown intended, has been closed. Nowadays, one slinks in at the back via the stables.

But all this seems in keeping with Appuldurcombe's character. While many great houses in England have managed to keep their parks, internal decoration and even furnishings more or less intact, here instead we have one that is typical of the many marvels that have been lost, through war or bankruptcy or sheer lack of appreciation. Except that Appuldurcombe is not quite lost. It has its own special atmosphere. Some find it eerily sinister, others deeply romantic.

Wrest Park

BEDFORDSHIRE

REST PARK is a real treat and quite unique, a single garden cradling three hundred years of rare surviving features – canals, parterres, serpentine waterways, formal woodland compartments, intriguing buildings and classical statuary. That all this survives is thanks to many generations of one garden-loving family, each of whom added their own stamp yet also preserved the contribution of their predecessors.

At Wrest's heart is a long, straight, Versailles-esque canal, known as the Long Water, which stretches down the main axis from the house. This was created for Anthony and Mary de Grey, the 11th Earl and Countess of Kent, who from 1671 were improving their home, medieval in origin, with a new classical front. In this they were helped by the Dowager Countess, Amabel, wife of the 10th Earl, whose

LEFT The early eighteenth-century pavilion makes a stunning end to the Long Water.
BELOW The view from the house over the nineteenth-century parterre and down the Long Water to the woodland gardens beyond.

signature is on the surviving bills for the building work. Amabel's money also allowed the parkland to be expanded to the north, south and west, and no doubt she was also involved in the creation of stunning formal gardens that included a grand walled garden, wildernesses for taking wooded walks in (one of blackthorn, one of yew), fountains, parterres, a terrace walk and, of course, the Long Water.

Anthony died in 1702 and was succeeded by his son Henry, raised to the title of duke in 1710. He had boundless enthusiasm for improving the gardens in a style appropriate to his status. It is thought that initially the garden projects were a collaboration between the duke, his gardener (John Duell) and designers Thomas Ackres, and George London and his partner Henry Wise, with later and more innovative works in the 1730s involving Batty Langley and Thomas Wright. The gardens at Wrest are widely recognized to have Dutch resonances, including the use of canals, topiary and walks, and this is not surprising given that Henry had visited the Netherlands and admired its gardens. Historians also argue convincingly that Dutch references such as statuary of William III (and of Neptune, who was often used to symbolize him) are part of a political iconography designed to convey sympathy for William and Whig politics.

The Dutch connection was compounded in 1729 when Henry married Sophia Bentinck, daughter of Hans Bentinck, the 1st Duke of Portland, who had been the Superintendent of William III's gardens in England and the Netherlands. Sophia came to have a great hand in the gardens' development and a letter of 1734 survives in which she gives a progress report to her husband in his absence:

> It has been a great pleasure to me my dear Lord when once you were gone to see you had such fine weather for your journey which I hope now will continue not only for your harvest but for getting your gardens in the order you desire which the people are very busy about. They are now cutting away the grass behind the Black-moors statues and I hope both that and the gravel slope will be done quickly. Carter was here yesterday about the iron gate at the bottom of John Duel's walk. He said that the gate you intended putting there would not do well and proposed doing it in another manner but that one way or another he could not possibly have it done this week so I thought it best to let it quite alone till after this week and till you can give directions about it yourself and wish he gets the gate done at the end of the terrace as he promises

to do by Friday but not being at work at it yet I was vexed to have them lose this fine weather towards finishing the painting it and sent after him again today.

Under Henry the far end of the Long Water, which had previously been punctuated with a decorative iron screen, was embellished with a baroque pavilion, in front of which stands a celebratory statue of William III in classical garb, possibly by sculptor John Nost. The pavilion is ornate, with a grey domed roof, steep stone steps up to a grand entrance, and a complicated arrangement of both curved and angular bay windows protruding from a central circular hallway. It was used for entertainments, sometimes even for breakfasting, and inside is a round room with little doors leading to smaller chambers on the outside, all beautifully decorated with wall and ceiling trompe l'oeil painted by French artist Louis Hauduroy, the only public examples of his work in this country. Painfully narrow twisting stone staircases lead up to tiny rooms, from where occupants can gaze over the surrounding gardens. All this was designed by Thomas Archer, an English architect heavily influenced by his own European travels. Archer also designed and built Hill House, a cruciform eye-catcher on the top of nearby Cain Hill, part of the Wrest Park estate. This was an important element of the gardens' design and the much-loved focus of many family diversions but was unfortunately demolished in the 1830s.

A glimpse into Wrest at this time, bustling with tree planting and construction projects, is given by a letter from the Earl of Harrold to Henry, written in 1716:

> [I] was very glad to hear of all the familys continuance in good health at Rest [sic], I cannot but think you must have found the stay there very agreeable, considering the fine weather which usually reigns in this month. My Sister Bell has amused me very agreeably in one of her last Letters, with an account of the sev'ral alterations so much for the better Yr Grace has lately made there, as the filling up on Mr Ackres cannal, and making a hansome terrass in the room of it answering to it on the other side, which leads to the Hill House; I must confess I was ever of Opinion that such a walk would be much more noble by reason that the Gardens are enlarged by it and must make things look more of a piece; I've heard nothing how the trees prosper upon Cane Hill, which I was often inquisitive about, as it is one of my favourite places and for which I

used to interest my self preferably to any of the others. In short I believe all will be so considerably changed, by the Growth of the trees, and the sev'ral improvements that have been made since my departure from thence, that I shall be able to entertain but a faint Idea of ye place.

At right angles to the Long Water Henry created sharply defined rectangular pools much enjoyed by his wife's ornamental wildfowl. That to the east was called Ladies' Lake and that to the west was the Bowling Green Lake. Adjoining the Bowling Green Lake was an amphitheatre, a fashionable eighteenth-century garden feature in which terraces were cut into the turf rather like huge earth sculptures. Later this flooded and merged into the lake, the ensuing shape inspiring a new name of Leg o'Mutton Lake, until English Heritage reinstated its original rectangle in the late twentieth century, taking the view that this area was most appropriately presented in its eighteenth-century form. By the side of the lake, reflected in its surface, is Henry's bowling green, surrounded with gravel paths and tall yew

hedges trained into arches. The focus of the green is a dainty white building in which bowlers would have taken refreshments, beautifully designed with a classical colonnaded front. This banqueting house's present appearance is believed to be the result of a remodelling by Batty Langley, who is also thought to be responsible for the amphitheatre, perhaps with help from his friend Lord Burlington of Chiswick House (see page 68).

Around the Long Water Henry set out a massive woodland garden through which formal allées splayed out in sharp lines, intertwined with serpentine paths. This whole was surrounded by more formal canals, and by the parkland beyond. Today, Wrest has matured into a mysterious realm where huge trees and rampant undergrowth frame paths beckoning into the distance. Alas, it often suffers from a mud problem, as the secrets of the gardens' complex but antique

BELOW The Bowling Green lake, with the yew-framed green beyond.

drainage system are largely shielded by undergrowth. The walks are punctuated with features such as the Hutton Monument, a tombstone-like commemoration of Thomas Hutton, a friend of the de Greys, as they liked to remember people special to them in the gardens. Some of these features are arranged within leafy compartments or 'garden rooms', particularly striking examples of which are the East and West Sand Rounds – large circular clearings then with a sandy surface, both with an urn in the centre. Also noteworthy is the Duke's Square, an open glade which was framed by clipped hedges with alcoves for urns and statues such as cherubs and pastoral figures, as well as a central obelisk dedicated to Henry himself.

In this period as others, statuary played an important role in Wrest's gardens, pieces being acquired from some of the age's most celebrated sculptors. Subjects included the seasons, Venus, Queen Anne, and a basin, with Neptune being supported by wyverns representing the Grey family – most probably a statement of the Grey family's support for William III.

In the west part of the woodland Henry created Lady Duchess' Square, an oval hedged glade which also contained urns, seats, busts and a striking central column with a pineapple finial. The main focus here today is a brick alcove with a seat (much appreciated by visitors, who can easily spend a day under Wrest's trees) and a statue that was probably added in the nineteenth century and is believed to be of Henry's granddaughter Jemima.

Henry died in 1740 and Wrest Park passed to Jemima, with a specially created title of Marchioness Grey. Jemima embraced the gardens, in which she had grown up, and rejoiced in adding new features to the existing structure, with the help of her husband, Phillip Yorke, Earl of Hardwick. Phillip and Jemima were married when they were still both young, mainly in order to satisfy her grandfather and inherit Wrest, but it seems they were well matched. One of their many common interests was a love of Wrest, evident in a letter from Jemima to Mary Gregory, a young relation with whom she grew up at Wrest, in which she describes Phillip's first encounter with it:

> We did not arrive here till Seven, . . . as the Sun was but just set & it was perfectly calm & fine, it was exactly the Time I think the most pleasant of the whole Day. The Sereneness of the Evening Light spread a peculiar Beauty over the whole Place. We had a short but a very pretty Walk by Owl-

Light & Moonlight together. Mr. Yorke desires I would assure you that what he has seen of the Garden he admired mightily, & should have been extremely glad if you could have shewn it him. He has been taking a Walk with Mr. Longueville whilst I was dressing, which I did not at all allow of, for I wanted to have been with him every Time he was to see anything in the Garden.

Jemima and Phillip also shared an intellectual sense of humour, which was reflected in some of the features they added to the garden. They created the Mithraic Glade, in which was placed a large flint and stone 'altar' to the Persian sun god Mithras, decorated with indecipherable markings. Accompanying the altar was a rustic root house built of stone and wood (now gone), which claimed to be the home of the Priest of the Altar, and Jemima also had plans for an 'Eolus's Harp to hang up among the Trees'. These ideas were very much in keeping with the contemporary enthusiasm for garden features with a 'Picturesque' quality, in which a romantically rustic atmosphere with a touch of classicism or mythicism was considered highly desirable. In 1748 Lady Anson wrote to Jemima with an anecdote of how visitors had been fooled by the altar's false antiquity, and no doubt this would have given the couple much amusement:

I must inform your Ladyship that the Duchess of Bedford, with a Party, have been at Wrest since you left it, in order to shew it to Lady Louisa Trentham. They were at the Hill-House by Day-light, they say, but walked over the Garden by Moon-shine; however they saw enough to excite their Curiosity extremely as to the Altar, & taking it for an Antiquity, at least in its shape & design, they went home & turned over Montfaccion & Kennet, but without success, & the Duchess had applied to me, since her coming to Town, for some explanation of it – But perhaps your Ladyship has heard all this already in Staffordshire.

In the same fantastical vein, Jemima and Phillip created a ruined bath house, a huddle of two rough ironstone huts in a watery setting among pools, a spring, a cascade and an elfin bridge. Although it still survives, now hidden behind the nineteenth-century orangery, little is known about the creation of this interesting building, with sources attributing it variously to 'Capability' Brown, Sir William Chambers or, most probably, Chambers's pupil Edward Stevens, using a design by his tutor.

Jemima also made one significant change to the gardens' structure, bringing in 'Capability' Brown to soften their edges by 'naturalizing' the outer canals into a more modern serpentine style. To commemorate the involvement of the famous landscape designer they erected the Capability Brown Column, a bizarre tapered Doric column, with two rusticated blocks seemingly wedged halfway up, and topped by a pineapple. Jemima did not have much affection for Brown, which is perhaps the reason for the slightly ridiculous

LEFT An urn acts as an ornamental focal point at the end of a woodland walk.
RIGHT The indecipherable Mithraic Altar was a great joke for Jemima and Phillip.

LETTER FROM WREST

Amabel Grey to her mother, Jemima, Marchioness Grey, 13 May 1774

Wrest is in high beauty, & look'd particularly well on Tuesday evening which was remarkably pleasant with us, & Ld. P. says was rather the contrary in town. But I must acknowledge, we are deficient in flowery shrubs, particularly lilacs. Those near the walk from the bridge, look as if they had been cut with the rest of the underwood, & bear no flowers. I shall ask about them. But as to nightingales we will stand the contest with Richmond, for we have several near the house, & the thicket on Cane Hill is full of them: one entertain'd us for a quarter of an hour on Tuesday evening. The Hill is cover'd with such a profusion of Cowslips, orchids & blue-bells, that it is more a garden than the garden itself. A large & fine magnolia is come & as we were afraid of its staying out of the ground, or rather Mr. Thorpe was afraid, it was planted in what would be the middle of my old garden, if the Sand Walk was away, without writing to you for orders. But Mr. Thorpe desires to know whether you would have that Sand-Walk be taken away, for my part I think it might, even though you did not divide the ground, according to the pattern you first intended. He wants to know whether you would have the four Burgundy Roses he has got, stay in pots or be put into the ground, but if they were, it would not be safe to move them, & perhaps you had better stay till you had fix'd upon a pattern for the flower beds. He could not get as many roses as you desir'd for this is not a time of the year when the gardeners have plenty: they are generally bought & sold in Autumn. A swan is setting near the water that runs from the bridge, & I suppose must be let alone, though I doubt whether her setting will succeed.

design of the column. In 1779 she wrote to her daughter, Lady Bell Polwarth:

> Indeed if he [Brown] does as he promises, consider of & mark trees for cutting both in the Grove & middle part, & look over the Kitchen Garden, it would take him up the Hours of Daylight, but I wish you was not to be troubled an Evening with him. I can only recommend that as he is Every Thing, Politician, (Divine for ought I know) Farmer, Architect, Lover of Virtue, you may set him upon any subject, or throw Books in his way, & show him your Sketches & Drawings, and there is besides a copious fund on the subject of Two Great Men of Luton & Hayes, whom he really does know a good deal of if he is disposed to be communicative. As to his Idea about the Grove what I could collect is that it must be left to him upon the Spot, but in general that he would try to Unsquare it, (as I should do) would take of Formal purpose, or cut through, irregularly, the corner towards the Old Park, & break in the Outlines, particularly towards the Parterre where the Shadows are so strong.

The naturalized canals provided the perfect setting for yet another of their inventive ideas: the re-creation of a willow pattern scene, no doubt as part of the fashion for chinoiserie (a pseudo-Chinese style encouraged by new explorations in that country). As so often seen on eighteenth-century chinaware, the composition was made of a gently sloping wooden Chinese bridge (rebuilt in rather un-oriental brick in the nineteenth century); a squat temple with a pointed roof, made using a design by William Chambers, a leading proponent of chinoiserie; a conch water feature in which a small waterfall dropped into a shell some 3 feet (almost 1m) wide; a languid willow tree (alas, lost to winds in 1950) and a tulip tree (*Liriodendron tulipifera*).

After Jemima's death in 1797, Wrest passed to her daughter Amabel ('Bell'), who had been much involved in the gardens during her mother's lifetime. Sadly, though, perhaps her most enduring legacy was to make the brave decision to sell off most of the original lead statues in order to raise money during a financial crisis at the beginning of the nineteenth century, partly to help support the poor. This process, not without mishap, was described to her in 1809 in a letter from Wrest's steward Lewis Harrison:

I am sorry to say, that most of the Images your Ladyship wishes to have remained, have been melted down, excepting King William & Diana at the Building & the two gilt Urns near the House. I clearly understood your Ladyship Queen Anne was one of the number desired to have been taken down, & the Bacchus & Plenty which were much disfigured & defaced. The third Diana at the head of the Little Canal is yet standing. I hope it will not be of much consequence the others were removed, and the more so, as they may be re-erected at half the expence of other materials should conceive, than the lead sold for. I think your Ladyship will call to mind having personally shewn me Queen Anne, & saying 'Let it go too'.

Amabel did, however, also make few additions, such as five antique 'Graeco-Roman' altars within one of Henry's woodland glades, very much in keeping with the traditions of her parents and great-grandparents.

When Amabel died, Wrest passed in 1833 to Thomas de Grey, her nephew. Thomas was a very accomplished amateur architect (founding President of the Institute of British Architects – now known as the RIBA) and must have had a fantastic time making Wrest his own. Thomas demolished the old house and built a new one in the style of a French château on the same axis but 650 feet (200m) further to the north, where there had previously been specimen tree planting. This allowed him to leave the Long Water and woodland, but add a French-style parterre that he had personally designed in order to link the new house to the older gardens. De Grey was to say of his creation here, known now as the South Parterre: 'The pattern of the French Garden is certainly rather out of the common course. Whether it will produce the good effect that the fertile brain of its author has contemplated remains to be seen; but at all events it is original and novel and not as yet hackneyed and common place.'

The parterre is a grand one with scroll-shaped flower beds, their bright flowers striking against the base of green grass, and lead statues (made to look like stone) of mythological figures: Venus and Adonis; Diana and Endymion; Aeneas and family; and Helen and Paris. A path leads down the centre to lawns marked with clipped Portuguese laurel (*Prunus lusitanica*), originally in ornamental planters and intended to be restored sometime in the future. It then meets a circular marble fountain in which four figures sit in the shelter of a shallow basin. Placed all around are statues of figures such as Ceres, Venus, Cato, Iris, the Tragic and Comic Muses, Flora and Pomona. Broad lawns, now partly used for croquet, then run down to

BELOW FROM LEFT TO RIGHT The ruined bath house, romantic creation of Jemima and Phillip; the Capability Brown Column; and the 'Chinese' temple, an essential component of a Chinoiserie scene.

the Long Water with the pavilion beyond. Needless to say, the view of this composition from the house's raised terrace is stunning.

To the west, and reached by another straight gravel path, is a glamorous orangery, to make which Thomas took down a Batty Langley greenhouse and built it on a slightly different footprint, raised on defined architectural banks. The style of this lovely building is complementary to that of the house, with a balustraded roof, grey domes at each end and high arched doors (although not high enough for the orange trees, which instead had to be wheeled in for the winter through concealed doors at the side). The trees were apparently good croppers, as well as highly decorative features, being arranged at the bottom of the banks in the summer.

Thomas also made a large 6-acre (2.4ha) walled kitchen garden, divided into different areas variously for ornament; vegetables, fruit and flowers; service buildings and glasshouses (of which the fig house survives); and frames and pits. The walled garden was a very smart affair indeed, with rather grand gates and a head gardener's house that looks like a little turret. This productive area was very close to the house, attached to the west end of which de Grey built a splendid conservatory, filled with fancies such as oranges, camellias, geraniums, cacti and fuchsias. In between the conservatory and the kitchen garden de Grey laid out an 'Italian' flower garden, so that his wife would have a lovely view from her conservatory seat across the flowers, through a little gate, and to the fruit and vegetables beyond. Running down one outside wall of the kitchen garden, linking the park to the front of the house to the gardens at the back, he made Strangers' Gate Walk, a turf path edged with a beautiful border of shrubs and herbaceous plants, with roses, clematis and honeysuckle climbing up the brick wall behind.

At the east end of the house Thomas made a tiny gabled wooden cottage with a small hedged front garden, called Le Petit Trianon, after Mme de Pompadour's château at Versailles. Next to this he also built an ornamental dairy in a

LEFT Thomas de Grey bought eighteenth-century lead figures (made to look like stone) for his parterre.

RIGHT ABOVE Thomas de Grey demolished the old house, of medieval origin, but built a new one 650 feet (200m) to the north, on the same axis.

RIGHT BELOW A collection of statues is displayed between the parterre and the Long Water.

BELOW The nineteenth-century orangery sits on a sharply defined bank.
OPPOSITE LEFT Lady de Grey had a lovely view from her seat in the conservatory, across the Italian flower garden and into the kitchen garden.
OPPOSITE RIGHT ABOVE Le Petit Trianon, a cottage designed primarily for play.
OPPOSITE RIGHT BELOW The ornamental dairy, intended more for fanciful entertainment than for serious food production.

Swiss style, making this corner of Wrest reminiscent of the Swiss Cottage and gardens created by Prince Albert at Osborne House on the Isle of Wight (see page 98).

Thomas died in 1859 and became the last burial in the family mausoleum at nearby Flitton church. This astonishing edifice is Tardis-like in the way that the exterior belies the interior: the outside is a simple if beautiful white building but the inside is an otherworldly chamber containing the tombs of the Grey family as far back as the 6th Earl of Kent, who founded the mausoleum in around 1605.

Wrest was inherited by Thomas's daughter, Baroness Lucas, widow of Earl Cowper, and although she did not use it as her main residence, it was the venue for lavish house parties, particularly those involving the Souls, one of the leading social sets of the time. From 1905 to 1911 the house

was let to the US Ambassador, who used the house as his country residence and also entertained many important guests there. During the First World War Wrest was used as a military hospital before being damaged by fire, but after the death of the 8th Baron Lucas – a fighter pilot, shot down over the trenches – it was sold out of the family to John George Murray, an industrialist from the north-east with colliery and brewing interests. In 1934 Murray sold parts of the parkland to the Essex Timber Company, sounding the death knell for Wrest's once leafy setting, as the majority of the park and avenue trees were felled for timber, leaving a rather barren landscape. Much of the statuary was sold to Philip Sassoon of Trent Park in Middlesex and finally in 1939 Murray sold the house, gardens and remaining park to the Sun Insurance Company as their wartime headquarters.

Eventually, though, Wrest was bought after the Second World War by the Ministry of Works, who rented it to the National Institute of Agricultural Engineering. As the Silsoe Research Institute it occupied the site until only very recently, but after extensive negotiations English Heritage is now in sole control of the house and gardens (much of the parkland is owned by local farmers). A thorough masterplan has been compiled to manage Wrest's future, with English Heritage determined to 'conserve and re-present Wrest Park in order to reaffirm its place as one of Britain's most beautiful and complete historic landscape gardens'. Restoration and improvement works are already under way and so the future is bright for this astonishing place and the many layers of its historic landscape.

Chiswick House

LONDON

*T*HE NAME of Chiswick House is one that resonates across the world, the influence of its architecture and garden design having been felt through many centuries and in many countries. Architecturally, this influence took the form of raising the classicist Palladian style to fresh popularity; in garden terms Chiswick was consistently ahead of its time, and is particularly important as a testing ground for the ideas of William Kent, one of the key figures of the English landscape park movement.

Credit for this must go to its owner-creator, a young aristocrat and patron of the arts, Richard Boyle, the 3rd Earl of Burlington. During his lifetime, creative figures such as Alexander Pope, John Gay, Jonathan Swift, David Garrick,

Georg Handel and William Kent all benefited from Burlington's friendship and support, making Chiswick a wonderfully vibrant and cultural place. Epic poet Alexander Pope refers to the wide influence of Burlington in his 'An Epistle to the Right Honourable Richard Earl of Burlington' of 1731, establishing Burlington as an exemplar of good taste against which not everyone matches up:

BELOW Lord Burlington's formal pools and temple, painted by Pieter Andreas Rysbrack, *c*.1728–31.
RIGHT An avenue from the house, lined with urns and clipped trees.

Yet shall (my Lord) your just, your noble rules
Fill half the land with imitating fools;
Who random drawings from your sheets shall take,
And of one beauty many blunders make,
Load some vain church with old theatric state,
Turn arcs of triumph to a garden gate;
Reverse your ornaments, and hang them all
On some patch'd dog-hole ek'd with ends of wall;
Then clap four slices of pilaster on't,
That lac'd with bits of rustic, makes a front.
Or call the winds through long arcades to roar,
Proud to catch cold at a Venetian door;
Conscious they act a true Palladian part,
And, if they starve, they starve by rules of art.

Richard Boyle had inherited the title of 3rd Earl of Burlington in 1704 when he was only ten years old and Chiswick became his when he came of age in 1715. It had been in the Boyle family since his grandfather bought it in 1682 and was essentially a Jacobean villa with gardens consisting of various separate walled enclosures, pleasant but unsophisticated. Burlington was to use it only as a part-time residence, a good base for entertaining (the main family home being Burlington House, now the Royal Academy of Arts, on Piccadilly in central London).

The Earl had just returned from a Grand Tour of Europe that incorporated France, Belgium, the Netherlands, Germany, Switzerland and Italy, where it is likely that he saw gardens belonging to the Italian villas Borghese, Mondragone and Aldobrandini, as well as those at the French palaces Versailles and Fontainebleau. This had fed but certainly not satiated an appetite for design and architecture, so his timely inheritance was an ideal recipient for his knowledge and ideas.

LEFT The Orange Tree Garden.
BELOW The *patte d'oie* with an allée leading to the Bagnio in the centre and another leading to the domed building that John Mackay called a 'Heathen Temple'. Painted by Pieter Andreas Rysbrack, *c*.1728–31.

In his new gardens Burlington did away with the Jacobean walled enclosures, introducing instead interpretations of the classical style of garden, possibly with help from landscape designer Charles Bridgeman (although historians' debate on this has so far proved inconclusive). To the west of the house alongside a natural source of water called Bollo Brook he carved from the ground two highly formal basins of water – long rectangular pools defined with angular edges and curved apsed ends. The pools were surrounded by lines of trees seemingly planted in cubic turf mounds and a contemporary painting shows one to be overlooked by a porticoed temple. Burlington also planted a grove of trees in a tight formation by the house, and built a rather smart little deer house that is still standing today, centuries after any animals used it, if indeed they ever did.

Burlington also created a now celebrated orange tree garden in which a crisp turf amphitheatre surrounded an obelisk in a circular pool, accompanied by an Ionic temple, as recorded by Flemish artist Pieter Andreas Rysbrack in *c*.1728–31. According to Rysbrack, the amphitheatre was dotted with dozens of standard orange trees in white wooden tubs (perhaps moved to the temple over winter), and specimen birds such as peacocks, pheasants and ducks added animation. Today this garden still remains, although the birds do not.

Lord Burlington's Chiswick was to be particularly notable for the way he ornamented it with little buildings, real

architectural treats. Most significant was the placing of such buildings at the end of a *patte d'oie*, a splayed 'goosefoot' arrangement of three allées of tall clipped hedges and uniform trees – possibly the first time (but certainly not the last) that this was done in garden design. In 1724 in *A Journey through England*, traveller John Macky described how 'Every walk terminates with some little building, one with a Heathen Temple, for instance the Pantheon, another a little villa, where my Lord often designs instead of his House, . . . another walk terminates with a Portico, in imitation of Covent Garden Church.'

The 'Heathen Temple' Macky mentions was a domed building with tetrastyle portico, rusticated bays and Corinthian pillars. It is not clear who the architect was, but candidates are James Gibbs or Burlington himself. The 'little villa' was in fact a *bagnio*, which Burlington himself designed in 1717. This was, as its Italian name suggests, intended as an amusing bathhouse, and was a rather splendid building, with two storeys topped by a lantern and ornamented with urns. Architect Colen Campbell published a clear drawing of it in his *Vitruvius Britannicus*, writing that the Bagnio was 'the first Essay of his Lordship's happy Invention'; and Burlington must have liked it very much because he used it as a drawing office in which to work on his many other architectural projects. The Rustic Arch is a small building with an arched entrance, whose crude 'rusticated' exterior belies an elegant interior including niches for sculptures. The Rustic Arch still stands today, but the domed temple and the Bagnio became victims to fashion and were both demolished by a later owner, only decades after they were constructed. To the side of the *patte d'oie* stood a Doric column topped with a copy of the Venus dei Medici and this too survives.

In 1727 Burlington was able to acquire Sutton Court, the estate neighbouring Chiswick, and could therefore create further gardens to the west of the villa. These were based around two more *pattes d'oie*, one of which still exists, spanning out from the Burlington Gate where there is an obelisk incorporating a classical relief that Burlington had owned since 1712.

In 1719 Burlington made a second trip to Italy, during which he met an English painter called William Kent. They hit it off so well that Kent ended his lengthy Italian stay to come back with Burlington to Chiswick, where he was to play a significant role, carrying out a great deal of work on the gardens. Indeed, it was largely through William Kent's involvement that the gardens of Chiswick came to be so influential, as having explored his ideas at Chiswick, he went on to be a major player in the English landscape park

movement that spread through England and then the world, changing the face of gardens from that of formality to a more naturalistic style. Kent's standing at Chiswick was such that when he died in 1748 he was buried in the Boyle family vault.

In 1726 Burlington began his largest garden building, the villa itself. His creation, the product of an informed yet original mind, is an exciting Palladian villa with a cream and slate octagonal dome rising from a relatively small building to which oversized staircases and a large Parthenon-esque portico add a quirky character. This was built next to the original house and later joined to it with a two-storey link building before the old house was eventually demolished in 1788. Ever since it was built, this villa has captured the imagination of all who see it, mainly because although of grand appearance it is actually diminutive and also rather

OPPOSITE FROM LEFT TO RIGHT The deer house built by Lord Burlington, the Rustic Arch and the obelisk at the Burlington Gate.
BELOW In 1727 Lord Burlington acquired his neighbour's land and was able to create more gardens to the west of his villa, shown in this painting by Pieter Andreas Rysbrack, *c.*1728–31.

ABOVE Lord Burlington's cascade, in an engraving of 1750.
LEFT The cascade, in full working order.

on Saturday to see the Chain pump work up the spring, the water comes in to the river very fast but it dry's [sic] up in a minute.' This cascade has recently been restored after falling out of use in past decades.

After a life in which his influence had established classicism, or Palladianism, as the dominant architectural style in England and in which he had sowed the seeds for a new style of gardening with his championing of William Kent, Lord Burlington died in 1753, leaving behind his wife, Dorothy, and daughter, Charlotte. The estate was inherited by Charlotte's husband William Cavendish, the 4th Duke of Devonshire and owner of Chatsworth in Derbyshire. Their son, the 5th Duke, then inherited in 1764 and decided to push the villa into a full-blown country mansion, adding new wings, while demolishing the lingering Jacobean house. Outside, he brought in Samuel Lapidge, once assistant to the more famous 'Capability' Brown, to continue Kent's work in easing the gardens away from

overt artificiality towards the fashionable landscape style. Lapidge toned down the formal allées and vistas, filled in the apsed basins and demolished ornamental buildings such as the Bagnio and Domed Building. Near the Bagnio's site was built a smart stone bridge with balustrading and a gracious arch over the river, probably designed by either James Wyatt or James Paine.

The 6th Duke of Devonshire inherited Chiswick in 1811 and enlarged it by acquiring the next-door estate of Moreton Hall. The hall had been built in the 1680s for Sir Stephen Fox, a wealthy and philanthropic official of Charles II. A fashionable brick building, it was probably designed primarily by Hugh May, a leading architect who was also an inspector of gardens at Hampton Court Palace and so is likely to have played a role in those at Moreton Hall. It is possible that green-fingered diarist John Evelyn played a part, as he was a friend of Sir Stephen and his wife, Elizabeth. Whoever was responsible, the result was pleasant compartmentalized gardens, combining productivity with ornamental effect. The novelist and traveller Daniel Defoe was sufficiently impressed by Moreton Hall to state in his travel letters of the 1720s:

Sir Stephen Fox's house at Chiswick is the flower of all the private gentlemens [sic] palaces in England. Here when the late King William, who was an allowed judge of fine buildings, and of gardening also, had seen the house and garden, he stood still on the terras for near half a quarter of an hour without speaking one word, when turning at last to the Earl of Portland, the king said, 'This place is perfectly fine, I could live here five days.'

The 6th Duke demolished the Moreton Hall building itself but kept and absorbed its immense walled kitchen gardens. He also developed Chiswick's pleasure gardens, contributing the huge 300-foot (91m) conservatory, which still survives. Built in 1813 by Samuel Ware, this is a very early and therefore important example of such glass structures, which only became widespread in later decades. It has a curved frontage and domed roof and is exquisitely beautiful. Its purpose was to house exotic fruits and also camellias, at that time believed to be tender and thus requiring indoor accommodation. Some of the original camellias survive in the conservatory today.

Around the conservatory the 6th Duke had his gardener, Lewis Kennedy, design an 'Italian' garden with formal geometric beds, and this corner is still enjoyed today, its bright bedding plants providing cheer among the trees. The 6th Duke also purchased land that he let to the Horticultural Society (soon to become the Royal Horticultural Society) for a demonstration garden, with a special door in the boundary wall so that the Devonshires could slip through and enjoy the society's gardens. The society stayed at Chiswick until 1903, when the RHS Gardens at Wisley were acquired.

The 6th Duke was very sociable and a wonderful account of Chiswick in this era is provided by a sparkling guest, Prince Pückler Muskau, who was on a tour of England from his German homeland:

A pretty effect is produced at Chiswick by a single lofty tree, the stem of which has been cleared up to the very top, and from beneath which you command a view of the whole gardens and a part of the park; – a good hint to landscape gardeners . . . The cedars here . . . are celebrated, and grow to the size of old fir-trees. Colossal yew hedges also show how long this estate has been an object of extraordinary care. The new conservatories do more credit to the taste of the present possessor than the pleasure-ground. It is strange enough that orange-trees nowhere reach any great size in England. They are very 'mesquin' here. On the other hand, the flower-gardens are magnificent. The beds are so thinly planted that each separate plant has room to spread, excepting those beds which are entirely filled with one sort of flower. In them, the chief aim is the perfection of the whole, and they are consequently by far the most beautiful. In the pinery I saw, for the first time, the great Providence pines, specimens of which have been produced of twelve pounds weight.

There is a menagerie attached to the garden, in which a tame elephant performs all sorts of feats, and very quietly suffers anybody to ride him about a large grass-plat. His neighbour is a lama, of a much less gentle nature; his weapon is a most offensive saliva, which he spits out to a distance of some yards at any one who irritates him; he takes such good aim, and fires so suddenly at his antagonist, that it is extremely difficult to avoid his charge.

Chiswick has unfortunately only stagnant slimy water, which is sometimes so low that the elephant, if he were thirsty, might drink it up at a draught.

Alas, Chiswick's happiest times were drawing to a close and when the 7th Duke of Devonshire inherited in 1862, he decided to rent it out, leading almost inevitably to its gradual decline. The 4th Marquis of Bute was one impressive tenant (as was the Prince of Wales, later Edward VII) but, at the same time as Bute was resident, large parts of Chiswick's parkland were sold for housing, creating the villa's distinctly suburban setting of today. After Bute left in 1892, things continued to get worse, with Chiswick being used as a private mental hospital. In 1918 Gertrude Jekyll published many pictures of a neglected Chiswick in her book *Garden Ornament*, describing 'The fine stone bridge at Chiswick House with beautiful urns on the piers, all cruelly overgrown with Ivy'.

Eventually, in 1929, the 9th Duke sold the whole estate to Middlesex County Council, which did not immediately save it from decay but did at least protect it from further development, although it demolished the extensive stables. The villa soon passed into the hands of the Ministry of Works (which evolved into English Heritage) because, as the 1958 guidebook earnestly proclaims: 'After the war heavy expenditure on repairs was found to be necessary and in view of the architectural importance of the house it was felt that this should be the responsibility of the Government.'

In the mid-twentieth century Chiswick once more began to benefit from positive attention when a society of passionate experts, the Georgian Group, led a campaign of restoration. The villa's wings (post-Burlington additions) were demolished and in the gardens the formal *patte d'oie* recreated, although aligned slightly differently from how it was aligned in Burlington's day.

Yet in spite of this surge of energy, Chiswick continued for many years to struggle. The gardens were managed by Hounslow London Borough Council as a public open space and declined along with most of the nation's parks in the last decades of the twentieth century, because of drastic cuts in funding and gardeners when local authority funding was reprioritized following the introduction of compulsory competitive tendering for services rather than the retention of a skilled in-house staff dedicated to particular sites. Nevertheless, it continued to be very popular with over 1 million visitors per year. The villa meanwhile passed into the responsibility of English Heritage after its formation. Then in 2007 Chiswick, long exalted by garden historians, received an immense grant from the Heritage Lottery Fund. With both villa and gardens now in the ownership of the Chiswick House and Gardens Trust, it is returning to the state of its glory days.

Marble Hill House

ᴧᴜ

LONDON

*I*NTELLECTUAL SOCIETY in the eighteenth century was vibrant and fashionable and largely focused around a large clique of talented friends, composed of a heady mix of poets, architects, aristocracy and royalty. The chief focus of their creative thought was a passion for the arts and particularly classicism, and they cultivated an Arcadian life of cultural endeavours against a pastoral backdrop.

Much of royal life was at that time focused on Thameside Richmond and Twickenham, near London, as the Prince and Princess of Wales (later George II and Queen Caroline) occupied Richmond Lodge as a summer residence. The area was thus quite a social and cultural hub, becoming the haunt of wealthy, influential and creative personalities such as Lord

Ilay (a founder of the first Royal Bank of Scotland and enthusiastic tree collector), politician James Johnston, Lady Mary Wortley Montagu, the Duchess of Queensberry (who famously boasted of being able to milk a cow, a great pastoral achievement), landscape designer Batty Langley (then gardener at nearby Twickenham Park), and writers John Gay, Jonathan Swift and Alexander Pope. The latter in particular was at the heart of the area's spirit; as the translator of

BELOW Marble Hill House, seen from the River Thames in the 1740s.

RIGHT Almost the same view from the River Thames today.

Homer's *Odyssey* and *Iliad*, Pope was a great admirer of classicism, and had used it as inspiration in creating beautiful and influential gardens for himself in Twickenham.

As in the classical age that they so admired, many of these movers and shakers devoted great energies to their homes and gardens, developing a beautiful environment on the curving banks of the River Thames. Here they could enjoy each other's company, living out the pastoral Arcadian dream, playing at husbandry and creating gardens in a natural, informal style. At this time, the writer Daniel Defoe was inspired to write of Twickenham, situated on the banks of the River Thames to the south of London:

The banks of the Sein are not thus adorn'd from Paris to Roan, or from Paris to the Loign above the city: the Danube can show nothing like it above and below Vienna,

or the Po above and below Turin; the whole country here shines with a lustre not to be describ'd; take them in a remote view, the fine seats shine among the trees as jewels shine in a rich coronet; in a near sight they are meer pictures and paintings; at a distance they are all nature, near hand all art; but both in the extreamest beauty.

Today many such jewels still survive, houses such as those of Ham, Syon, York and Orleans, although sadly Pope's was demolished long ago. Nevertheless, from this cauldron of ideas the English landscape garden style grew and then spread across the world, and its legacy is still powerful today.

Henrietta Howard was a great friend of Alexander Pope's – he called her a 'pastoral lady' – and thus a central figure in the pursuit of Arcadia. She was a courtier who had been the mistress of George II for many years and when he began to tire of her (and, indeed, as she began to tire of court life), she was unusually fortunate in that he made her a number of generous gifts as a way of funding her future. A sensible woman, she used these to gain a new independence from her violent and profligate husband, Charles Howard, 9th Earl of Suffolk and owner of Audley End (page 86). Her chief requirement was, of course, a home and so in 1724 she set about building herself one, with Twickenham being the obvious choice of location.

Henrietta's talented Twickenham friends were eager to help in the creation of her new home, Marble Hill. The Earl of Ilay helped acquire the site (much of which was owned by Thomas Vernon of Twickenham Park, who was rather uncooperative towards Henrietta) and provided trees from his nearby Whitton Park, including a black walnut that survives today as one of the oldest in the country. The 3rd Earl of Peterborough was almost childlike in his enthusiastic support, while the 1st Earl Bathurst sent lime trees and the lambs so crucial to pastoral husbandry. In particular, Alexander Pope was greatly involved in designing the gardens, although Henrietta also had help from Charles Bridgeman, who was working as royal gardener to Queen

LEFT ABOVE Henrietta Howard, painted by Charles Jervas, c.1724.
LEFT BELOW The north front of Marble Hill House.
RIGHT ABOVE The black walnut tree that was given to Henrietta Howard by her friend the Earl of Ilay.
RIGHT BELOW Henrietta Howard's shell grotto, the decorative shells long gone.

Caroline at Richmond Lodge and also drew up designs for Audley End, Claremont, Blenheim and Stowe.

The result was magnificent. The villa was a Palladian gem created by architects Colen Campbell, Roger Morris and the Earl of Pembroke (the 'architect Earl' of Wilton in Wiltshire) as a practical but elegant symmetrical box with squat roof and diminutive doorway. The front of the house was edged with a curving wall to make an oval frame around the carriage circle, suggestive of two arms open to embrace and receive its many visitors. The outlook was on to a 'Great Field' down to Richmond Road, now a suburban thoroughfare but then a quiet lane linking Twickenham to Richmond.

A second front – visitors would have been likely to arrive both by river and by road – opened on to a terraced lawn framed with lines of chestnut trees that ran down to the Thames, giving a clear vista of the water, and giving the occupants of passing pleasure boats a clear view of the house. Within groves to the side were an ice house and fashionable grottoes, one of which Henrietta and her niece personally covered in shells to give it a romantic rustic look. Today the ice house still remains, tucked among some woodland daffodils, as does one of the grottoes, a flint stone cave – shells long gone – which nestles below a ring of box hedge and shielded from view by shrubberies of laurel and other evergreens. Later in life Henrietta became friends with the charismatic art critic Horace Walpole, a new resident of

the area at his quirky Gothick home Strawberry Hill, and he encouraged further development with features such as the Priory of St Hubert, a fanciful edifice purpose-built as a romantic feature.

Henrietta steadily increased her holding of the land around Marble Hill, for example in 1748 buying a parcel to the north-west that allowed the creation of the Sweet Walk, in which sweet-smelling flowers surrounded a serpentine avenue of trees planted to screen houses in neighbouring Montpelier Row. In 1756 she created to the south-east of the main villa an ornamental cottage called Little Marble Hill, whose pretty charm made it much recorded by the many painters who have flocked to the riverside.

Henrietta died at Marble Hill in 1767 and for the next fifty years the house was let to various tenants, including Maria Fitzherbert, wife of George IV through a secret and illegal marriage, and Charles Augustus Tulk, a founder member of the Swedenborg Society.

In 1824 it was sold to an army agent, Timothy Brent, who had been living at Little Marble Hill cottage. Brent's heirs demolished the cottage and sold its grounds. The main villa meanwhile had been sold by Brent to Captain Jonathan Peel, a younger brother of Sir Robert Peel and a soldier, politician and racehorse breeder. The Peel family turned out to be loyal owners of Marble Hill, either living in it or renting it out for the next sixty years, and even acquiring the Little Marble Hill land to return to the main estate. The memory of Henrietta Howard has lingered with Marble Hill for all of its life, but Jonathan Peel, who was eventually made a general, made many changes of his own, including a new stable block (which survives today as a tea room), an access drive to the house through the Sweet Walk and a flower garden on one of the terraces down to the river (now grassed over once more).

General Peel died in 1879 but his wife continued to live at Marble Hill until her own death in 1887. The house and estate were then put up for sale with little success, until in 1898 they were bought by the Cunard family of shipping magnates, who lived near by in Orleans House. Business-savvy, the Cunards set in motion plans to develop a housing estate on the land around the house, accordingly felling trees and laying roads. This, of course, inspired outrage among Twickenham's influential local people, not least of all because Marble Hill focused prominently in an internationally famous Arcadian view of the Thames from Richmond Hill (painted by luminaries such as J.M.W. Turner, T.C. Hofland and Augustin Heckel) and a public

campaign to save it was launched. Eventually, an Act of Parliament was passed to protect the view (the first to do so), £72,000 was raised and ownership of Marble Hill passed to London County Council, who then ran it as a public park and tea room.

In the mid-1960s Marble Hill passed to the Greater London Council (GLC), who held it until the GLC's abolition in 1985, when the property passed to English Heritage. Today Marble Hill is used largely as a local park by the Richmond community, and many of its historic features have been hidden by sports fields, playgrounds, car parking and tree planting. The Thameside Arcadian idyll as a whole is undergoing a tremendous rebirth, though. This is thanks to the innovative Thames Landscape Strategy, a hundred-year blueprint which since 1994 has ensured that the Thames from Kew to Hampton is managed in a coherent way. The villas, their gardens, the river and the surrounding landscape are once again becoming a symbiotic whole, their landscapes and the visual connections between them being carefully managed to achieve just the right pastoral effect.

Audley End

ESSEX

IN TWENTY-FIRST-CENTURY ENGLAND we are well used to placing a high value on our homes and the image they present to the world, but we are by no means the first to do so. In the seventeenth century, the Earl of Suffolk succumbed to a desire to impress that led him to create a monstrously expensive house at Audley End, Essex, its cost contributing to his ruination and guaranteeing the house itself the most insecure of futures. 'We are told that fools build houses for wise men to live in, but of Audley End it may be said not only that Suffolk was a fool to build a palace that strained his resources to create and left him insufficient income for upkeep, but also that the wise were very chary of inhabiting it.' So wrote H. Avray Tipping in *Country Life* magazine of 26 June 1926. The expense of Audley End continued to dog the Earl's descendants on and off for generations to come, until eventually it was passed to the state (and thus to English Heritage) in 1948 in order to pay death duties.

Like many of his early seventeenth-century peers the 1st Earl of Suffolk, Thomas Howard, was desperate to have a home that would not only persuade James I to make a royal visit but would also impress upon him its owner's wealth, status and good taste. The existing house had been built by his grandfather, Thomas Audley (Lord Chancellor of England from 1533 to 1544), and was a conversion of the abbey of Walden. In 1605, though, the 1st Earl started building a huge house, stables and formal gardens to replace that of his grandfather. These new gardens were in many places enclosed by high brick walls and were arranged in a neat rectilinear pattern surrounding the house. They included a wilderness, a popular feature of the time in which a wooded area was punctuated with formal allées to provide views and walks; a bowling green; a courtyard; and a mount garden, where an elevated bank with brickwork bastions provided a walkway with views over the garden. In addition, the passing River Cam was diverted and a large monastic fishpond remodelled to

LEFT Pod the Peacock surveys his gardens at Audley End. Pod was a popular sight for many years until he was killed by a car.
RIGHT The stable block, built in 1605.

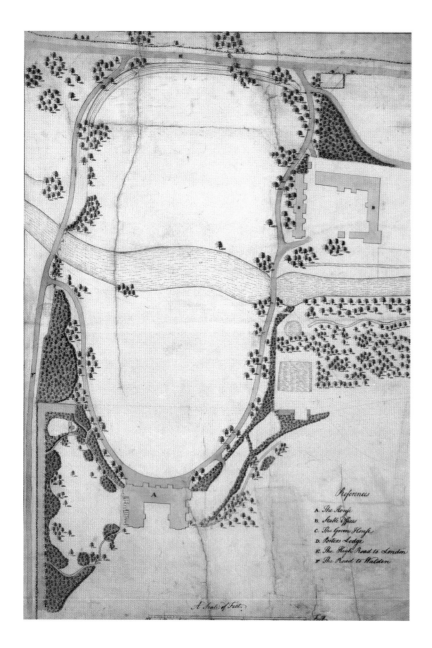

some of the park to Charles II. Christopher Wren, architect of St Paul's Cathedral, advised on improvements but otherwise the royals did not show much interest, beyond using it as a convenient base for the Newmarket races, although Catherine of Braganza held court there in 1668. In 1701 Audley End was returned to the Howards. Henry, the 6th Earl of Suffolk, then followed advice from architect Sir John Vanbrugh and demolished a large part of the outer court of the house in order to make the remainder a more manageable size.

In 1722 Audley End was inherited by Charles Howard, who became the 9th Earl in 1731 on the death of his older brother, Edward. He gained a certain amount of fame as husband of Henrietta Howard, mistress of George II and creator of Marble Hill (see page 80). Charles tweaked the landscape into fashion with details such as new clipped evergreen hedges and walks in the Mount Garden, a lawn in place of the now-dated wilderness and kitchen garden (or 'cellar garden', as it was known) and the removal of the last buildings of the mansion's outer court. It is thought that the mastermind behind this may have been Charles Bridgeman, who also worked at Marble Hill.

In 1745 the 10th Earl died without children, striking another blow to Audley End, which was still struggling from a lack of resources. The estate was split between four heirs, threatening its survival as a single designed landscape, but fortunately one of these, Elizabeth, Countess of Portsmouth, managed to buy the house and part of the park from a co-beneficiary, Lord Effingham, to add to her share. She demolished yet more of the house, and in the grounds moved the kitchen garden from near to the house to its present location, some distance to the north-west. Within the park she judiciously removed trees from the earlier formal avenues (admittedly already much plundered for their valuable wood) in order to create fashionable clumps rather than the ordered lines favoured by earlier styles.

Lady Portsmouth's heir, Sir John Griffin Griffin (later Baron Braybrooke), held Audley End from 1762 to his death in 1797. He added much to its gardens, hiring landscape architects 'Capability' Brown and Richard Woods (see pages 89 and 45). Brown was chiefly responsible for giving the western garden the strikingly beautiful look it has today, pulling down the

make straight ornamental canals. In the park, formal avenues of trees stretched out into the wider landscape.

Thomas's creation was so lavish as to have cost £200,000, around fifteen times the cost of many other large houses built at the time. A gigantic palace of immense proportions, the house was financially demanding and in 1619 the family's fortunes became impossibly slim when Thomas, by now Lord Treasurer, was convicted of embezzlement (resulting in a spell in the Tower of London, a fine of £30,000 and a fall from royal favour).

By the time Audley End had passed to James Howard, the 3rd Earl, the best solution seemed to be to sell the house and enclosing walls of the Jacobean courtyard to create an open sweep of lawn, currently enjoyed mainly by the Audley End Cricket Club. Across the lawn he reshaped Thomas's formal Cam-canal into a serpentine curve, complemented by gracious curved carriage drives. Along the ridged hills on the horizon he added a tree belt to create the illusion of Audley End's nestling in a secluded valley. This was, in fact, far from the truth, as public roads have always run surprisingly close to the front of the house, making for an exciting view for travellers but a shortage of privacy for the occupants. Brown created an informal flower garden for Lady Griffin Griffin from a seventeenth-century bowling green and the Mount Garden (although the walkway element of this remained). Eventually, though, Sir John and 'Capability' Brown were to fall out when Brown took the liberty of charging interest on the bill for his work, which had run over schedule.

Richard Woods's work was chiefly on the Elysian Garden, where he submitted a design to take a watery area previously occupied by monastic and seventeenth-century mills and create something very special. The finished garden probably owed much to Italian architect Placido Columbani, who oversaw the work and is thought to have submitted an alternative surviving plan, but Woods's influence is clear. The effect must have been wonderful. Visitors would walk down a dark evergreen-lined path through an archway to a suddenly open glade, where a pleasant circuitous walk was decorated with a jaunty refreshment tent; there were also a rustic cascade (definitely Woods's design), ornamental gateways and statues, and the Tea Bridge, in which visitors could play cards and take tea by the water. All this was set against a backdrop of scented and colourful plants including hollyhocks (*Althaea rosea*), carnations (*Dianthus*), marigolds (*Tagetes erecta* and *T. patula*), potted oranges, Persian lilacs (*Syringa persica*) and magnolias (*Magnolia grandiflora*, *M. tripetala* and *M. virginiana*). Visiting Audley End in the 1820s, international traveller (and playboy!) Prince Pückler Muskau described the Elysian Garden as being a 'large oval, surrounded with a thick natural evergreen wall of yew, laurel, rhododendron, cedar, cypress, box, holly, etc.; a brook, adorned with a grotto and water-fall, flows through the velvet turf, on which the rare and splendid plants and flower-beds of every form of colour group themselves most beautifully'. Alas, this enchanting idea soon proved to be frustrating in reality, as it was created in a frost trap in which the plants struggled. Today the bones of the Elysian Garden remain, including the brook, cascade, Tea Bridge and yew,

'CAPABILITY' BROWN

Lancelot 'Capability' Brown, the most famous of England's garden designers, is estimated to have worked at more than 120 sites, all over the country. This astounding productivity is sometimes viewed critically because his designs largely destroyed the formal gardens of earlier periods, leaving us with few examples today. This should not, however, detract from Brown's legacy of landscape parks, distinctive for motifs such as large lakes, swards of turf, clumps of ornamental trees such as elm, oak, beech, fir and pine, as well as focal points of cedar.

Brown was born in 1716 in Kirkharle, Northumberland. He left in 1739 to work at Wotton, Buckinghamshire, then moved to the gardens created by William Kent at Stowe, home of Lord Cobham. While there, Brown married Bridget Wayet and had four children. He began to take on commissions for garden improvements elsewhere, such as Warwick Castle. He earned his nickname through his habit of looking at a site and assessing its 'capabilities', by which he meant its potential to be improved by one of his designs.

The Browns moved to Hammersmith, then a village on the edge of London, where he made valuable contacts among the local nurserymen and their main clients, the great landowners. Over the following decades Brown took on commissions at estates such as Croome Court (Worcestershire), Burghley House (Cambridgeshire), Longleat (Wiltshire), Blenheim Palace (Oxfordshire), Alnwick Castle (Northumberland) and Holkham (Norfolk). In 1760 he became Surveyor to George III's Gardens and Waters at Hampton Court Palace and moved with his growing family into Wilderness House in the park. Commissions elsewhere continued, with Claremont (Surrey), Syon House (London) and Harewood House (Yorkshire), until his death in 1783.

'Capability' Brown and English Heritage: Wrest Park (page 56), Audley End (page 86), Appuldurcombe House (page 50) and Old Wardour Castle (page 42).

but it is far shadier than ever intended, and the array of flowering plants and ornaments is long since gone.

The Elysian Garden's Tea Bridge was designed by Robert Adam, who also created many other elegant garden buildings at Audley End. These included a classically arched bridge to take the public road across the River Cam; a column known as Lady Portsmouth's Column to provide a focal point in the north-east of the park; and the Temple of Victory, a small circular building with columns and domed roof, placed on top of Ring Hill to the west of the house. This temple made for an appealing eye-catcher from the park, and also served as a place where visitors could take refreshments when walking or riding round the estate. Near the temple was a Gothick menagerie where, following an eighteenth-century trend, was housed an entertaining collection of birds (ranging from eagles to goldfinches). Both these buildings are still standing but are now privately owned so cannot be visited.

Towards the end of his life, John Griffin Griffin built the Temple of Concord on the slopes to the other side of the house, in the East Park. This rather striking 'Grecian ruin'

commemorates George III's recovery from madness and was built largely of Coade stone, an artificial stone made from a ceramic composite by Mrs Eleanor Coade in her Thameside London factory. Griffin Griffin also used Coade stone to make the lion that tops the arched Lion Gate on the main approach to Audley End, adding it as part of a remodelling of a gate built by the 1st Earl in 1616.

The next heir to pay serious attention to his landscape was the 3rd Lord Braybrooke, who inherited in 1825. It was during this decade that Prince Pückler Muskau visited Audley End and his letters record a favourable impression of what he found there:

Audley-End, belonging to Lord Braybrooke, claims a place among the finest in the country. The road lies through the middle of it, with a deep ha-ha on each side, which secures the park and yet leaves a full view into it. You see, at first, an extensive green landscape, in the centre of which is a broad, river-like, and beautifully formed piece of water, which unfortunately, however, has too little motion to

LEFT The Elysian Garden with its cascade and refreshment tent, seen from the Tea Bridge, painted by William Tomkins in 1788.

ABOVE The Tea Bridge in the Elysian Garden, painted by William Tomkins in 1788.

RIGHT The Tea Bridge still stands but the Elysian Garden struggled in a frost trap and has mostly disappeared.

ABOVE *Audley End from the West* by Edmund Garvey, 1782. This clearly shows Lady Portsmouth's Column to the left and the Robert Adam bridge across the River Cam.

LEFT The bridge designed by Robert Adam stretches over the River Cam to the western garden.

RIGHT John Griffin Griffin's Temple of Concord commemorates George III's recovery from madness.

prevent its being covered with duckweed [the Audley End gardeners curse this problem to this day]. Near to the opposite shore stands the splendid gothic castle, which was originally built by the Duke of Suffolk, and was then three times as large as it is now. The multitude of its towers, projecting angles, and lofty many-formed windows, still give it a very imposing and picturesque appearance.

Regretting the loss of the Elysian Garden to frost, the 3rd Lord Braybrooke brought in designer and author William Sawrey Gilpin to help lay out a formal flower garden or parterre to the east of the house, replacing 'Capability' Brown's more informal arrangement. The inspiration for the new parterre was Braybrooke's interest in the Audley gardens of his ancestors (he was a keen historian), but he worked from a seventeenth-century design found in a book rather than any plan specific to Audley and so the result was an evocation rather than accurate re-creation of the gardens of the past – in fact, this area was used as a bowling green in the seventeenth century. Gravel paths surrounded grass cut

with an ornate pattern of flower beds filled with roses trained into low tunnels and colourful flowers, mainly herbaceous rather than the carpet bedding of later garden styles. According to an 1884 magazine article, the beds were planted with flowers such as violas, pelargoniums, gladioli and scabious and would have absorbed some 50,000 plants each year. Separating the flower garden from the park to the north, Gilpin designed shrubberies as an evergreen backdrop, using plants such as the Savin juniper (*Juniperus sabina*) and false olive (*Phillyrea angustifolia*) for green shading, and the flowering quince (*Chaenomeles speciosa*) and red escallonia (*Escallonia rubra*) for touches of colour. Between the garden and the eastern park was, and is, a clean view interrupted only by a bank inset with a flight of steps and the 'Capability' Brown ha-ha so that the parterre provided a colourful band between the house and park.

Lord Braybrooke also made many improvements to the kitchen garden, including adding a large (170-foot/52m) vine house in 1802 and an orchard house. This was essentially a squat but delicate glasshouse on low brick walls, built in order

We are fortunate to have another first-hand account of Audley End, this time written not by a member of the nobility but by William Cresswell, a young man working in the kitchen garden in 1874. Cresswell's handwritten diary was 'found' on an antiquarian bookstall in 1990 (it has since been published by English Heritage) and is a wonderful link with Audley End's past. Cresswell stayed at Audley End for less than a year but during this time he wrote a daily record of his work there, leaving us details of how he had to pot literally thousands of geranium cuttings in one day; of crops of 'Roseberry' Brussels sprouts, Asiatic cauliflowers and kidney beans; and of horticultural fancies such as the arum lily (*Zantedeschia aethiopica* – listed by Cresswell as *Richardia ethiopica*), miniature tree fern (*Blechnum gibbum* – listed as *Lomaria gibba*) and poinsettias (*Euphorbia pulcherrima* – listed as *Poinsettia pulcherrima*); monthly wages of £3 9s. 4d.; and, more infrequently, stories of a rather appealing life – such as his entry for Monday, 24 August 1874: 'Practising cricket in evening for Match next Thursday on lawn. Lord B-k bowling part of time, ball once knocked into river by Mr Holdham.'

Today the kitchen garden is run by Garden Organic, a leading organic gardening charity. Once again visitors can stroll down tidy gravel paths bordered with low box hedges (created from over 8,000 plants), admiring glimpses of healthy vegetables through iron frames of espaliered fruit. Wherever possible, historic varieties are grown, such as apple 'Claygate Permain' (a variety dating from 1823), fig 'White Ischia' (1865) and peach 'Dr Hogg' (1865). Thanks to the dedication of Garden Organic's staff and volunteers, organic methods are always used.

In the area between the Elysian Garden and the kitchen garden, in around 1865 the 5th Lord Braybrooke created the Pond Garden, which is reached via a small bridge covered with a romantic honeysuckle arch. Here two square ponds and a rockery were made on a secluded strip

to grow peaches and other stone fruit. It was installed by Thomas Rivers, the day's leading fruit horticulturist, who conveniently hailed from nearby Sawbridgeworth. Having been run as a successful commercial nursery business in the second half of the twentieth century, the kitchen garden inevitably lost much of its historic character but was the subject of a restoration in 1999. The Orchard House was completely rebuilt, using as a guide the surviving brick base and the original plan, which Thomas Rivers had fortunately recorded in an edition of his book *The Orchard House*. Today it contains a healthy stock of peaches, including a variety of *Prunus persica* known as 'Early Rivers'. The Vine House has been extensively repaired but still boasts over 60 per cent of its original timber, making it one of the earliest survivors of its type, proudly housing productive vines believed to date from its beginnings. Also restored were the range of backsheds, including the potting shed, boiler house and bothy.

LEFT The Temple of Concord is striking when seen from the house across a ha-ha.

RIGHT ABOVE The kitchen garden is neat and productive with lines of espaliered fruit and box borders.

RIGHT BELOW FROM LEFT TO RIGHT Garden Organic grows flowers as well as edible produce at Audley End; an orange tree flourishes in the Orchard House; citrus trees in the restored Orchard House.

of land running between the kitchen garden's walls and a straight brick-lined channel, through which an atmospheric torrent could be made to rush, with a series of sluices. One of the ponds accommodated Lord Braybrooke's pet otter, Paddy, and the other was used for fish. The rockery was made of Pulhamite, another imitation stone, and, judging from an entry in *The Garden* magazine of 1877, it must have been very attractive:

> The blocks from long exposure, are weather stained and mossy and the crevices are filled with the true Shamrock (*Oxalis acetosella*), *Cotyledon umbilicus* and the smaller growing ferns, etc. Overhanging are wide spreading branches of the English yew, and the recesses and various of the more salient points are occupied by fine specimens of hardy ferns and shrubs such as *Berberis Darwinii*, etc., arranged and planted by someone who evidently had studied natural, or in other words, true artistic effects.

This garden is planted with roses and climbing shrubs growing up both the kitchen garden walls and also along frames bordering a drop to the brick-contained canal, making for an appealing corner.

On the other hand, the high-maintenance Gilpin parterre to the east of the house did not manage to hold the interest of Braybrooke's heirs and went into decline from his death in 1858. Over the years it became more and more simplified until the last beds were finally removed in the mid-twentieth century. But in the 1980s the garden became the subject of an influential restoration by English Heritage, with help from landscape consultancy Land Use Consultants and other leading professionals such as Brent Elliott (librarian at the Royal Horticultural Society's Lindley Library and specialist in nineteenth-century gardens).

First, archival searches produced gems such as a nineteenth-century planting list and plan. Then there were extensive archaeological works, using techniques such as geophysical surveying, where sensing equipment can 'read' beneath the ground surface without invasive digging, and archaeobotany, where plant remains are studied to see what would have grown and where (in fact, the earth at Audley End is so dry that little was found with this technique). The topsoil was stripped away and the flower beds excavated (uncovering parts of the medieval abbey underneath). All this archaeological work was crucial in revealing that the garden had not been created exactly as it had been designed on paper. Once the findings had been carefully studied, the paths were restored and the pattern of the parterres re-marked and re-planted by the Audley End garden staff, the post of Audley End head gardener having been reinstated specifically to fulfil this purpose. Unsurprisingly, this restoration is now recognized as one of the best of its kind, largely because of the quality of the research, and has set the standard for projects across the world.

Osborne House

ISLE OF WIGHT

MONG THE MANY BRITISH MONARCHS who were keen and knowledgeable gardeners Queen Victoria and her husband Prince Albert of Saxe-Coburg and Gotha were, until modern times, rivalled only by William and Mary in their enthusiasm. As well as embellishing existing royal gardens, they created two new private ones: Balmoral in Scotland and Osborne on the Isle of Wight. As though to test their gardening skills, these were at opposite ends of the kingdom – one cold, one warm – and in both places the queen let everything be decided by the Prince Consort.

Albert's interest in horticulture was life-long. As a child, he and his brother had their own garden at Rosenau, his family's summer residence in Bavaria, and one of his last public acts before he died was to save what is now the Royal Horticultural Society from a financial crisis, help it obtain a royal charter and attend the opening of the garden at its headquarters.

After Victoria married Albert in February 1840, the young couple naturally made changes at Buckingham Palace, but they found it noisy and the London air polluted. In 1843, after the arrival of their first three children, they began to discuss buying somewhere more suited to family life. The Prime Minister, Sir Robert Peel, told them that the estate at Osborne on the Isle of Wight was for sale. Thanks to the arrival of the railway at Portsmouth, the island was only four hours from London or Windsor and Victoria had happy memories of holidays she had spent with her mother at Norris Castle, a James Wyatt house just to the west of Osborne. So in 1844 Albert was sent to look at what was on offer.

He found a plain late eighteenth-century mansion – 'a very nice clean, dry and warm little house', he told his wife, to which 'a few rooms' could easily be added. About the estate he reported, in his not totally perfect English: 'The

situation of Osborne is very beautiful, the grounds are undulated and the views very fine.' He commented favourably on the fact that the property could not be overlooked, but added: 'The Park of Osborne is dreadfully neglected and will require much draining and fencing . . . The Trees look sickly and are scanty.'

On his next visit, Victoria went with him. They stayed for several days, exploring the area, and decided to go ahead with the purchase. On 1 November the prince, acting as 'a Trustee for her Majesty', bought the Osborne estate from the owners, Lady Isabella Blachford and Miss Blachford. He paid just under £28,000, plus a further £31,700 for four surrounding farms, 'with monies issued and applied for the use of her Majesty's Privy Purse' – her own money, not state funds. Albert was sure Victoria would find Osborne 'a source of amusement, comfort and satisfaction' – and he was right.

To advise on enlarging the house they called in the London builder-cum-architect Thomas Cubitt. He told them

LEFT Mature trees now mask the Pavilion Tower.

RIGHT A wheelbarrow with pelargoniums in the Walled Garden.

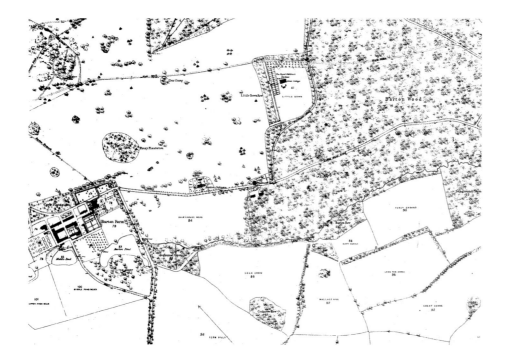

it would cost no more to pull it down and start again than to alter it, and as Cubitt, although a 'spec' builder, was a man of integrity, they agreed to his suggestion. Albert sat down with him to plan a new house. The first part to be built was the Pavilion wing, a relatively unpretentious villa with a square tower, built of brick rendered to look like stucco in a sort of semi-vernacular Italian style. Its setting and gardens, though, were rather more ambitious.

The foundation stone was laid on 26 June 1845 and construction went ahead quickly. Because the house was set on a series of terraces, massive retaining walls were required; and in order to profit from the view down to the coast and then across the Solent back to the mainland, the land had to be considerably remodelled. Yet, in spite of the amount of earth moving and terracing that had to be done, by 15 September the following year, Queen Victoria, the Prince Consort and their now four children could move in.

The house was expanded throughout the queen's reign and the landholdings around the house were also gradually increased until the estate eventually comprised 2,000 acres (810ha). Most of this was farmland, which under Albert's guidance was worked in model fashion by various tenant farmers. As early as October 1846, thirty-three men were working outdoors, five of them employed in the 'Gardens and Pleasure Grounds' at a wage of 12 shillings a week, and there was also a boy who did the weeding and was paid 5 shillings.

Albert remained fond of Rosenau, taking his wife there in the year they began Osborne. Set in a wooded landscape, it had a small formal garden on a terrace overlooking the valley of the River Itz and was to some extent the model for the grounds the prince laid out at Osborne. Even more influential were the tours he had made in central and northern Italy before his marriage. The young couple made frequent visits to King Leopold of the Belgians, who was uncle to both of them and lived at Claremont in Surrey, one of the foremost English landscape gardens. At Chatsworth in Derbyshire they had been impressed by Paxton's Great Conservatory, while at Trentham in Staffordshire, owned by their friends the Duke and Duchess of Sutherland, the glories of the latest 'Italianate' style were on display.

With impressions of all these gardens to call upon, Albert set about designing four interlocking terraces on the north-east side of the house at Osborne, looking towards the sea. Two were on the level of the main reception rooms and two on a lower level, and they were to be filled with formal parterres, fountains and statues, and edged with balustrades topped with vases and tazzas. Cubitt advised on structural matters, while on style the prince had the guidance of Professor Ludwig Gruner, an artist and expert on Raphael from Dresden, who had accompanied him on his Italian journeys. Gruner had recently worked at Buckingham Palace and been appointed the Queen's official advisor on art.

Starting in 1846, they created the Pavilion Terrace, immediately outside the bay window of the Drawing Room. It was dominated by the Sphinx Crator, a vase designed by Gruner, who took four sphinxes made in artificial stone, gave them wings and set them round a flat bowl. Numerous flower beds, mostly in complicated quadrant or crescent shapes, contained summer bedding plants, and around the central bed were granite benches. The ensemble was punctuated by statues and urns, and the various elements were linked by gravel paths. Next, in 1847, at a right angle to the Pavilion Terrace, came the much larger Main or Upper Terrace, which also had a central fountain, this time with a statue of Venus, and flower beds in curvilinear geometric shapes, set in plain areas of grass, again connected by paths.

From here, steps led down in two directions to the Lower Terrace. A curving double flight on the axis of the Main Wing debouched through an arch in the embanking wall on to the Orangery Terrace, irregular in shape and less formal in layout than the terraces above. It had various beds filled with shrubs and one circular bed, containing a Chusan palm tree, now named *Trachycarpus fortunei* but then called *Chaemaerops excelsa*. Planted by Victoria on 24 May 1851, her thirty-second birthday, this is said to be the first Chusan palm planted out of doors in Britain. The tree died in 2002 but the present queen planted a new one in May 2004.

Connected to the Orangery Terrace through the arches of a pergola is the Andromeda Terrace, with its large circular fountain. In Albert's clever plan, this area is also linked back to

the Main Terrace above by a straight double flight of steps. These two final terraces were completed by about 1851.

It was Gruner who designed the Venus and the Andromeda fountains, while the actual statue of Andromeda, made for the Great Exhibition of 1851, is by John Bell. The sea monsters around the fountain are by Queen Victoria's favourite sculptor, William Theed, a pupil of Thorwaldsen.

Some of the statues were presents from the royal couple to each other. Victoria, for instance, gave Albert a massive Juno for Christmas in 1852. One or two, such as the Venus, the Andromeda and the statue by John Francis of Eos, the prince's favourite greyhound, were in bronze, but Albert, with economy in mind, favoured zinc, electro-plated to look like bronze, a speciality of Geiss of Berlin. Many were bought from catalogues: those representing the four seasons on the Pavilion Terrace, for instance, came from Miroy Frères in Paris, and the four sphinxes round the Crator from Austin and Seeley in London. Others, such as the busts of Jupiter and Ocean, were copies of antique models in less noble materials. Indeed, the artificial stone Medici Lions, set where the lowest terrace linked to the Broad Walk, were also from Austin and Seeley and widely available in all sorts of materials. The balustrades edging the terraces, and the vases, tazzas and decorative balls on top of them, were made by Cubitt in a cement mixture, not real stone, and the plinths for the statues were initially only made of wood. Such apparent penny-pinching was perhaps engendered by a desire, particularly after the excesses of George IV, still well within living memory, not to attract criticism of royal expenditure.

After much research the four terraces have recently been reinstated in their full Victorian splendour. Much of the statuary had survived, though some had walked around a bit. Many electro-plated items had been damaged by the salt sea air but are now coated in an acrylic compound to preserve them. The planting resembles as far as possible what Queen Victoria would have known. In her day, all the bedding plants – as many as 60,000 – were raised on the estate; the annual schemes did not change and the most elaborate ones were on the Pavilion Terrace. Geraniums or pelargoniums,

LEFT ABOVE One of the Medici lions.

LEFT CENTRE Fine trees in the park.

LEFT BELOW A large bowl planted with heathers created a turning circle for carriages at the entrance to the house.

RIGHT The pergola links two terraces with views to the sea.

heliotropes, stocks, jasmine, gladioli, roses and peonies are all recorded in the queen's journal, and brighter-coloured annuals, such as lobelia, calceolarias and salvias, were also used, each being placed to contrast with its neighbours.

Standard roses, hollies and bays gave height to the centre of the beds, while trees, shrubs and perennials, such as pampas grass, yuccas, agaves, palms, lilacs and camellias, were planted elsewhere, and orange trees were brought out of the Orangery. Twenty more camellias were added in 1853 at a cost of £35 (some survive), and heathers, equally loved by Albert, were included. There was also the famous Osborne myrtle, which descends from a sprig in a nosegay given to Victoria when she visited Albert's ancestral Gotha in 1845 and still survives.

On the pergola were climbing roses, wisteria and vines, with euonymus at its base and jasmine and honeysuckle climbing elsewhere on the walls. Against the wall on the Lower Terrace, Albert planted a *Magnolia grandiflora*.

Victoria does not seem to have had a spring planting scheme, though there was one after her death, with narcissus, hyacinths and tulips, arabis, wallflowers and forget-me-nots ; nowadays there is always a spring scheme.

Once he had finished the terraces in 1851, the prince constructed an enormous lawn north-west of the house to be used for festivities. It had at its heart a porphyry vase on an equally vast scale, a gift from the King of Sweden. Much levelling was done to improve the views, and the resulting spoil was used to create a raised area. Known as the Mount, this supported a reservoir which supplied the fountains; on its banks Albert planted his favourite evergreens and some yuccas, and made paths to reach the fine views from the top.

Elsewhere on the estate, Albert worked within the already mature eighteenth-century landscape park and pleasure grounds, but using Italian elements: laurels, poplars and myrtle. It was a green landscape, with trees and shrubs rather than flowers. There was a circuit walk, the Ring Walk, which followed eighteenth-century boundaries and now takes in historic features such as an ice well built by Cubitt in 1846, ornamented with a classical entrance in 1853 and secreted in a grove of rhododendrons.

Albert's energy was extraordinary. As well as all this (and organizing the Great Exhibition), in 1851 he made a new entrance drive. This was lined with a double row of cedars and evergreen oaks, and much straighter than the old serpentine one, though with a sharp bend at the entrance to ensure privacy. Carriages entered a courtyard and drove

round a circular 'basket' 5 feet (1.5m) across, made of cement, today planted again with heathers as Albert liked it. (Modern visitors, though, enter the estate at the tradesmen's entrance and take the old curving eighteenth-century drive.)

If Albert's statuary was commonplace, his plantings were considerably more rarefied. For almost twenty years the Royal Botanic Gardens at Kew sent him numerous specimen shrubs and trees and occasional bulbs and perennials. Some of these offerings came fresh from the expeditions of Joseph Hooker and other plant-hunters. Often they had not even been properly named when they arrived at Osborne; sometimes they came with a name that is not recognisable today – *Ajuecca filimentosa*, for instance.

Away from the house, a three-quarters of a mile (1.2km) walk or buggy ride along a ridge towards the sea, lies the Swiss Cottage with its surrounding gardens. This two-storey timber chalet, assembled in 1853–4 and filled with scaled-down furniture and even a little kitchen, was a place where the royal children could play at being ordinary. Yet here was no Marie Antoinette-style frivolity, nor even nostalgia for the garden that Albert and his brother had enjoyed at Rosenau: like most of what the Prince Consort did, this had a serious purpose.

In 1850, three years before the foundation stone of the Swiss Cottage was laid, he had marked out for each of his seven oldest children a plot near where it was to be built. Each plot was a rectangle, about 12 by 5 feet (3.6 by 1.5m), divided into four by paths, and designated in order of age, from Vicky, aged nine, to Arthur, then a baby. Each child had a little wheelbarrow and a set of scaled-down tools with his or her initials on (copies of the tools can be seen in the nearby thatched summerhouse), with clogs and smocks to wear while working; for here they were to grow soft fruit and vegetables, which their father would purchase from them at the market rate, so that they would learn the value of work and money. (These were virtually the only vegetables grown on the estate; almost everything else for the household's consumption came by train from the kitchen garden the royal couple had set up at Frogmore, near Windsor, leaving Osborne's Walled Garden to grow fruit and cutting flowers.) Later, an orchard for the children was made to the north of their gardens; this has recently been restored with apples, pears, plums and cherries of suitable period varieties.

In 1857, the last two children were given gardens (again the youngest, Princess Beatrice, was only a baby), but by then each plot was sub-divided in a more complex way, with fourteen beds set in two parallel rows. The first two beds contained flowers, such as roses, fuchsias, mignonette, sweet peas – and violets, their mother's favourite flower. The next eight held soft fruit – strawberries, raspberries, gooseberries and currants – and in the final four beds vegetables were grown. This pattern never changed, even when the royal grandchildren gradually took over the plots, and almost to the end of Victoria's life the fruit of their labours would be served at her dinner table. The layouts of the children's gardens were recently reinstated and pupils from nearby Whippingham School replanted them, with everyone dressed in Victorian costumes. Today, flowers, fruit and vegetables flourish there once again.

Clearly, the little gardens must have looked been after by the staff when the royal family was elsewhere; but we know that the family visited Osborne at least four times a year: for a period in March and April; for Victoria's birthday in May; from mid-July until after Albert's birthday on 26 August; and for a few days just before Christmas. When in residence, they lived a life as close as possible to the ordinary, much of it outdoors. Victoria would take her breakfast in the open air if the weather permitted, and then deal with her correspondence or paint watercolours in one of the many arbours and summerhouses, where she could sit sheltered from the wind. Later she would walk or ride around the estate, often to watch Albert planting trees. An entry in her journal for 1847 notes that 'we walked out with the children, & they helped, or at least thought they did, in planting some trees . . .'

Albert would skate with the children on Barton Pond in winter and sail with them in summer; occasionally he went over to Farringford, near Freshwater, to see Tennyson, the Poet Laureate. But planting trees was his chief interest, thousands of them, many grown on in his own nursery. He planted them as single specimens (the magnolia outside the kitchen garden, for instance, which the queen mentions him planting in 1846), in clumps, in avenues, and in substantial woods. Where the trees were intended to be part of the landscape seen from the house, he would get the workmen to place flags where the trees might be planted and then he and his head gardener would climb to the top of the tower to see whether they looked right or would be better elsewhere.

In the past, monarchs had created gardens and landscapes as a way of making evident their power and taste. What Albert created at Osborne for Victoria still had a message, but a very different one: that of model domesticity, modest but far from puritanical or 'Victorian' in the modern pejorative sense. On the contrary, it was rather sensuous. The queen would listen to the nightingales in the trees and watch the moonlight on the sea, and the prince compared the view to that over the Bay of Naples. Benjamin Disraeli, visiting Osborne as Prime Minister, likened it to 'A Sicilian palazzo with gardens, terraces, statues and vases shining in the sun'.

When Albert died at Windsor in December 1861, aged only forty-two, a desolate Victoria rushed to Osborne to find consolation. She spent the first three months of her long widowhood here, returned regularly and died here on 22 January 1901. Her eldest son, Bertie, who became Edward VII and whose tastes were much more urban, soon gave the property to the nation (though he liked the huge Swedish vase enough to have it moved to Buckingham Palace). A golf course and a naval college were constructed in the park, and the house was subsequently used as a convalescent home for officers, the gardens offering a therapeutic environment. Both house and grounds were gradually opened to the public and the Royal Parks took over the running of the estate.

On the terraces, the parterres were simplified and some turned into rose beds, which required less maintenance; later they were grassed over. Other changes were made, not only to save money or labour. The children's gardens, for instance, were turned into mixed borders, with spring bulbs followed by forget-me-nots and wallflowers, and then summer flowers such as fuchsias and delphiniums, penstemons and asters. Edward VII is said to have wept when he saw these alterations, so he must have had happy memories of gardening there. The hedge to the east was removed and a wild garden made in the paddock, which had trees such as various Crataegus and Prunus and a *Pawlonia imperialis* underplanted with primroses, wild flowers and thousands of bulbs planted in the grass.

After that there were no major changes to the gardens until English Heritage took over in 1984. Both the house and the grounds were then thoroughly researched with a view to restoring them to how they had been towards the end of Queen Victoria's life – the last decade of the nineteenth century.

An unusual aspect of the restoration was the need to trace and identify the numerous 'memorial' trees which had been planted by successive royal owners and their distinguished

guests to celebrate events such as weddings or visits. The first seems to have been planted by Prince Albert in 1845 and later the children planted an avenue to mark his death; Victoria planted a tree on every possible occasion, the last only a few months before she died. Her mother, the Duchess of Kent, planted what was then called *Cryptomeria lobii* on 25 May 1857 (her grand-daughter Helena's eleventh birthday), and the eldest princess, Vicky, planted several. In 1859, for instance, she chose a *Chamaecyparis nootkatensis* to go near the Swiss Cottage and commemorate her marriage the previous year to Prince Frederick William of Prussia; and in February 1897, by which time she was Dowager Empress Frederick of Germany, she planted a *Cupressus lambertiana*. (Vicky's eldest son was the German Kaiser whose armies

RIGHT ABOVE The childrens' gardens in front of the Swiss Cottage.
RIGHT BELOW Each royal child had a wheelbarrow and set of scaled-down garden tools.

fought Britain in the First World War and in 1917 all the labels of memorial trees mentioning German names were tactfully removed and stored by the Office of Works.)

This tree-planting tradition continued after Victoria's death. On 30 November 1911, for instance, her grandson George V and his wife Queen Mary each planted a *Quercus robur*, then referred to as a British rather than English oak; and, in an indication, perhaps, of changing horticultural fashion, the present queen planted a more decorative *Acer grosseri* var. *hersii* on 26 July 1965 but, unfortunately, a poor position had been chosen and it did not survive.

Over the years, many of these 'ceremonial' trees died and were replaced, often with something different. Others survived, but not always in the most suitable place either for their own good or in terms of the aesthetics of the landscape. So one of the restoration team's tasks was to inventory them and take decisions about which could stay where they were.

Deciding on the fate of these particular trees was part of a much larger project that considered every single tree on the

estate, whether in a wood, in a grove, in a clump or an individual specimen. Those that had been there in 1901 were, where possible, to be preserved, while those that had been planted or self-seeded later would be cut down or moved. In the long term, all this work will enable future generations to enjoy not only the parkland, with its fine trees, but also the historic vista from the terraces across the Solent. Other sea views, such as those from the path leading to the Swiss Cottage, have already been opened up once again.

After the restoration of the terraces and the parkland, the late eighteenth-century walled kitchen garden had to be considered. A classic 1 acre (0.4ha) in size, it was originally divided into quarters by four paths, probably edged with box, which intersected in the centre at a well. We know there were cucumber frames, and that asparagus was grown, but there is no evidence about other vegetables or fruit in the eighteenth-century. When Victoria and Albert bought Osborne, there were also a camellia, vineries and melon grounds here and the sale particulars describe the garden as 'stocked with choice standard and other trees'. The queen commented in June 1846 on the beauty of the pinks and fruit trees that flourished in the shelter of the garden's walls, and in March 1849 she noted that the camellia was in full flower.

At first, Albert used the Walled Garden for storing plants he had bought or been given, but in 1847, as it was not needed for vegetables, he and Victoria decided it should become a decorative fruit and cutting garden. Over the next few years, they had the walls raised about a foot (30cm) and ornamented with pilasters and a cornice; and, when the old house was demolished in 1848, its portico was set in the east wall to make a fine entrance. The queen liked these improvements well enough to sketch them in 1850 and the portico can also be seen in Cyril Ward's 1912 *Royal Gardens*.

A new octagonal well with a pump was made in the centre and two greenhouses for propagating were placed on either side of the northern path. Then the old vine house was replaced by a range of cast-iron greenhouses, over 90 feet (27m) long, manufactured in Birmingham by Henry Hope. Set along the north wall, they caught the sun from the south but, even so, were heated by gravity-fed hot water.

They connected to the so-called Long Building on the outside of the wall, which combined boiler room, tool shed, potting shed, space for storing fruit and gardeners' bothy. Two further glasshouses were erected outside the walls to the north, one of which may have been a fernery, and three

OPPOSITE Evening light on one of
the magnificent trees.

LEFT A watercolour by Cyril Ward,
published in his 1912 book *Royal
Gardens*, shows colourful beds
outside the Walled Garden.

glassed pits were built for raising bedding plants to set out on the terraces. The eighteenth-century melon pit was kept in use, and there was also a special covered pit on the outside of the west wall for growing the queen's violets.

In 1885 Victoria complained about the lack of flowers in the greenhouses, even though Vicky had obtained a collection of exotic South African plants which were displayed in one of them. An article in the *Gardeners' Chronicle* in 1897 mentions an orange tree, which 'fruits well upon a wall', and a photograph taken in the late nineteenth century shows this orange tree growing in the open. Unusually, because it was espaliered against a wall and not in a pot, it could not be taken indoors in winter but, protected by a special wooden cover, it survived. The royal accounts indicate that the cover was removed well after the latest frosts could have been expected and not put back on until well into winter; and that in December 1899, 'Repairing and fixing covering to orange tree in Kitchen Garden' cost 3s. 11½d.

There were also Tea roses, which flowered all year round and were exhibited at the local Ryde Flower Show; late-flowering chrysanthemums (also exhibited); and winter-flowering carnations. And even at Christmas there were violets to please the queen. In the same year another magazine listed orchids, ferns and palms growing in the glasshouses, and mushrooms 'splendidly grown' in an outhouse.

The facilities in the Walled Garden were continually updated throughout the queen's reign. For instance, new piping to access the reservoir on the Mount was installed in 1886, which involved replanting the entire garden; a new boiler was installed in 1892 and the two propagating greenhouses were replaced in 1895, by which date they were being used as vineries. In about 1895 the Duke of Connaught and Princess Louise presented their mother with an Italian well head, made in iron, for the centre of the garden. (This has since disappeared.)

It was not to be expected that the same standard of excellence would be maintained in the Walled Garden after the queen's death in 1901, although the convalescing officers apparently appreciated the shelter of its walls when sent out for walks in the winter. During the Second World War it became a plant nursery, and this use continued when the Royal Parks took over management. Although the lean-to glasshouses survived, in about 1976 the two vineries were replaced with slightly wider aluminium greenhouses, and at some point a modern oil-fired boiler was installed.

When English Heritage took over in 1984 it laid most of the beds to grass, having decided that bedding plants for the terraces would be bought in rather than grown on site (although the lean-to glasshouses were repaired and used to propagate and overwinter plants for the house). The public

ABOVE LEFT An old photograph of the espaliered orange tree in the Walled Garden, which survived outside all year round.
ABOVE RIGHT By 1976 utilitarian modern greenhouses had replaced Victoria's vineries.
OPPOSITE A view through the Contemporary Heritage Garden created within the Walled Garden.

was not allowed access. Ten years later, English Heritage began to consider what could be done with the Walled Garden to make it an additional attraction for visitors – and perhaps one that might bring in some extra income to the estate. Traditional kitchen gardens had been in decline all over the country for most of the post-war period because growing fruit and vegetables was so labour intensive; but towards the end of the twentieth century, spurred on by a television series and the present Prince of Wales's kitchen garden at Highgrove in Gloucestershire, a number were restored and put into working order again. This solution was considered for Osborne, with the added possibility of using the glasshouses for plant sales and the Long Building as a shop and cafeteria, but it was rejected.

In 1999 Deborah Goodenough was appointed head gardener, and it was decided that the Walled Garden would, with the Moat Garden at Eltham Palace, be one of the first two of English Heritage's Contemporary Heritage Gardens (see page 200). Five eminent designers – Rosemary Verey, Elizabeth Banks, Jill Billington, Xa Tollemache and Rupert

Golby – were invited to submit ideas for 'an imaginative and decorative planting scheme . . . that will recreate the spirit of Queen Victoria and Prince Albert's fruit and flower garden and which will also provide cut flowers and foliage for Osborne House'. They had to retain the structure – walls, doorways, paths – plus the well in the centre, the violet frame and the lean-to glasshouses on the north wall; and they had to devise 'a design solution' that would incorporate the rectangular footprints of the two glasshouses that had been taken down without damaging their still-surviving decorative tiled floors. The labour, additional structural elements and plants were to cost under £35,000, to which professional fees would be added. All the plants chosen must have been available in 1901, an obligation that seemed somewhat contrary to the 'contemporary' spirit of the competition and also meant using old varieties of fruit, even though they are notoriously subject to disease, rather than the better modern cultivars.

The five were given just over a month from 15 April to 24 May to submit their designs and the judges met on 27 May to consider the proposals and interview the designers. The competition was won by Rupert Golby, who seems to have been the first professional garden designer ever to work at Osborne (although Golby does not like the 'designer' epithet, preferring to describe himself as a 'gardener who plants'). His approach was that the public should be shown a working space where plants were clearly growing – from germination through to fruiting or flowering. He thought there need not be anything formal, as that was provided by the parterres on the terraces. In the two largest plots, a formidable quarter of an acre (1,012m²) each, he wanted 'a market garden feel' and suggested maize and sunflowers at their centres, for height and colour. But everything, he said, could well be different in future years to emphasize the changing nature of all cultivation.

Touring the house, Golby found the royal couple's personalities so omnipresent that he decided to exploit the Victoria and Albert theme in the Walled Garden. The terracotta pots bear their initials, as does much of the ironwork; he also planned coronets for the tops of the arches, in the end omitted for budgetary reasons. He chose as many plants as possible with appropriate names: 'Royal Sovereign' strawberries, rhubarbs called 'Prince Albert' and 'Queen Victoria', 'Prince Albert' apples – and Victoria plums,

of course; while the Walled Garden's amazingly gentle micro-climate, even milder than the rest of the very balmy Isle of Wight, allowed the famous orange tree to be replaced.

The Walled Garden was opened on schedule in July 2000, and it has since matured delightfully: roses and espaliered fruit trees now cover the walls and curve over the arches, peonies, lilies, agapanthus and nerines bloom in the borders and the glasshouse range is filled with tender shrubs and, echoing Vicky's collection, South African plants such as proteas.

By insisting on period plants in the Walled Garden, English Heritage remained faithful to its intention of restoring the pleasure gardens at Osborne to their state during the last decade of Victoria's long reign. Although Prince Albert had been dead for nearly forty years by the time she died in 1901, Victoria never forgot his influence on the house and gardens, and it is still there for modern visitors to appreciate.

Bayham Old Abbey

)X(

KENT

AYHAM ABBEY was founded in about 1207 by the Premonstratensians, a relatively rare order in England, often known as the Norbertines or White Canons. One of the first wave of monasteries to be dissolved by Henry VIII, it was leased to Sir Anthony Browne, the king's Master of the Horse, who was also given Battle Abbey (see page 166). After various changes of ownership it was bought in 1714 by Sir John Pratt, a lawyer and founder of a dynasty of lawyers and politicians, who built a small house in the grounds. This was later extended by his grandson, another John Pratt, and, unsurprisingly, as it was an early example of the Gothick style, it was admired by the aesthete Horace Walpole.

This John Pratt made a garden round his new house, and probably realigned the monastic fishponds to make a pool. The abbey ruins became a feature in the view and it may have been at this point in the mid-eighteenth century that part of the abbey gatehouse was turned into a summerhouse.

In 1799 John Pratt III's cousin, John Jeffreys Pratt, who had become 2nd Earl Camden, called in Humphry Repton to landscape the grounds, and the following year Repton produced one of his best Red Books (see page 117). Calling his plans the 'Application of Gardening and Architecture united, in the formation of a new place', he advised pulling down the house and replacing it with a *cottage orné*, and then building a larger house to the north. There would be a new lake, and the ruined abbey and *cottage orné* would become eye-catchers, visible from afar across a fresh landscape made from the surrounding farmland.

Camden ignored Repton's suggestions about the new house and made quite modest alterations to the existing one.

RIGHT The abbey ruins can be admired from the windows of the Gothick Dower House.

OPPOSITE Groves of rhododendrons still frame the view back to Bayham Abbey House.

So far as the landscape was concerned, at first he only followed the Repton plan by damming the little River Teise to make a lake, though one less serpentine in form than Repton had suggested; but fifteen years later (and by now 1st Marquess Camden), he decided on other improvements. Repton visited Bayham again in 1814 and suggested a different site for the possible new house. He died in 1818, disappointed that 'nothing seems to have been done in consequence of my former opinion. It will perhaps be said that the water has been formed but it has never been completed.'

By about 1820 a landscape had been made in the valley, but it is not clear whether this was to Repton's plan. His ideas about a new house were again ignored and the existing one was enlarged once more, and surrounded by gardens. Later in the century, these gardens became quite opulent in style, with walks, a summerhouse and a sundial – and exotic plantings that were continued up to and within the ruins. The old abbey was turned into a sort of English Ninfa: its ecclesiastical walls were covered by creepers and the soil at their feet was ornamented with flower beds.

In 1870 the Camden family decided that they did need a new house, and had a mansion in Tudor style built where Repton had suggested in 1814 – on a hill above the lake. Named Bayham Abbey House, it had terraces and gardens leading down to the lake, which included a rock and water garden, a maze and groves of rhododendrons.

The ruined abbey was still an eye-catcher, but from a different viewpoint. The architectural historian Nikolaus Pevsner commented that 'only the Aislabies of Studley Royal had a better ruin than Bayham. Theirs was Fountains Abbey.' (He might also have mentioned the Arundells and Wardour Old Castle.)

But as early as 1897 the estate began to be broken up and by the end of the twentieth century most of the land surrounding the abbey, including the new house, had been sold off. A small area, including the abbey ruins, the Dower House and some land around them (just 35 out of 909 acres, or 14 out of 368ha), was placed in state hands by the Camden family in 1961, and this has been managed by English Heritage since 1984. Part of the old house (known as the Dower House although it was lived in by the Camdens' chaplain) became the ticket office, while its grander rooms provide an attractive venue for weddings.

Repton's lake, rather silted up, is still visible, as are some of the later shrubberies and lawns. The Victorian plantings on the abbey ruins have all been removed except for the beech tree growing out of the altar, which seems to symbolize new life emerging from dereliction. Sadly, half of it was lost in the Great Storm of 1987 and the remainder is dying and will soon have to be removed before it falls. But for the moment it provides the most compelling image of this evocative place.

RIGHT A beech tree growing out of the altar seems to symbolize new life, but is now dying.

Kenwood

LONDON

ESTLING ON THE SLOPES of Hampstead, overlooking London from the north, Kenwood is today much enjoyed for the view, from its terrace, of what appears to be a semi-rural lake almost enclosed by trees. The trees are, however, relatively recent and largely uninvited, being self-seeded, and the view from Kenwood was for many centuries nothing short of spectacular in its far-reaching grasp of London, now reduced to a tantalizing glimpse, bringing fame and the admirers who make Kenwood's story so vibrant. One such admirer was the architect Robert Adam, who wrote in *The Works in Architecture of Robert and James Adam* (1773–9):

> Over the vale, through which the water flows, there is a noble view let into the house and terrace, of the city of

London, Greenwich Hospital, the River Thames, the ships passing up and down, with an extensive prospect, but clear and distinct, on both sides of the river. To the north-east, and west of the house and terrace the mountainous villages of Highgate and Hampstead form delightful objects. The whole scene is amazingly gay, magnificent, beautiful and picturesque.

This famous terrace, and a house alongside, was created in the seventeenth century when the Caen Wood estate,

OPPOSITE The long-famous view of London behind Kenwood's estate, now partly hidden by trees.
BELOW Kenwood's south front and popular terrace.

ensconced in ancient woodland, belonged to royal printer John Bell. By the eighteenth century it was owned by the Earl of Ilay and his brother-in-law James Stuart, the 2nd Earl of Bute. They let it to a gentleman called George Middleton, partner in what was to become Coutts Bank, who planted a lime avenue as a continuation of Bell's terrace. A century later the poet Samuel Coleridge was to write that this was 'one of the finest in England, a grand Cathedral Aisle of giant Lime Trees'. The avenue still provides a shady walk today, although the original trees were felled in 1960, so the current ones are clones, propagated from a nearby sucker of Middleton's originals.

By 1746 the 3rd Earl of Bute, John Stuart, had inherited both his father's and uncle's shares of Kenwood. Stuart carried out much work on its landscape, in spite of being busy having five children (twelve in the course of his lifetime) and becoming Lord of the Bedchamber to Frederick, Prince of Wales. He was eventually to become (an unpopular) Prime Minister. At Kenwood he had formal gardens stretching down the bank from the south of the house to a line of formal fishponds. Noted as a plantsman, he filled the gardens with a wonderful collection of plants, many only recently introduced to Britain, that included varieties of staphylodendron, saxifrage, verbascum, muscari, chrysanthemum, pulmonaria, monarda, sedum,

ajuga, menispermum (moonseed vine), erythronium and rhamnus (buckthorn).

However, Kenwood never attracted much loyalty from its owners and in 1754 Bute sold it to William Murray, a Scottish lawyer who was later to be made the 1st Earl of Mansfield. An important personality in the eighteenth century, Mansfield is particularly notable for a ruling that made slavery illegal in England. He made a great many important changes to Kenwood, including the purchase of neighbouring land, which more than doubled the estate's size to some 232 acres (94ha). More land was rented from the Bishop of London, who owned a vast area to the north, making a total of 1,500 acres (607ha).

The Earl of Mansfield invested no small effort in his house, hiring Robert Adam to remodel it with a new library wing, a third storey, an imposing portico and stucco ornament on the south side. The Earl brought his grounds into current fashion by replacing the divided formal gardens with lawns. The fishponds enjoyed by Bute were modified to make Wood Pond and the Thousand Pound Pond (its name reflecting its cost), which as well as having an ornamental effect acted as a reservoir for the people of north London. Thousand Pound Pond had a sham bridge masking its end, whereby an elegant long 'bridge' with low arches and tall balustrading gave the impression that it must have crossed a considerable stretch of water. Landscape designer Humphry Repton was rather unimpressed by the Sham Bridge, calling it 'a deception so frequently liable to be detected, I think it is an object beneath the dignity of Kenwood', but it survives today, having been restored in 1992.

Thanks mainly to J.C. Loudon, writing in *Arboretum et Fruticetum Britannicum* (1844), we know that the earl also planted a great many shrubs and trees, including many beech, a *Robinia pseudoacacia* (black locust) and a *Quercus suber* (cork oak). In particular, on the terrace he was said to have planted with his own hands what became a magnificent cedar of Lebanon.

The earl also made pleasant grass and gravel walks through the woodland, and on the slopes to the north he created a beech mount, where specimen beech trees were planted on a raised bank to create an arboricultural eye-catcher from the house. Today this area still provides stunning autumn colour but the tree growth was so great that the crucial visual link between the house and the mount had been lost for years. The garden staff recently took the plunge and strategically felled a few trees (using crane platforms to ensure that they chose the right ones!) to open up the view once again.

When the 2nd Earl of Mansfield inherited in 1793 the work did not stop. Humphry Repton was brought in and made important changes to the north of the mansion. Repton wrote in the Kenwood Red Book (a Red Book was the portfolio of proposed changes that he always presented to his clients):

> The house is at present encumbered and surrounded on every side by red brick walls and old buildings, that it is difficult to give any just representation of it upon paper, especially as I have at present no accurate plan of the premises, but the preceding drawing represents the garden and orchard to the east, with the walls sloping down into a deep valley . . . where I conceive there is sufficient space for all the home offices, or those which ought to be contiguous to the dwelling. When this valley is brought to the same level, partly by filling up and partly by digging, the offices as they will range several feet below the level of the house, will very easily be hid by a screen of plantation.

Repton's works nudged the road further away from the house and removed a walled forecourt, creating instead the

HUMPHRY REPTON

During his glittering landscape design career Humphry Repton worked on some important estates, but he very nearly did not become a designer at all. He was born to middle-class parents in 1752 and as a teenager was sent from the family home in Norwich to study in Holland. On his return he was apprenticed to the textile trade.

When his parents died in 1778, though, he decided to set up on a small Norfolk country estate with his wife Mary. This new life was not wholly smooth or successful, although various abortive employments helped to build an impressive bank of contacts. By the age of thirty-six Repton had moved to a cottage at Hare Street in Essex and decided to set himself up as a landscape designer.

On a steady path at last, he found work at nearby estates such as Catton Park and Holkham and then further afield at Welbeck Abbey (Nottinghamshire) and Sheffield Park (Sussex), Attingham (Shropshire) and Tatton Park (Cheshire). One of Repton's skills was marketing, namely in the Red Book portfolios in which he used watercolours with 'before and after' flaps to persuade clients of the dazzling improvements he could make to their properties. Many of these survive today.

By the nineteenth century a fashion was growing for embellishing landscape parks with a flower garden near the house. A leading light in this movement, Repton worked not only on large country parks but also on smaller garden areas, as at Woburn Abbey (Bedfordshire), Endsleigh (Devon), Ashridge (Hertfordshire) and the Royal Pavilion in Brighton. Also in this period he planned Russell Square, Cadogan Square and Bloomsbury Square (London).

In 1811 Repton suffered spinal injuries caused by a carriage accident when he was returning home from a ball one snowy night. He never fully recovered but lived on until 1818.

Humphry Repton and English Heritage: Kenwood (page 114) and Bayham Old Abbey (page 110).

Half Moon Lawn. This aspect of Kenwood house is sadly often overlooked by visitors today, as they flock to enjoy the sunny terrace with its views across London, but it was designed to be an impressive and memorable frontage and so is well worth a visit. Repton also suggested that lodges were needed at the estate's entry points but it is not clear what design input, if any, he had into the resulting octagonal East and West Lodges. These still stand intact today, tiny cream buildings with pointed slate roofs and central chimneys, but alas they are virtually invisible among the detritus of modern access arrangements, swamped by road signs, tarmac and four-wheel-drive cars.

To the immediate north of the mansion is an ancient ridge of woodland area known as Prospect Hill, through which Repton created a circuit path. Today this path is little used, a rare quiet spot within the estate. Its beautiful collection of trees have earned it a Site of Special Scientific Interest (SSSI) designation, although the beeches are struggling with climate change (the ground is too dry) and grey squirrels (who gnaw away at the young trees).

Repton also converted the kitchen garden at the west front of the house to a flower parterre with nineteen crescent and circular beds. It is believed that the plantings included a number of early rhododendron introductions, so extensive research is being carried out into the various specimens still scattered around Kenwood. In 1816 estate steward Edward Hunter wrote to Lord Mansfield, 'I think there is a finer bloom in the rhododendrons this year than I ever saw both in the Flower Garden and in the Wood. But they are a month later than usual.' Particularly admired by visitors are two splendid examples in the flower garden – *Rhododendron* 'Sun of Austerlitz', with bright pink blooms, and *R.* 'Mrs J.G. Millais', which has large paler pink flowers with a bold yellow centre.

However, by 1838 this parterre arrangement seems to have been unsatisfactory, J.C. Loudon writing in the *Suburban Gardener* that

> we may remark that the flower-garden at Kenwood is the only defective part of the place. It is naturally shaded and confined by a lofty lime avenue on the one hand, and by a rising hill of oak wood on the other; and the area of the garden contains by far too many small trees and shrubs among the flowers: in consequence of this, the turf is almost always damp on the surface; and the flowers come up with slender and etiolated stems, and pale colours.

> Most of the flower beds, also, are too large; and they do not combine to form a whole.

Loudon accompanied his description with a sketch that suggests that Repton's nineteen beds had already multiplied into thirty-eight smaller ones. This garden underwent many more changes over the years and is now a plain lawn, surrounded by shrubs and much loved by picnicking families.

A replacement kitchen garden was built to the east of the stable block. This was unusual in that it had walls on only three sides, the south one remaining open to the view of London in order to allow fresh warm air to circulate through the area. This garden still exists, but unfortunately most of it is out of English Heritage's hands and is used as a maintenance yard.

Also created in this period was a 200-acre (81ha) model farm, or *ferme ornée*, which would have supplied Kenwood with fresh produce very much in keeping with the 'escape to the country' role of such a property. The centrepiece was a delightful farmhouse with an octagonal farmyard and much of this remains today, having been used by Express Dairies in the twentieth century, although the farmyard has been lost and is marked only by the low wall of its foundations.

Near by is an enchanting ornamental dairy arrangement comprised of a central dairymaid's cottage, flanked by a buttery and a little room where those playing at being dairymaids could take tea. Sitting on a raised mound looking over what would have been rolling meadow filled with picturesque long-horned Warwickshire cattle, these three buildings huddle together, looking almost impossibly sweet with their overhanging eaves, exaggeratedly pointed roofs and staring windows. They were later joined together to form one quirky structure (and in the 1950s converted to residential use), but the three distinct shapes can still clearly be distinguished. In the shade of the trees behind is a trapdoor down to a well-preserved ice well, in which a narrow passage leads to a huge round brick pit. This would have been filled with ice primarily to cool the buttery above. This buttery has an ornately patterned floor with tiled walls using an almost Islamic motif, while stone counters run around the inside of the room with channels cut through them for the excess milk to drain. Operations at the dairy were supervised by Dido Belle, the half-caste illegitimate daughter of Lord Mansfield's nephew, conceived while he was in the Caribbean with the British Navy (the Mansfields'

primarily as a home for his spectacular collection of paintings and furniture but died before the paintings were even hung. Philanthropic in death as well as in life, Lord Iveagh left his art and also Kenwood to the nation, dictating that it should preserve the 'atmosphere of a gentleman's park'.

Managed by London County Council, Kenwood quickly became a popular visitor destination, not least when coupled with the adjoining Hampstead Heath, the large historic manorial grazing land adjacent to Kenwood, whose 240 acres (97ha) had been bought in 1871 for £45,000 from the Manor of Hampstead by the Metropolitan Board of Works. Thus the life of Kenwood became that of a public amenity, much valued as an open space within a busy city.

During Kenwood's early years as a public park, the head park keeper was Frederick Oxford, who lived with his young family in what is now known as Mansion Cottage, a pleasant house by the service wing. His son, Arthur, was ten years old when his family moved to Kenwood and he still likes to return as often as he can to reminisce and check on progress. His memories are wonderful, packed with stories of skating on the ponds, resident peacocks (encouraged to squawk outside the windows of less-popular staff), wartime wheat harvests, rabbit shooting and unexploded bombs on the terrace. At that time many of the staff and their families lived on site, enjoying an atmosphere of camaraderie that must have been similar to that when the estate was a private one. His memories perhaps dictated by a child's priorities, Arthur particularly remembers the old tearooms, run by Mrs Waller and her daughter, who lived in the flat above and would give the staff's children any cakes that were left over after the bank holidays. Today the restaurant still occupies the same area, the Old Brew House of the service wing, but it now includes what was the Mansion Cottage garden, laid out for diners as pleasant flowering terrace gardens by the garden designer Arabella Lennox-Boyd.

Writing in *Country Life* in 1950, architectural writer Christopher Hussey said: 'The Parks Department of the London County Council, which has been responsible for carrying out the decision to rehabilitate Kenwood, have certainly earned the gratitude of Londoners and visitors from overseas for making this ever-enjoyable jaunt for a summer's day possible again.' Among the attractions then were outdoor concerts begun as part of the Festival of Britain in 1951. These continue now, the musicians playing across the water from the south bank of the Thousand Pound Pond.

Both Frederick Oxford and Lord Mansfield would be pleased to see that today Kenwood is lively and thriving. Nature may have taken over a little more than Humphry Repton would have liked, but Kenwood is still appreciated as a retreat from London, now for a unique mix of mums and buggies, eccentrics, North London celebrities and dog walkers, all seeking sanctuary from the noise of London just as their historical counterparts did hundreds of years ago.

LEFT The Sphagnum Bog is home to a rare moss.

RIGHT ABOVE A pleasant veranda overlooks what was once a Humphry Repton flower garden.

RIGHT BELOW Mansion Cottage, which in the mid-twentieth century was home to the head park keeper and his young family.

Belsay Hall

NORTHUMBERLAND

'IN THE COUNTY OF NORTHUMBERLAND, about fifteen miles north-west from Newcastle-upon-Tyne, and eighteen miles from the sea, is a group of abrupt hills or crags, formed by the upheaval of sandstone strata into the form called "Crag and tail", the crags facing towards the west', wrote Sir Arthur E. Middleton, Bart, in 1910. Amongst these crags sits Belsay Hall, Sir Arthur Middleton's remote home, whose spectacular gardens are among English Heritage's finest.

For many years this part of the world was considered to be the border between England and Scotland and so it saw its share of warfare. Not surprisingly, when the Middleton family built themselves Belsay Castle at the end of the fourteenth century (having owned the land since the thirteenth), the design was very much focused on defence, the castle being a chunky stone tower house. By the seventeenth century the area was relatively stable and so Sir Thomas Middleton was able to convert the castle into a gentleman's country house. In time, this house was also given an ornamental park and formal gardens. A 1728 engraving by Samuel and Nathaniel Buck (brothers who made it their business to engrave many of the sights of England and Wales) shows the forecourt to be enclosed by walls on two sides and railings to the front, with rows of shrubs clipped into standard cones and balls running round the outside of lawns and along a path up the middle of the garden.

LEFT Belsay Hall, gardens and park from the air, with a vibrant show provided by the rhododendrons planted by Sir Arthur Middleton in the first decades of the twentieth century.
BELOW Belsay Castle, shown in a 1728 engraving by Samuel and Nathaniel Buck.

The captivating place that we find today, however, is largely the work of Sir Charles Monck (the 6th Baronet, who had to change his name from Middleton in order to inherit the Lincolnshire estates of his maternal grandfather, Lawrence Monck, as well as those of the Middletons) and, in turn, his grandson Sir Arthur Middleton, the 7th Baronet.

Sir Charles was a quirky but determined man who, like so many eighteenth-century gentlemen, travelled extensively as part of a Grand Tour to see the cultural sights of Europe. He was accompanied by his wife and baby son, Charles Atticus, who was born during the trip, in Athens, and made some of the journey on horseback, lying on a cushion on his father's knee.

Greece in particular made a great impression on the young Sir Charles, so his notebooks, written throughout his life, are peppered with references to Greek culture, including long passages in Greek, a language which he strove to learn. Sir Charles's work on the estate began almost immediately on his return in 1806, his travels inspiring him to build a new hall in Greek Doric style (actually almost modernist to our eyes). To emphasize the Mediterranean tone Caledonian pines were planted as a backdrop, park lodges built in a complementary design and the park itself tweaked into the current style. The park is today owned and managed by the charitable Belsay Trust, and they do a good job of keeping it peaceful, tidy and beautifully rural.

There is nothing worse than having your own good taste let down by your scruffy neighbours, though, so Sir Charles also rebuilt (and relocated) the village of Belsay, creating golden sandstone cottages with low, open recessed porches that beg

to be enjoying Mediterranean sunshine. Not all Sir Charles's plans came to fruition, however. He intended to place a lake between him and the village but, according to a relative's telling, he may have let his enthusiasm carry him away:

Sir Charles decided to fill up the dene [by the] village and carry the road straight across and make a lake of 80 acres behind the dam. The lake would have run back to the Frogpond and make [sic] an island of Swanstead; the farmers did some of the casting and the soil was dug off the north side of the present village lake. To [turn] the water off if required he arranged a plunge and a rod to work it in the middle of the dam and a channel from the lake. The road authorities asked for guarantees so did people down the town, Sir Charles found this arrangement was unsafe and blocked the channel with a large stone from the quarry . . . Finally he made a much smaller lake and this was again reduced by Sir Arthur who cut out the back to a lower level . . . Before Sir Charles muddled with the lake it went from the Frogpond to the west edge of the present village wood.

Sir Charles was a serious gardener with a particular interest in fruit cultivation. Indeed, his personal notebooks show him to have been almost obsessed: they are relentless in their recording of the fruity delights that he cultivated – pears, peaches, nectarines, oranges. A sad entry in his 1811 Commonplace Book, the notebook in which he recorded any useful information, says: 'Guavas ripe in the store (*Psidium Pyriferum*). It is a rank smelling and tasting fruit, most like strawberries, but not near so good – it is not worth cultivation.'

Always experimenting with new techniques, Sir Charles brought hot-wall technology to the kitchen garden at Belsay. Such technology was relatively unusual for northern gardens. Belsay's hot walls involved lighting range fires within the base of brick and stone walls to encourage the exotic fruit that grew up them (peaches, figs and the like), as described in this letter from Sir Charles to the Horticultural Society (later to become the Royal Horticultural Society):

A few years ago a Fig House was built here . . . last autumn [I] took down the back wall, and rebuilt it with a flue of three ranges in a wall of ten feet high . . . I caused the facing bricks to be set on edge, so that the wall, between the smoke of the fire and the inside of the house, was only two and a half inches thick . . . to obviate the weakness of the wall, I caused the ranges of the flues to be covered with a two and a half inch cover of fire stone, and upon that again another such plate of firestone, to serve . . . the range of flue above, so that the two courses of bricks bound the thin wall of facing bricks to the park part of the wall which was of stone work . . . I procured cast iron eyes of three quarters of an inch capacity, with shanks of six inches long, and caused the shanks to be sunk in the under side of the soles above mentioned, so that when the wall was built the eyes appeared in horizontal rows at one foot distance from each other . . . through these eyes rounded oak rods, as long as the wall is high, were drawn perpendicularly.

Sir Charles left many personal jottings and through them all shines his passion for Belsay and its natural life. On 24 April 1820, for instance, he wrote: 'wild cherry trees in full flower. Beeches leafing. Thorn hoofs leaved. Hack thorn (*Prunus silvestris*) in flower in hedges. Saw swallows.' The weather is scrupulously recorded (10 January 1814: 'I think the coldest day I ever felt. Frost very severe, wind due South'), as are his various enthusiasms, including the breeding of silkworms (16 June 1811: 'Silkworms kept upon lettuce in the store are spinning'), and horticultural experiments (6 August 1817: 'Walnut leaf tea very strong will kill worms in the earth of flowers which grow in garden pots or oblige them to come up, and not injure, but rather invigorate the plants'). Revealed most clearly is his attentive passion for plants and their comings and goings from season to season: 13 January 1819: 'fine open weather, not a shower of snow yet. Stocks yet in flower on the borders of the Garden with Polianthus, wall flowers, some hepaticas. Single snowdrops up and show flowers but do not yet hang their flowers down. *Pyrus japonica* out in flower against garden south wall.' In contrast, he makes only passing mentions of events such as his daughter's wedding! By the 1820s trips away from Belsay are barely acknowledged except for what they show him about different growing conditions: London, 11 May 1825: 'Horse chestnuts at Chelsea College in full bloom', followed by (24 May 1825) 'Oaks mainly in full leaf about Dorking in Surrey. Horse chestnut flowers just past full.'

GARDEN NOTE

Sir Charles Monck kept copious notes on gardening, including one on 'Unnecessary Expenses of Gardens':

1 Large areas of machine kept turf.
   Remedy Mow it once or twice a year. Plant it with bulbs or spring flowers.
2 Needless multiplication of walks which require weeding and the edges keeping.
   Remedy In some cases grass mown walks will be easier kept.
3 Too many drives or approaches.
   Remedy Use the high road and place the lodge at the nearest convenient point to the House.
4 Large areas of Greenhouse and Vinery &c&c.
   Remedy Have less and buy Fruit and Flowers when wanted. NB Plants under glass require constant attention, and therefore time and labour.
5 Large areas of Bedding out both spring and autumn.
   Remedy Reduce the area and so reduce the greenhouses required for raising the bedding plants. Plant in disused beds that cannot be well done away with: small shrubs and Hardy Heaths.
6 Large areas of Herbaceous plants.
   Remedy Plant small shrubs and heaths if the beds must remain. Roses require less attention. We have filled a border with lavender.
7 Large areas of fruit and vegetable garden.
   Remedy Reduce area and only grow fruit and vegetables that you cannot easily buy. Those not easily bought are Green Peas (those sold are often hard and old), cauliflowers if you are far from market, fresh cabbages, spinach, lettuce, brussel [sic] sprouts and buy beetroot, onions, carrots, Jerusalem artichokes, potatos [sic], turnips, spring lettuces. Buy in Northumberland apples, pears, damsons. Grow your own cherries (maydakes and morellos). Those bought are hard and unripe. If ripe they do not travel well. The same with strawberries if you are not near market and with Raspberries.

To the south of the Hall Sir Charles made smart terraces, in which lozenge-shaped parterres burst with plants, giving way to a lawn which then disappears with a deep walled ha-ha (incorporating stylized arching deer shelters underneath) dropping precipitously to the parkland below.

For many, though, Sir Charles's greatest creation, and certainly the most astonishingly imaginative, was the Quarry Garden. This huge crevice, the source of the new hall's stone, was carved through the older house's formal gardens to form a rugged landscape in which rocky walls and arches towered over the garden below. Sir Charles planted it in the most naturalistic way with ferns, of which he was a serious collector (in 1854 he listed a huge number of hardy ferns in his possession, including a *Cystopteris fragilis* (brittle fern); *Adiantum pedatum* (Virginian maidenhair); *Onoclea sensibilis* (a 'sensitive fern from Canada'); and the *Osmunda regalis* (royal fern). By contrast though, he also chose a few more exotic-looking plants such as a *Buddleja globosa* (orange ball tree) and *Piptanthus nepalensis* (evergreen laburnum), which were both killed by frost during the great winter of 1866–7; a *Chamaerops excelsa* (hardy palm); a *Yucca filamentosa*; and a *Trachycarpus fortunei* (Chusan palm) that still survives today by a huge rugged stone arch that stretches over the Quarry's canopy. Along the top he planted yews and pines to build shelter and height: these have given the Quarry a wonderful microclimate but also created something of a looming atmosphere.

At the end of the Quarry Garden visitors emerged blinking, both today and in Sir Charles's time, into the more open setting of the old Belsay Castle, now a ruin overlooking a grassy field where only the lumps and bumps testify to the eighteenth-century formal gardens. That this is such a spectacular eye-catcher is no accident, as to encourage its ruined appearance Sir Charles pulled down part of it and turfed over the formal gardens. Indeed, it would have been even more spectacular in those days, when Sir Charles could not have imagined that his own newly built house would eventually compete as an equally empty shell.

LEFT Rhododendrons and ferns shelter under the Quarry's rocky walls.

RIGHT ABOVE A walk through the Quarry Garden feels like an intrepid adventure through a ravine.

RIGHT BELOW The Quarry Garden is a haven for ferns, which Sir Charles collected.

Sir Charles died in 1867 and as his son Charles Atticus was already deceased, Belsay was inherited by Sir Arthur Middleton, the 7th Baronet who so beautifully described its setting at the beginning of this chapter. Like Sir Charles, he lavished knowledgeable attention on its gardens. He, too, was a serious plantsman and nudged the Quarry into being a sheltered spot for tender plants, creating the exotic jungle atmosphere that is so memorable today. Into this ravine squeeze masses of species rhododendrons, originally hailing from the Himalayas and China, which between them provide flowers from November, when *Rhododendron arboreum* var. *roseum* offers pinky-red blooms, to high summer, when *Rhododendron auriculatum* produces large white flowers. Sir Arthur also added a pocket handkerchief tree (*Davidia involucrata*) shortly after it was introduced to Europe from China in 1897 and today a seedling of this one continues to flower at Belsay, drawing large crowds to see its beautiful drooping white flowers. In contrast, he also created the West Quarry, which is gardened with the lightest touch to focus on natives such as primroses and foxgloves. At the entrance of the Quarry Sir Arthur began a meadow garden, where there is now a beautiful spread of snowdrops, but he also added many trees (parrotia, *Cryptomeria japonica*, acers and magnolias) that have struggled for survival in this difficult spot.

Sir Arthur also created two gardens between the Quarry and the hall – the Yew Garden and the Winter Garden. The Yew Garden is a delightful spot in which a tiny paved area with yew cylinders and colourful tulips is enclosed by a yew and Lawson cypress hedge (planted by Sir Arthur in 1897 as a shelter belt but never removed).

The Winter Garden provides yet another memorable scene, where a walk of heathers and other flowering plants frames what Sir Arthur created as a sunken tennis court but is now used as a croquet pitch by the Belsay Croquet Club. This immaculate lawn drops into deer-grazed parkland using a ha-ha less subtle than those we are used to. Watching over it all is a huge Douglas fir (*Pseudotsuga*

LEFT FROM TOP TO BOTTOM Today Belsay Castle is ruined, an atmospheric incident in the gardens; the Yew Garden, where yew cylinders are surrounded by lupins and alliums; the Belsay Croquet Club in action in the Winter Garden.
RIGHT The West Quarry is gardened with a light touch to give a naturalistic feel.

triffid amongst the brash rhododendrons). Anyone desperate for a glimpse of laburnum can get a fix by the old castle, where the approach from the Quarry Garden is delightfully framed by its yellow flowers.

Sir Arthur died in 1933 and, like so many large houses, Belsay Hall was requisitioned by the army during the Second World War. It stayed within the ownership of the Middleton family, however, and they were able to live in it for a while after the war. But Belsay is really too large and too grand for modern-day living so in the 1960s Sir Stephen Middleton, Arthur's grandson, moved to a smaller home near by, leaving the hall with a skeleton staff of one gardener. One can only pity that poor gardener as he struggled helplessly against the tide of nature and it was not long before the gardens were desperately overgrown. The title of Baronet Middleton eventually became extinct in 1999 on the death of Sir Lawrence, the 10th baronet.

In 1980 Belsay was taken into state care and it has since been restored by English Heritage. Thanks to a proficient and enthusiastic staff, its gardens now thrive in the tradition of Sir Charles and Sir Arthur, and are a hub of activity with visitors drawn to this remote spot by occasional art exhibitions, beautiful plants and, of course, an excellent tea room!

Witley Court

WORCESTERSHIRE

*I*F ANY GARDEN could echo, then those at Witley Court certainly would. Having been one of the country's largest and most opulent homes during the Victorian and Edwardian eras, the substantial hall suffered a fire in the mid-twentieth century and was then stripped to a skeleton for architectural salvage, the gardens being left to slip away into decline. In recent decades, though, Witley Court has been receiving the care and attention it deserves and so the gardens are gradually returning as a blend of naturalistic lake, ornamental woodland and stunning formal parterres, all watched over by the hall's magnificent shell.

Witley can be traced back at least as far as 1086, when it is recorded in the Domesday Book as a manor belonging to Urso d'Abetot, a cousin of William the Conqueror. By the second half of the seventeenth century it had been bought by Thomas Foley of Stourbridge. The Foleys were rich and important: Thomas's father had made great innovations in the mass manufacture of nails (even

conducting industrial espionage in Sweden) and Thomas had further increased the business's success by supplying cannons and ballistics in the Civil War, and by marrying the daughter of a major gun manufacturer. Over the next two centuries, Witley Court was to be owned by no fewer than eight Thomas Foleys (made into lords in the early eighteenth century), who variously bought neighbouring estates to create a huge property of over 2,600 acres (1052ha), as well as making improvements to the house and surrounding park and gardens.

In the mid-eighteenth century the fourth Thomas (2nd Lord Foley) made many changes, including damming a brook to create Front Pool, a lake to the north of the hall, across which were built two causeways, making for a scenic approach. He also rebuilt the medieval church by the house, and for at least some of the work used James Gibbs, designer of St Martin-in-the-Fields in Trafalgar Square. He died without heir in 1766 and so the title of baron was lost, while Witley passed to his second cousin, the 5th Thomas.

LEFT An early nineteenth-century painting of Witley Court's south front, before W.A. Nesfield created his famous parterres.
RIGHT The ruined Witley Court makes a striking backdrop to the South Parterre and the Perseus and Andromeda fountain.

In the late eighteenth century the Foleys created a 'wilderness' to offer shaded walks along the banks of the Front Pool and the brook that fed it. Unfortunately, the 6th Thomas was rather feckless and Witley Court suffered as a result of his financial difficulties, but in the early nineteenth century the 7th Thomas Foley was able to resolve things by marrying a daughter of the 2nd Duke of Leinster. He engaged the architect John Nash to make improvements to the house, including the addition of huge stone porticos that humble the visitor even today. He also created an octagonal walled kitchen garden that still survives, and the octagon theme was repeated in a collection of eight-sided dog kennels with pointed roofs, now private residences in the wider park. These were designed by George Stanley Repton, an architect with experience of quaint designs, who was also asked to introduce an element of formal garden around the house, with flower beds, terraces and balustrading. It is believed that his more famous father, the

ABOVE The northern front of the hall overlooks Front Pool.
LEFT The now-ruined Samuel Daukes orangery is still host to a splendid camellia.

landscape designer Humphry Repton, was consulted on the park, although regrettably there is little surviving information on his involvement.

After all these improvements, the reign of the Thomas Foleys at Witley Court finally came to an end in 1837 when, in order to pay off huge debts accumulated through gambling, the 8th Thomas sold it for £890,000 to William Humble Ward, the 11th Baron Ward of Birmingham and the youthful heir to millions earned through mining and industry. As Ward was only a minor, the house was rented out for a period, most notably from 1843 to 1846 to Queen Adelaide, widow of William IV. Lord Ward finally took up residence in 1846 and, like so many of Witley's owners, set out to improve his new property, transforming it into a quite fabulous example of the Victorian taste.

Architect Samuel Whitfield Daukes was brought in to pull the house into the fashionable Italianate style so famously used by Queen Victoria at Osborne House on the Isle of Wight. He clad the entire hall and neighbouring church in Bath stone, adding towers, new wings, balustrading and a huge orangery leading to the gardens via grandly curving staircases.

The era's must-have designer, William Andrews Nesfield, was given the job of transforming the gardens in 1856, and it is the skeleton of his astonishing work that we can see today. W.A. Nesfield was arguably the most successful designer of the early Victorian period, working at hundreds of prestigious properties. His special skill was to create complex parterres in which the main attractions were not so much flowering plants but rather the intricate patterns in which the beds were arranged, rather like a piece of embroidery. The beds were edged in box, and between them was sprinkled coloured glass or gravel. Nesfield spent three days at Witley Court before designing what he was to describe as his 'monster work'.

To the east a rectangular garden stretching away from the hall was filled with a delightful parterre around a fountain depicting Flora, the goddess of spring. This garden was described a few decades after its creation in the *Gardeners' Chronicle* (although the writer's description of gravel 'walks' is inaccurate, as they were actually for viewing only):

There are practically three gardens – a central one, flanked by a smaller one upon either side. The gardens are partly laid out in Box and in grass; the former are flowing scroll designs, with walks of red and white gravel, which will

W.A. NESFIELD

William Andrews Nesfield was born in Durham in 1794, the son of a rector and a gentlewoman. As a boy he was educated at boarding schools before studying maths at Trinity College, Cambridge, and then moving on to Woolwich as an army cadet. His studies eventually completed, he then fought in the Peninsular War in Spain, and later in Canada to defend it from the Americans.

Through all of this Nesfield was a keen watercolour painter and so, when he left the army, he decided to become a professional artist. This proved to be a successful career choice and he enjoyed both critical acclaim and high prices.

In 1834 Nesfield married the daughter of an archbishop and they moved to London, living in a house designed for them by Anthony Salvin, his brother-in-law. The garden that Nesfield designed for his family in Muswell Hill attracted some attention, being reviewed in the *Gardener's Magazine*, and he and Salvin began to work together on projects in which they were able to design both house and garden.

Nesfield became an extremely fashionable garden designer, known for his ornate parterres with vibrant bedding schemes. Over the next three decades he worked at 250 of the country's most impressive estates, including Eaton Hall (Cheshire), Castle Howard (Yorkshire), Alton Towers (Staffordshire), Inverary Castle (Argyll), Regent's Park (London) and Sudeley Castle (Gloucestershire).

Unfortunately for Nesfield, the inevitable decline in popularity of his high-maintenance designs happened during his lifetime, so he had to suffer the indignity of watching his creations fall from favour and then either decay or be dismantled. He died in 1881 and today relatively few Nesfield gardens can still be seen.

LEFT FROM TOP TO BOTTOM
W.A. Nesfield's East Parterre,
photographed in *c*.1920; Nesfield's
South Parterre, photographed in
c.1920; his 'Monster Work',
photographed in *c*.1920.
RIGHT One of the pavilions in the
South Parterre.

doubtless have a good effect in winter, but are now eclipsed by the gay colours of Pelargoniums, Ageratums, masses of Mangles' variegated Pelargonium, and Viola Bluebell, beds of Coleus margined by *Cinerania compacta*, and splendid groups of *Tropaeolum Hunteria*.

From the south portico the view must have been heart-stopping. A grid of formal paths punctuated with clipped evergreens, standard trees and smart flower beds dipped down and then stretched upwards to 900 yards (823 metres) of stone balustrade surrounding the gardens, dividing them from the deer park beyond. On either side were pavilions that Daukes designed with an exotic flavour, giving them curved steps, bell-shaped roofs with a scale-covered finish and beautifully decorated ceilings as a reward for those venturing inside. In case it was needed, extra colour was provided by masses of flowering plants in large stone vases known as tazzas. The *Gardeners' Chronicle* described

the oval groups of flowers on the slopes in front of the terrace, other Rhododendron and sub-tropical beds comprising Cannas (very dark kind), variegated Maples, and Ailanthus glandulosa. The ovals are designed in Box – a very pretty group of figures, tastefully planted with walks alternately of dark and light gravel, each figure being bordered with Lonicera variegata cut close, inside the Box edging, and having a very pretty and chaste effect. The group of Rhododendrons are edged with ornamental stone and golden Yews, trimmed, trained Hollies, and large stone vases with garlands of flowers draping their sides and affording infinite variety, while Nature's broad expanse of dense green carpet is the groundwork upon which the artificial objects are introduced or placed only in so far and in such proportion as they ornament and improve. The carpet bedding is very suitably on a grass terrace upon the south side of the large fountain – the prettiest piece of carpet bedding I have seen during the whole season.

The most memorable part of this scene was, and is, undoubtedly a central fountain that shows the Greek hero Perseus rescuing Andromeda from Poseidon's sea monster by slaying it with a spear, surrounded by dolphins, shells and armed Nereids. Carved of Portland stone, it is one of the largest pieces of sculpture that you will ever see – indeed, a photograph from the 1880s shows a lady of the family

rowing in it (the basin is 180 feet by 120 feet/55m by 37m and the central piece rises 26 feet/8m above the water). This magnificent feature was designed by Nesfield, carved by James Forsyth and engineered by James Easton, costing £20,000 to build.

The *Gardeners' Chronicle* writer said in 1881: 'It was a sight not easily forgotten as I leisurely ascended the second slope and looked down up on the dashing spray blown by the wind and glistening with sunbeams, for a moment sparkling like jewels, now silver, and anon passing with golden drops as the last flash of light grew dim before the shadow of a passing cloud.' Each minute that the fountains fired, 4,000 gallons/15m³ of water were needed to satisfy their 400 jets. Fortunately, they were generally fired only twice a week, and then only when the owners were in residence. The success of the fountains' operation was thanks to gravity: from the ponds to the north, water was pumped uphill, using a horse-powered steam pump, to reservoirs half a mile away. The height of the second reservoir was such that it provided enough pressure to rush the water through pipes to the fountains at 4,500 gallons/20,500 litres each minute. Uniquely, some of the dolphins were fitted with reeds on their water nozzles, with the result that they played notes as the water passed through and could be arranged to produce different tunes. The sheet music for these still exists, although sadly the recent restoration of the fountains did not stretch to the reeds.

In 1862 ornate golden gates were introduced at the furthest point of the garden as an eye-catcher, in a position

OPPOSITE FROM LEFT TO RIGHT
Rhododendrons frame woodland walks to
the lake; part of the Wilderness is now
maintained as a beautifully shaded
streamside meadow; a cascade – raised in
recent years to prevent flooding – tumbles
down the eighteenth-century dam from the
Front Pool.

where Nesfield had suggested a belvedere. These were later sold and moved to Arizona, America.

Lord Ward's first wife died in childbirth shortly after their marriage but in 1865 he married the beautiful Georgina Moncrieffe and went on to have seven children. The eldest of these inherited Witley and in 1885 became the 2nd Earl of Dudley (a titled revived for his father). He took up residence in 1888 on reaching the age of twenty-one and the gardens were at the centre of his coming-of-age celebrations. At the various parties for dignitaries and estate families the drives were lit with hurricane lamps, fairy lights were used to decorate the lawns and the fountains were illuminated after dark.

This was a particularly opulent time of Witley's history and the Prince of Wales, later Edward VII, was a regular guest, attracted largely by the earl's shooting parties. This lifestyle took its toll on his marriage, though. He had many children with his wife (Rachel Gurney, a Norfolk banking heiress) but apparently there was little else in common between them and while the earl was partying, the countess carried out 'good works'. In 1908 they separated, the countess being allowed to use Witley as her residence. The gardens were very important to her and she laid out a topiary garden by the church, known as My Lady's Garden, in which clipped birds, spirals and arches added a note of gaiety. The family finances were by now as shaky as the

marriage and the earl had to mortgage the estate. In 1920 the countess was drowned in a swimming accident in Ireland and the earl then sold Witley Court.

Witley's next owner was a wealthy carpet manufacturer, Sir Herbert 'Piggy' Smith, but the glory days of Witley Court were well and truly over. Piggy installed electricity but used only a small corner of the building and controversially reduced staffing in the hall to just half a dozen maids and a butler (the Dudley family had had over a hundred staff).

In 1937 a fire broke out in the south-east corner of the house, in the basement bakery, and the tiny number of staff meant that any fight to put it out was a hopeless one. Large parts of the house were gutted and as the insurance money was insufficient to pay for the rebuilding, Witley was put up for sale once more, the house going for only £4,000. In 1954 it passed into the hands of an antique dealer who stripped it of everything it held – even the timber from the roof – so that it quickly became totally ruinous, with trees growing within its walls. The garden suffered, too: its ornaments were auctioned, the Perseus and Andromeda fountain was both plundered and struck by lightning and the pipes that had supplied it were sold as scrap for £2,000, while the parterres gave way to a desert of rough grass punctuated with overgrown trees and box. Many of the beautiful

Brodsworth Hall

SOUTH YORKSHIRE

THE GARDENS of Brodsworth Hall, near Doncaster in South Yorkshire, are now regarded as among the most remarkable Victorian gardens in the whole country. Yet when English Heritage took over the house in 1990 no one had any idea of the historic value of what surrounded it. Today, the bedding plants and bulbs in the formal garden glow brilliantly in spring and summer, while the Grotto or Fern Dell, with over a hundred varieties of ferns, provides cool contrasting shade. With the scent and soft colours in the Rose Garden, the clipped precision of the evergreen shrubberies, the spectacular laburnum arch, wildflower meadows, a historic geranium collection, hundreds of shrubs and autumn colour from the ornamental trees, there are horticultural treasures at Brodsworth to please all tastes. Even winter is a delight, as marble statues and 200,000 snowdrops gleam white amidst the dark yew and holly trees.

Brodsworth has a strange history. Peter Thellusson, a banker of Swiss origin, bought the estate in 1791, at which point it comprised a mid-eighteenth-century house surrounded by substantial acres of farmland, including parkland, and perhaps as much as 20 acres (8.1ha) of gardens, including a grove, a bank and pleasure grounds. When Thellusson died in 1797, his children found that most of his property had been left to his descendants in trust. This was quite normal for the time, but he had imposed the extraordinary condition that nothing should be handed over until all of his male descendants who were alive at his death had themselves died. For nearly sixty years this will was the subject of costly litigation and even the cause of an Act of Parliament. Possibly it was the inspiration behind Charles Dickens's satirical case of *Jarndyce v. Jarndyce* in his novel *Bleak House*. Finally, in 1859, Peter Thellusson's property was divided in half and Brodsworth was inherited by his great-grandson, Charles Sabine Augustus Thellusson.

Charles decided to put the bizarre circumstances of his bequest behind him. He would demolish the Georgian house and spend part of his fortune on building, decorating and furnishing a new mansion on a different but nearby site. Perhaps because he had been born in Florence, Charles wanted an Italianate house, even though by the 1860s this style was becoming less fashionable in England than it had been in the '40s or '50s. An Italian, Chevalier G.M. Casentini, has often been credited with the design and certainly he

LEFT Snowdrops and statues abound at Brodsworth.
RIGHT This watercolour probably formed part of architect Philip Wilkinson's project for the house.

visited Brodsworth and supplied statues for the house and garden; but it now seems more likely that a London architect, Philip Wilkinson, was given the commission.

The work, begun in 1861, went ahead at a great pace and was completed by 1863. The new Brodsworth Hall was a substantial house, with thirteen bays on the garden side. A balustrade crowned with urns added to its impressive appearance, as did the rustication of the ground floor. It was approached by a carriage drive curving through shrubberies to arrive at a vast lawn in front of the *porte cochère*. A noble cedar of Lebanon in the middle of the lawn had been a feature of the eighteenth-century park and Charles may have intended its retention to emphasize that there was continuity as well as novelty in his plans for the Brodsworth estate.

Who designed the extensive gardens that surround the house is not known. Probably it was Charles himself, with his head gardener, Samuel Taylor, and since Casentini supplied the statuary, he may have had a hand in the layout too; but, as with the house, although the formal parts are Italianate, they are in a style that was by then rather dated and there is little of the real spirit of Italy.

To some extent the layout seems to have taken into account the pleasure grounds and park which had been laid out in the eighteenth century, although Charles made the parkland outside the gardens larger by grubbing up hedges. The Industrial Revolution would not affect this part of Yorkshire until the end of the nineteenth century, and there was no need to screen any mines or factories. Agriculture was still the chief engine of the local economy, so the 8,000 acres (3,239ha) of arable and grazing land owned by Charles which surrounded the house offered much the same pastoral backdrop in the 1860s as they would have done over previous centuries.

Charles and his wife, Georgiana, had six children but any hopes that the Thellussons had put all problems of inheritance behind them, and that a whole dynasty was waiting to succeed, were to be dashed. After Charles died in 1885, his sons – Peter, Herbert, Charles and Augustus – inherited in turn. The only one of

ABOVE Charles and Georgiana Thellusson with one of their babies.
BELOW LEFT Frederick Larner, head gardener from 1913 to 1941, with his team of gardeners.
BELOW RIGHT George Freeman, one of the garden staff in Victorian times.

Brodsworth's archives, unfortunately, contain no plans for the gardens, but the accounts for the estate give many hints as to how work proceeded. Charles seems to have kept the old head gardener, William Swift, on for a couple of years after he took over the estate, but in November 1861, soon after work began on the new house, Samuel Taylor was appointed and the following January Swift was pensioned off. In 1861 expenditure on the garden was only £169 18s. 11d. but by 1862 it had risen to £496 12s. 11d. and a note in the accounts explains that this was 'not for the ordinary work of the Garden, but for laying it out afresh, for formation of terraces round Hall &c. &c.' The following year £782 15s. 2d. was spent, which did not include the gardeners' wages.

Once the gardens become more established, it is the small details of the accounts that give the flavour of the daily routines in a Victorian garden. Take 1870, for instance. There are regular payments for blacksmith's work, for gravel and for the coal and coke used to heat the 'Gardens and Gas House'. Other items indicate that plants were bought as well as grown on site. On 27 July £3 16s. was paid to Thomas Milan for 'Seeds April to June' and on 14 December James Veitch's famous nursery was paid £117 5s. for 'Plants Bulbs to July to Dec [sic]'. These may be the plants that cost £2 19s. 6d. for carriage on the railway in November. Sundries such as 'Thermometers and Silver Sand' were also bought from Veitch, costing £1 18s. for 'Jany to April'.

Sometimes bare figures suggest a personal story. Samuel Taylor died on 21 September 1870 and in October his widow was paid his wages from 1 May to 1 November – a total of £37 10s. On 2 June that year John Applin was reimbursed £7 17s. 9d. for the expenses of getting himself and his wife and their belongings to Brodsworth. They must have arrived at the beginning of the year because on 29 June he was paid £38 15s. as salary for '2 quarters'. The second quarter was paid at a slightly higher rate, so presumably he worked well. Other items indicate that he was empowered to pay out money (for example, £3 16s. for guano in June) and to receive it (£2 10s. 'from the Sale of an old boiler'). He was acting,

in effect, as head gardener. But on 22 November we find a note of £10 for his salary to 3 November plus '3 months extra in lieu of notice to quit'. Two fares to London costing £2 2s. were bought for him and his wife and £5 was paid for the carriage of their belongings – which seems quite generous and probably an indication that he had not been dismissed for misconduct but brought in as temporary cover for the ailing Samuel Taylor.

William Chuck then took over as head gardener and in November he paid for his wife's travel to Brodsworth. In that year J. Veitch & Sons were again the major suppliers of seeds and plants. Chuck had at least seven gardeners under him, often more, and a garden boy (and in 1884 the accounts show a woman as well); he could also call on labourers who, as on other estates, doubled up in different roles.

As well as keeping the pleasure gardens looking good, the gardeners looked after the kitchen garden. Charles had kept its eighteenth-century shape – not the classic square but a long rectangle – and had the stone walls rebuilt in brick. Here his staff were expected to produce not only enough fruit and vegetables to feed the family and indoor servants but also a surplus that could be sold. The quality must have been excellent, as Augustus Thellusson once found peaches from Brodsworth on sale at Fortnum and Mason's up-market grocery store in London. Flowers such as lily-of-the-valley were also sent down to London by rail for Covent Garden market. The head gardener received 10 per cent of what the kitchen garden earned. In 1894, for instance, William Chuck earned an extra £9 2s. 6d. in this way to add to his £95 annual salary – a useful perk. With rent-free accommodation, as well, in a handsome new house within the walls of the kitchen garden, this was an excellent post.

Another important aspect of the gardeners' work was to provide flowers and plant arrangements for the house, particularly for special events. When Peter Thellusson celebrated his coming of age, the local paper reported on 5 January 1872 that the walls of the ballroom 'were literally dressed in evergreens and flowers, the arrangements being due to Mr Chuck the head gardener'.

their generation who had children was the youngest sister, Constance. She had married a distant relation, Horace Grant-Dalton, and it was their son, Charles, who took over when Augustus died in 1931.

As late as the 1920s, the head gardener, Frederick Larner, had a dozen gardeners working under him but gradually Brodsworth began to suffer, like most similar estates, from the social changes that made it increasingly difficult to find the troupes of servants and gardeners such large properties required for their maintenance. Charles Grant-Dalton and his wife, Sylvia, had no option but to retrench, and decided to rent out most of the huge kitchen garden.

During the Second World War, Brodsworth was requisitioned by the army, but although as many as 1,000 men were billeted in the park and estate buildings after Dunkirk, they caused no significant damage. One good point was that the kitchen garden was cultivated once again to provide food for the soldiers. When the war was over, the upkeep of such a large property became more and more difficult, even though Charles Grant-Dalton mowed the lawns himself. So after he and Sylvia died, their daughter Pamela took the decision to hand the house and pleasure gardens, though not the farmland, over to English Heritage. The transfer was made in 1990 and Brodsworth was the first new site acquired after EH was set up in 1984. The remarkable ensemble of mid-Victorian furniture, paintings and other contents were purchased by the National Heritage Memorial Fund and then transferred to English Heritage.

Both house and contents were in a poor state and the interesting decision was taken not to attempt to restore everything to how it would have been when Charles Thellusson first decorated his home in the early 1860s but to 'conserve as found' wherever possible and, apart from crucial repairs, to present the house as it had been at a time when it was generally well cared for, if a little shabby.

The gardens were in an equally sad condition, as recent maintenance had consisted of little except mowing the lawns in front of the house. Everywhere was overgrown and some areas were almost impenetrable. But, although a certain melancholy pleasure can sometimes be gained from wandering through a garden on the verge of dereliction, this taste is not shared by everyone and it was decided to make the gardens a real amenity for visitors by reviving their Victorian splendour. This was felt to be a particularly appropriate solution, as there had been no dramatic

changes since Charles Thellusson's time – something which made regenerating his garden easier once the jungle had been cleared.

Work on the gardens had to wait, though, until 1994 because all available funds were needed for the house, to make it waterproof and deal with the effects of the subsidence caused by coal mines which ran underneath. This delay proved beneficial in the end, as the real importance of the gardens as an example of mid-Victorian taste had not been realized when the gift of the property was made. A considerable number of Thellusson papers had been handed over with the contents, making Brodsworth one of the best endowed with archive material of all English Heritage houses. Photographs and account books give an idea of how the family lived, and life 'below stairs' for their employees is particularly well documented. Research here and in local records by a dedicated team of volunteers, working with the curator, revealed details that helped the garden team when they began work. Then clearing the paths of undergrowth uncovered further features whose existence had not previously been known about, including plants such as a rare variety of thyme – *Thymus praecox* subsp. *arcticus* 'Hazel Camplin' – and a new type of fern, *Asplenium scholopendrium* 'David Avery', which was named after the then head gardener.

Sadly, amidst all the wealth of detail, the owners, Charles and Georgiana Thellusson, remain shadowy figures. They left no diaries, their letters have not survived and the only pictures are rather posed and formal ones. But now, thanks to the restoration work, it is possible to envisage what they would have seen as they took a morning constitutional around their gardens, and how their children might have enjoyed playing there.

If the Thellussons left the house through the south hall, they would have found themselves on a terrace, which runs round the two sides of the house. Comprising strips of grass either side of a path, it has no balustrade (further evidence, perhaps, that the gardens were not laid out by an Italian) but connects with the lawns at the lower level by grass slopes. The children would surely have run – or rolled – down these banks, while for more sedate adults access to the lawns and gardens was by marble steps placed directly outside each exit from the house, including the French windows. The sides of these steps were ornamented by marble greyhounds, an animal which formed part of the family crest. On this south side of the house, Charles probably planted the formal tall yew hedge, the plants trimmed, at intervals along its length, into niches to contain statues. Intended to enclose the pleasure gardens and separate them from the land beyond, this was a very nineteenth century approach to laying-out a garden as it destroyed the uninterrupted views over the estate which eighteenth century owners would have wanted. Only one gap was left where it was possible to see over the metal fence behind the hedge and look out to the stands of trees in the parkland and to the woods beyond.

From there, Charles and Georgiana would have taken a path which runs in front of the hedge along to the parterres of the Flower Garden, with their dramatic bedding. In teasing fashion, these were not placed directly in front of the west front of the house but separated from it by wide croquet lawns and then further cut off from immediate view by formal shrubberies. Dominated by two monumental specimens of *Cedrus atlantica*, and so now known as the Cedar Beds, these contain an extraordinary range of evergreen trees and shrubs in dozens of shades of green and gold – yew, bay, viburnum, Portuguese and Japanese laurels, box, holly. Today these are all clipped into geometric shapes – spirals, domes and magnificently crisp and chunky obelisks. The present immaculate appearance of this area, with its play of colours and shapes, is a marked contrast to how it looked before the restoration began, when it was overgrown and full of self-sown trees.

At last, Charles and Georgiana would have reached the bright colour of the parterres. This was the part of the garden most altered in the twentieth century, when, to make maintenance easier and cheaper, modern roses and tall cypresses replaced the annual flowers; but, luckily, the elaborately cut parterres were not simplified. They had possibly been modelled on shapes in Robert Thompson's *The Gardener's Assistant*, which was published in 1859 just before the Brodsworth gardens were begun.

The parterres are particularly labour intensive. In Victorian times the bedding schemes would have been changed three or four times a year; even today the gardeners set out 10,000 plants and bulbs twice a year in the beds and in four superb tazzas: pansies, forget-me-nots, polyanthus,

RIGHT ABOVE Pamela Grant-Dawson on one of the marble greyhounds which ornament the steps.

RIGHT BELOW Her father, Charles Grant-Dawson, mowed the lawns himself.

hyacinths and tulips in spring; blue petunias, perhaps, with begonias and French marigolds in summer, dotted with such exotics as banana trees. This changing rainbow of colour is punctuated by more geometric topiary and dominated by two magnificent monkey puzzle trees (*Araucaria araucana*) and the three-tier marble Dolphin Fountain which plays in the centre. These parterres are a living contradiction to those who still sneer at 'Victorian carpet bedding'. With unusual plants such as gingers used for dot planting, and 'White Pet' roses grown as standards, there is nothing vulgar here, and considerable subtlety.

The twin Cedar Beds on the house side of the Flower Garden are duplicated on the far side; and here there are also a few specimen trees, such as *Arbutus unedo*. Between the two beds, lined up on the axis of the Dolphin Fountain and the garden front of the house, is a laburnum arch, which drips with bright yellow racemes in late spring. Unlike most of the metalwork in the gardens, this was made recently in order to add colour for visitors. It rapidly became a favourite feature – though purists might object that it blocks the original uninterrupted view from the library of the house through to the fountain, which Charles and Georgiana would have seen silhouetted against the dark yew hedge beyond.

If they had taken the wide path which the arch now covers, they would have reached the Grove, a complex area of the gardens, where traces of the eighteenth-century layout are most evident. At its entrance, filling a corner

between two paths, an overgrown rock garden has recently been cleared and replanted with plants from the USA, Scotland, Norway and the Alps – *Saxifraga oppositifolia* and *Dodecatheon poeticum*, for instance – which recall the Thellussons' frequent travels to mountainous places abroad. After passing it, Charles and Georgiana would have strolled under a metal bridge – again now restored – and climbed winding steps up the Mount to the stone Summer House – also recently restored – constructed in 1866 in the shape of a classical Doric temple. Standing under its portico, they could gaze down admiringly over the formal areas and back to the house – though probably they never even peeped into the tool shed so conveniently placed in the basement.

The poignant Pets' Cemetery, containing the graves of favourite dogs and of Polly the parrot, which now lies behind the Mount, was only begun in 1896 by their son Peter, so the Thellussons' garden tour would have followed a path leading this time over the metal bridge and into one of the surprises of Brodsworth – the Grotto, or Fern Dell as it used to be called. The site is an old quarry (though not, as is often stated, the one from which the stone for the eighteenth-century

BELOW FROM LEFT TO RIGHT 'White Pet' roses bloom by the Dolphin Fountain; Alpine plants in the rock garden; the Summer House on top of the Mount.
RIGHT The laburnum arch is resplendent in late spring.

scolopendrium), survived the years of neglect, while many of the others here today were from the collection of Wing Commander Eric Baker, to which were added some mature tree ferns (*Dicksonia antarctica*). A tiny cascade tumbles down through six little pools and the severity of the stone and the green of the ferns are enlivened by lilies, yellow and blue asphodel, and creeping plants such as ajuga – as well as by autumn bulbs such as sternbergia and colchicum.

This area is well labelled in botanical terms, but perhaps the most interesting label is the one on a wooden seat in an alcove, which commemorates John and Gladys Jones, who met and married in the 1930s when she was working at Brodsworth as a housemaid and he was one of the gardeners.

The middle path around the Grotto is edged by posts and chains covered with trained ivy. Like all the paths at Brodsworth it was made in what, in the 1860s, was the expensive but maintenance-free new material called asphalt to provide a smooth surface for a dog cart to take invalids or small children around the grounds, while Charles and Georgiana could have walked through a tunnel under this path and arrived in a part of the Grove known as the Target Range. This was used for archery – *the* fashionable garden sport, with croquet, in mid-Victorian times, before lawn tennis was invented. In 1871 Charles bought three terracotta statues to stand here; cheaper than Casentini's marble ones, they were badly damaged and are awaiting restoration.

At one end of this long narrow lawn lies the Target House, with its classical façade and Palladian window. Like the Grove, it possibly dates to the eighteenth century but, strangely, the Thellussons seem to have turned it into a Swiss chalet, where they could take tea. Today it houses an exhibition about the gardens and the vista from its windows looks back to an eye-catcher at the far end of the Target Range. A bit of *trompe-l'œil* fun, this simply represents a pedimented doorway and two windows which give the impression of having been blocked up, as though in response to the window tax, as many windows were in the eighteenth century.

Photographs taken in about 1915 show irises growing on either side of the Target House, but the site would have been unsuitable for such sun-loving plants. Today modern plantings ornament the banks of the Range – mostly ferns on one side, with some wild strawberries, and herbaceous perennials on the other: bergenias, peonies, hellebores, hostas, Japanese anemones, aquilegias, phlomis, acanthus, dicentras, forget-me-nots, geraniums and yellow poppies – the whole made dramatic by the trees growing high on top of the banks.

house and the Thellussons' Summer House was extracted) and, as at Belsay Hall (see page 124), the owners decided to turn the crater into something aesthetic, which would add to the horticultural appeal of their garden. Started by 1864, the work was by a Joseph Barron, who may have been the son of William Barron, who had carried out the famous rock work at Elvaston Castle in Derbyshire. (Joseph probably also made the rock garden at the entrance to the Grove.)

The Grotto has three main levels with wide paths leading round the edge and under and over each other, linked by winding stone terraces. At its bottom lies a walk of bright white gravel, symbolizing a river flowing through this mini-canyon. The rocky sides were filled with ferns, enjoying the shade created by the depth of the quarry. A surprising number, including the hart's tongue fern (*Asplenium*

The Thellussons would probably not have ventured into the walled kitchen garden and this treat is also denied to modern visitors, as it is in separate ownership. They could have made their way back to the house along more winding paths edged by evergreen shrubs, where a backdrop of larger trees such as sequoiadendron and beech is punctuated – one can scarcely use the word 'animated', so languid is their air – with statues. (Like those in the Cedar Beds, the greyhounds on the steps by the house, the Dolphin Fountain and the tazzas in the Flower Garden, these were supplied by Casentini, who was paid a total of £2,750.) Or they could have taken the path, edged with tall yews, along one of the high Spine Banks. These were ridges in the Grove which were made from rubble when the area was quarried in the eighteenth century. Between them runs a valley which has recently been planted with acers such as *A. shirasawanum* 'Aureum' and *A. palmatum* var. *dissectum*, which change from

yellow or purple in spring to all shades of red, yellow and orange in the autumn.

Charles and Georgiana seem to have stopped work on their garden by 1871, and she lived to enjoy the spectacular results until 1883 and Charles for two years more. Frustratingly, it is not clear whether one of the most original areas was created in their lifetime or added by their eldest son, Peter. The magnificent Rose Garden next to the Target House runs on either side of a curving pergola 150 feet (45m) long, which in summer is smothered with roses, such as 'Gardenia' and 'Climbing Cécile Brünner', interspersed

OPPOSITE ABOVE Favourite dogs lie alongside Polly the parrot in the Pets' Cemetery.
OPPOSITE BELOW The Target House, where the family took tea.
BELOW The Grotto has paths at different levels.

with honeysuckle and vines. This pergola can be perceived as the main vein of a rose leaf, with the paths to each side as the smaller veins. The five box-edged beds to the north were certainly laid out by 1893 and the matching five to the south were added in the 1990s to create symmetry and increase the effect of a leaf. More is not clear at present, but whatever future research may yield about its history, this area today is one of the most attractive parts of the whole garden.

The beds have been planted with about a hundred Old Garden roses – pink, yellow, red and white, and all of them in cultivation before 1900. There are many Portlands such as 'Indigo', 'Comte de Chambord', 'Pergolèse', 'Rose de Rescht' and, of course, 'Duchess of Portland'; there are Bourbons such as 'Bourbon Queen' and 'Louise Odier', and Centifolias, such as 'Blanchefleur' and 'Fantin-Latour'. In summer their intense fragrance hangs over a wide area, while the bright red hips linger from autumn into winter.

Along one edge of the Rose Garden, and following its curve, is a long crescent-shaped herbaceous border. Although laid out in the twentieth century on the site of the old dog kennels, when it was restored in 2006 it was decided to restrict the plants to those which had been introduced into Britain before Queen Victoria died in 1901. Edged with box and divided into nine compartments by yew buttresses, this garden is entirely cared for by Brodsworth's team of ten or so volunteer gardeners. Two of them were asked to do planting plans and carefully devised a plan for each of the nine sections for colour, shape and continuity, so that the border has something to show from late spring, when pink peonies burst into flower, through to autumn with rudbeckias. Gradually, over the summer, iris, geums, agapanthus, lupins, day lilies, achillea, geraniums, dictamus and many more herbaceous plants flower in sequence, backed up by the occasional shrub, such as hibiscus, large fuchsias and clematis trained up metal obelisks.

Another area none of the Thellusson family would have seen is the Rose Dell, a very recent creation. In the winter of 2004 about three-quarters of an acre (3,036m²) of woodland adjacent to the Rose Garden was cleared of ivy and self-sown

trees. New trees, including hornbeams, oaks and a copper beech, were planted, as were over a hundred varieties of species roses, such as *Rosa primula*, *R. moysii*, *R. blanda*, *R. gallica*, *R. pendulina* and *R. sericea* f. *pteracantha*, with its extraordinary translucent red thorns. All were chosen because they actually prefer the poor shallow soil in this, the lowest, part of the quarry. In spring the ground here is white with wild garlic, but in early summer its pungent scent is superseded by the more delicate perfume of the roses.

As well as roses and ferns, the gardens at Brodsworth contain several other major plant collections – of hollies, for instance. Many of these, such as the camellia-leaved holly (*Ilex* x *altaclerensis* 'Camelliifolia'), date from Victorian times and those which were badly overgrown have been carefully revived by pruning and cultivation.

Another recent innovation is the adventure playground that has been constructed on the northern edge of the gardens; but even here the Thellussons are not forgotten, as children can play on a boat reminiscent of one of the yachts they so much enjoyed sailing in.

Since the house and gardens were opened to the public in July 1995 by HRH Princess Margaret there have been some setbacks, particularly a severe storm in January 2007 when mature trees, including a chestnut and a turkey oak (*Quercus cerris*) that probably belonged to the Thellussons' garden, were brought down. But modern visitors, approaching the house and seeing the ancient cedar of Lebanon in front of it, can wander on and appreciate the 15 rich acres (6ha) of Charles Thellusson's restored gardens as much as he would have done – and enjoy the numerous recent embellishments as well.

OPPOSITE ABOVE LEFT Sylvia Grant-Dalton under the rose pergola in July 1959.
OPPOSITE ABOVE RIGHT *Rosa* 'Comte de Chambord'.
BELOW Climbing roses, honeysuckle and vines cover the rose pergola while Old Garden roses grow in the box-edged beds below.
RIGHT An ancient cedar of Lebanon stands in front of the house.

Down House

KENT

T HE GARDEN at Down House represents two opposite poles of the horticultural world: it is a real family garden and at the same time a place of international importance which has been nominated for UNESCO World Heritage Site status. This seeming contradiction comes about because Down House is where Charles Darwin, the great nineteenth-century naturalist and author of *On the Origin of Species*, lived for forty years. Its garden and the surrounding meadows were for Darwin the scientist an open-air laboratory and a place where he could walk and think out his theories on evolution and natural selection; while for Darwin the devoted family man they were a source of relaxation and pleasure.

In 1836 the young Darwin returned from his five-year voyage on HMS Beagle to find himself a celebrity. He soon married his cousin Emma, a member of the famous Wedgwood dynasty, and by 1842 they had two children and another on the way. Fame and fecundity meant that Charles and Emma needed to find a property with a rural atmosphere where they could bring up their family and he could work in peace. They chose Down House, a small Georgian residence, with a garden of about 1 acre (4,000m²) and a further 18 acres (7.3ha) of meadow, on the outskirts of the village of Downe in Kent, some 16 miles (25km) from London. (The final 'e' was added to the name of the village only in the 1860s and Darwin retained the original spelling for his home.)

Emma described Down House as 'a place which had no great charms', though she commented on 'A row of very good lime trees . . . and a fine mulberry'. Charles, writing to his sister Catherine in July 1842, portrayed the house as having 'somewhat of a desolate air' but a 'very distant & rather beautiful view'. Already he had inventoried the trees, for he goes on to list 'a really fine beech', walnut trees, yews, a Spanish chestnut, pears, 'some very old (very productive) cherry-trees . . . quinces & medlars & plums with plenty of fruit, & Morells-cherries, but few apples'. He also noted 'old larch, scotch-fir and silver fir, & old mulberry-trees making rather a pretty group . . .' but the mulberry Emma had noticed does not seem to have attracted his attention, although it stood (and still stands, cropping copiously) close to the house outside the room which they made their nursery and later the schoolroom. A purple magnolia which flowered 'against the house' was

LEFT ABOVE Looking back to Down House across the flowerbeds.

LEFT BELOW The sundial Darwin used to set his clocks stands just outside the veranda.

RIGHT FROM TOP Charles Darwin and his wife, Emma (née Wedgwood).

Charles's only mention of a purely ornamental flowering tree or shrub.

Over the years, as the number of inhabitants grew to include several more children and a number of servants, Down House was much enlarged, its character gradually changing to that of a rambling Victorian villa. Extra land was bought or rented, and the garden was laid out, planted and equipped with greenhouses.

The house was set right on one side of the estate, close up against a lane; so, the moment the Darwins moved in, changes were made to give them greater privacy. The lane in front was lowered about 2 feet (60cm) and a wall built along its length. This was a huge undertaking and the spoil removed was used to create mounds behind the 'row of very good lime trees' on the northern boundary, and so provide some shelter from the biting north winds. Most of the little garden between Down House and the road was laid to lawn, but Emma grew a few plants there, including ivy and Russian vine on the walls. Today, the climbers are back on the façade, while plants such as bergenias and spring bulbs add interest to the beds.

Behind the house, the aspect was much more open and agreeable, with an extensive lawn and the group of fine mature trees which Darwin had noted when he bought the property. Outside the drawing-room windows six

ABOVE Charles Darwin later in life, sitting in a wicker chair on the veranda.

LEFT A watercolour of Down House by the feminist writer Julia 'Snow' Wedgwood, Charles and Emma's cousin.

rectangular flower beds were made, with smaller circular beds to the sides, which were mounded up in the centre, as had been the fashion in the earlier years of the nineteenth century. Emma, who cared little for style but very much for plants, was responsible for choosing what grew here, as elsewhere in the ornamental gardens. Her daughter Henrietta describes the phloxes, lilies and larkspur planted in the middle of each bed, while lower-growing flowers such as portulacas and gazanias grew around the edges. Today the soil is less mounded up in Emma's old-fashioned way, but the beds still offer a mixture of Victorian formality and casual charm: wallflowers, bellis daisies and forget-me-nots flourish in spring, with phormiums to give height. Near by is the sundial used by Charles to set the clocks.

The garden was far from immaculate: indeed, it tended to the overgrown and scruffy – which was how Emma and Charles both liked it. Emma did some of the gardening herself, and grew a number of plants, such as mignonette and hollyhocks, from seed; but she complained that her ideas about pruning were 'diametrically opposite to the rest of my family'. Once she wrote to Henrietta that she planned to 'work my will on the old acacia'. Her daughter commented, 'This meant cutting it down. She was always more revolutionary in the matter of tree-cutting than her children.' Emma liked flowers inside the house, too, and her husband particularly admired the azaleas she massed in the drawing room.

In 1873 a veranda was added outside the drawing room, which could be accessed through a French window. Furnished with wicker chairs, and with white clematis trained along the rafters and plants such as the Scarborough lily (*Cyrtanthus elatus*) planted in a trough, it provided a link between the house and the flower beds and lawns, and then with the countryside visible beyond. The family loved to gather and read or talk in its shelter.

Because of Darwin's fame, particularly after the publication of *On the Origin of Species* in 1859, some of his numerous visitors felt it worth describing his surroundings. One mentions Down House being covered with ivy on the front, another the creepers on the back. (Many of the walls eventually had panels of diamond-shaped wooden trellis attached to them, and the plants that grew high with its help were vital to Charles's studies of climbing plants.) One American commented on 'the greenhouse with a mixed collection of plants', while another describes in detail the experiment being conducted on the revolving movements of climbing plants (what Darwin called in an 1863 letter to Joseph Dalton Hooker, then Assistant Director of the Royal Botanic Gardens at Kew, 'the irritability of tendrils'). Much later, in 1892, the Revd O.J. Vignoles wrote: 'The lawns are spacious and beautifully kept, and there was a profusion of flowers on all sides, and some magnificent trees and shrubs . . .'

In fact, the lawns close to the house were not always as well manicured as the Revd Vignoles described, even though the family played croquet on them. They were full of *Hygrocybe* or waxcap fungi, which only grow where fertilizer, or even manure, have not been used, and today this relative neglect means that the lawns and their waxcaps have been designated a Site of Nature Conservation Interest by Kent Wildlife Trust. Darwin would surely have been intrigued by the idea of part of his garden becoming an official site for scientific study, for he himself regarded the whole garden very much as a laboratory where he could satisfy his scientific curiosity. As well as his writings on geology and animal biology, there are many dealing with plant subjects – not only on how climbing plants move, but on how orchids are adapted for cross-fertilization by insects; on insectivorous plants; and particularly, in 1876, on *The Effects of Cross and Self Fertilisation in the Vegetable Kingdom* – all of which were researched by observation at Down House.

Indeed, there were few areas that Darwin did not study meticulously for research purposes. Even a plain hawthorn hedge he had planted received his attention: he noted it grew, over a twenty-nine-year period, to include twenty-one more species, such as field maple, spindle, beech and privet.

Charles's urge to measure and record spread to other members of the family. In the group of trees beyond the flower beds, set in the grass underneath a noble Spanish chestnut (*Castanea sativa*), visitors can see what looks rather like a small millstone. This is the Worm Stone, by which Darwin and Horace, his second youngest son (*b.* 1851), measured the rate at which the soil settles as earthworms continuously turn it over. The circular stone moves down in the earth in relation to two fixed metal rods, which descend over 8 feet (2.4m) into the earth from a hole at its centre – moving only about 2mm a year but enough to prove the point. (Charles's final published work was on earthworms, while Horace went on to become a scientific instrument maker, and his company made replica rods for the Worm Stone when it was reinstalled in 1929.)

At the side of the lawn was a gravel path which Darwin took at about midday in all but the worst weather. It ran from the house, past the six formal flower beds and along to a rose arbour. On the left were shrubberies filled with the evergreens the Victorians so loved. They probably included the twelve *Rhododendron thomsonii* given to Charles by his friend Joseph Dalton Hooker. Over the years, these all disappeared, but recently one has been propagated by layering from a specimen at Castle Howard, which had also received a batch of the original plants from Hooker.

To the right of the path lies a series of mixed borders now containing shrubs such as azaleas and lilacs, with herbaceous plants including geraniums, pulmonaria and centaurea. This area, planted before Gertrude Jekyll or William Robinson advocated natural drifts of plants, may have been inspired by John Claudius Loudon's *Encyclopaedia of Gardening*, for in Darwin's copy, now in Cambridge University Library, Loudon's phrase 'mingled borders' has been marked. Perhaps Charles's sense of gardening style was more advanced than Emma's.

The path from the house led eventually to the kitchen garden, which, far from being the classic square walled 1-acre (0.4ha) plot, was long and narrow and just a third of that in size. It was walled on only three sides, perhaps to maximize light in the awkward space. Darwin described it as 'a detestable slip' when he bought the house, but soon it was providing fruit and vegetables for his family and servants as well as cut flowers for the house. Strawberries, raspberries, gooseberries, currants and rhubarb; potatoes, onions, carrots, celeriac and parsnips; asparagus, lettuce and radishes; Brussels sprouts, beans of different kinds, broccoli, spinach, peas and several sorts of cabbage were grown. There were also hazel, almond and walnut trees, and several figs, which were grown in pots, and peaches on the wall. If the main purpose of the kitchen garden was to provide for the household, its secondary aim was scientific. There were, for instance, fifty-four varieties of gooseberry, so that Darwin could compare them.

LEFT ABOVE The Worm Stone.

LEFT BELOW Primulas growing in the Kitchen Garden replicate one of Darwin's experiments.

RIGHT ABOVE The greenhouses in the Kitchen Garden contain many of the plants Darwin grew.

RIGHT BELOW FROM LEFT TO RIGHT The comet orchid (*Angraecum sesquipedale*); a Venus flytrap; a cymbidium cultivar.

In recent years the head gardener was Toby Beasley, who had previously been in charge of Queen Victoria's Walled Garden at Osborne (see page 108) and has now returned to run the whole of the pleasure gardens there. At Down he was passionate about finding the correct period varieties and traced – and grew – 28 of the 41 varieties of pea grown here in Darwin's day as well as the rare 'Mr Turner's Cottage Kale' (though he failed to find seeds of Darwin's favourite broad bean 'Johnson's Wonder', which has disappeared from cultivation). Herbs such as sage, melissa, mint and angelica also flourish, as does an attractive mixture of stachys, asphodel, irises, roses and currant bushes. At one end, where Darwin placed his experimental beds, are rows of primulas to replicate one of his studies, and there is also an extensive collection of Pimpinel or Scots roses, and other old roses such as 'Rose de Rescht' and 'Village Maid'.

Against the north wall of the kitchen garden are set the greenhouses. The first, erected in 1856, was unheated; but in 1863, because he was interested in comparing tropical plants with temperate ones, Darwin began what was eventually a considerable range with a three-part hothouse and two unheated glasshouses, which he would inspect every day. Three sections survive, each now kept at a different temperature, and, together with a cold frame, they serve to demonstrate some of his experiments – all of which led to ground-breaking books. Orchids are grown, and various climbing plants, and carnivorous plants, such as the sundew (*Drosera rotundifolia*). Many parties of schoolchildren visit Down House and seeing this sort of practical experiment fascinates them and makes the subject of science more real.

Darwin's experiments were continually collated with similar research at Kew. Parcels of plants and books would go back and forth, and sometimes Kew would put in a few bananas for the Darwin family's enjoyment. Usually even the 'priceless treasures' for which Charles thanked Hooker were sent by post, though once a rare orchid in flower could only be entrusted to the safe hands of Joseph Parslow, the Darwins' butler. Other plants and seeds for experiments came from a wide circle of friends and correspondents around the world or were obtained from nurseries. Darwin often patronized one at nearby Westerham, or Thomas Rivers near Sawbridgeworth in Hertfordshire, and particularly the great Veitch nursery in Exeter (which, to Darwin's embarrassment, sometimes sent orders as gifts).

In the orchard grew more fruit trees – crab apples, apples and pears, and perhaps plums – and Darwin kept as close an eye on this area, as on every other part of his estate. The pear trees were by far the most fruitful: in October 1852 he wrote to his second cousin, the naturalist William Darwin Fox, saying, 'we have had lots of Beurre d'Alenbery, Winter Nelis, Marie Louise, Passe Colmar & Ne Plus Meuris but all off the wall; the standard dwarfs have borne a few, but I have no more room for trees, so their names would be useless to me.' Recently, cuttings taken from an 'Allington Pippin' apple tree planted by Darwin have been successfully grafted so that the orchard can be restored with some original stock.

At the far end of the property, accessed by a small gate in the kitchen garden, lies a narrow strip of land about 300 yards (274m) long which bordered, on the left, a 15-acre (6ha) meadow which Darwin owned and, on the right, one which he leased. He made a path of gravel bound with the local red sand, wide enough for two people to walk abreast, and planted a hedge along most of its length, under which Emma encouraged wild flowers such as bluebells, anemones and primroses. About a third of the way along, a loop, known as the Sandwalk, went off to the left, and ran through a small copse of about 2 acres (0.9ha), before returning near the end of the main path. Here Darwin planted hazel, alder, lime, hornbeam, birch, privet, dogwood and holly, making the loop cool and shady (and so known as the Dark Side); and he would make several circuits of it as part of his daily constitutional before setting off back along the path between the fields with its view across to the valley (the Light Side). At the beginning of the loop he kept a pile of flints and would move one across the path every time he completed a circuit.

Walking in a familiar place helped him to think, and here too he would make scientific observations, for instance on the viability of long-buried seed when disturbed by digging; but, although the Sandwalk was crucial to his meditations (and is later sometimes referred to as Darwin's 'thinking path'), he also liked his wife or friends to accompany him and talk as they went along. And neither were the children kept away from it. Darwin was an excellent father, taking great pleasure in the company of his sons and daughters and allowing them to interrupt him even in his study; so they used to play in the sand in the wood, and a rustic arbour or

RIGHT The Sandwalk still invites contemplation.

many years, and the thousands of letters he wrote or received. Emma's diary and letters and her notes for the garden also survived. In addition to descriptions by visitors, family members of all generations left reminiscences. Among the most evocative are those of the artist Gwen Raverat, the Darwins' grand-daughter, who knew Down House as a child after Charles's death. By her time the greenhouses were empty, but everything else had probably changed little. In *Period Piece*, her ever-popular memoir published in 1952, she remembers foxgloves and wild orchids, the swing between the two great yew trees on the lawn, blue salvias in the formal beds 'whose flowers we used to suck for the honey that is in them', 'tall syringa and lilac bushes' on the way to the kitchen garden and the roses there 'imprisoned behind high box borders'; and particularly 'the plop of the ripe mulberries as they fell to the ground'.

More importantly for the research, there were lots of photographs. William, the Darwins' eldest son, was given a camera in 1857 and became a keen photographer, and Leonard, the fourth of the six boys, later took many pictures of the garden.

Darwin employed two or three gardeners, most of whom doubled up in other roles. Henry Brooks looked after the cows and pigs, while Comfort was also the coachman. Brooks was known by the family as 'the gloomy gardener' and the only time he was ever heard to laugh was when Charles threw a boomerang and broke a cucumber frame. There is a wonderful photograph, taken by William in 1859, of Brooks and his son-in-law Henry Lettington, who was an under-gardener, with a donkey-drawn mowing machine.

Although Parslow, the butler, won prizes for the vegetables he grew in his cottage garden, the other men had no particular skills and were not allowed to touch the experimental beds. To Darwin's horror, Lettington once potted up some tropical orchids in 'common earth', but he later became 'a skilful crosser' – and Charles himself was not immune from error. His apology to Hooker in 1864 that 'The little [Nepenthes] which you gave me, tho' treated with maternal care, both died' is one of many references to the death of precious plants.

Today, English Heritage employs only two full-time gardeners to look after the 4 acres (1.6ha) of garden, two woods and various meadows. They are helped by contractors who cut the hedges and grass, and twenty-five

volunteers, who are always asked to do a bit of weeding before they tackle anything more interesting, such as planting out or putting up pea sticks.

Of all the gardens in this book, Down House is the only one that looks delightfully like a private garden that has opened for the National Gardens Scheme. As in the Darwins' time, it offers pleasant vistas, pretty flower beds, fine trees and a homely and practical vegetable garden. You almost expect the family to be selling tickets at the gate. But dig a little deeper and you feel an intense sense of purpose, as though Charles and Emma's High Victorian seriousness still pervades the atmosphere and inspires the staff who work there today.

Battle Abbey

EAST SUSSEX

T HE BATTLE OF HASTINGS in 1066 is said to be the one historical date that almost everyone in England can remember, and many people also know that an abbey was built on the battlefield by the winner, William the Conqueror, with the altar of its church erected on the place where the vanquished King Harold is said to have fallen, pierced in the eye by an arrow. This makes the battlefield lying below the abbey one of our most important historic landscapes and English Heritage has created a promenade around it, with panels explaining the different phases of the fighting.

At the Dissolution Henry VIII gave the abbey to his Master of the Horse, Sir Anthony Browne, and the domestic buildings became Browne's family's house. He demolished the church and, where it had been, laid out a garden with a central fountain or pool, surrounded by yew walks. He also had some earthmoving done to create a terrace overlooking the battlefield, and a 1737 engraving by the Buck brothers shows allées of trees along it, though we do not know when they were planted. In the eighteenth century there was also a formal garden in the cloister and hothouses for growing vines.

BELOW A Buck brothers engraving from 1737 shows that by then allées of trees had been planted on the terrace.

RIGHT A plain lawn has replaced the formal garden in the cloister.

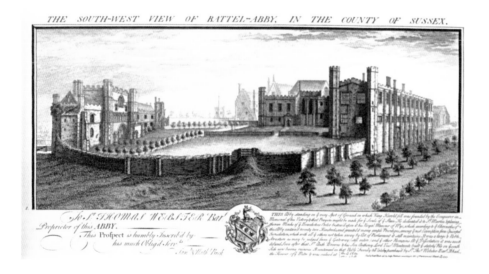

John Claudius Loudon, the author and garden designer, visited Battle in 1842 and noted the 'lofty elms' and other trees which stood close to the ruins, but he commented that the park had not enough old trees. He mentions 'a platform among the ruins, laid out symmetrically as a flower-garden, and very well planted and managed', which was probably the garden made by Browne on the site of the church, and to one side of it 'a covered yew walk, such as may sometimes be found in old French gardens', which presumably also dated back to Browne's day. But Loudon found most of the ground 'in a state of neglect' and he thought it would be improved by creepers on the ruined walls and 'a piece of water'.

A decade or two after Loudon's visit, different, more elaborate, gardens were made by the Duchess of Cleveland – not the famous mistress of Charles II but a later, more respectable lady. Catherine Lucy Wilhelmina had been born into the Stanhope family and first married Lord Dalmeny (their son became Prime Minister as Lord Rosebery). After his death, she married the 4th Duke of Cleveland, who bought the Battle estate in 1858 and allowed her Stanhope passion for landscaping (see page 186) to have a free reign.

The formal garden on the site of the church, made by Browne and observed by Loudon, was changed into something totally different: it became a wild garden in the newly fashionable style of William Robinson. A few exotic plants, such as yuccas, are there today, but it is unlikely that they are survivors from the mid-nineteenth century. The duchess created the Upper and Lower Terrace Walks, overlooking the battlefield, the upper one where the abbey's south guest range had been demolished in the late eighteenth century, and the lower one on Browne's simple terrace. Both were then copiously planted, but the Lower Terrace is left bare today. (Although the Upper Terrace retains some trees and shrubs, visitors have to take a route round the outside of the school within which it lies, so only glimpses are possible.)

The duchess also turned the horse pond into a lily pond (now overgrown and silted up), replaced the vineries with a more up-to-date conservatory (since lost) and made the cloister garden more elaborate, filling the box-edged parterres with bedding plants in typical Victorian fashion (now marked only by a square of lawn).

On the practical side, she retained an ice house and the octagonal thatched dairy that had been built for Sir Godfrey Webster in the early nineteenth century. As well as a large kitchen garden (sadly empty today), there was a small orchard, walled on the south side, to which she added fig and mulberry trees, while away from the house, in the park, she planted a number of fast-growing Turkey oaks (*Quercus cerris*).

The duchess died in 1901 and in 1922 the abbey's domestic buildings became a school, while the battlefield became public property in 1976. In common with many places in south-east England, Battle was hard hit by the Great Storm of 1987 and there has since been a programme of replanting the trees. Ten of the camellias in the duchess's walk survive against the precinct wall, as, remarkably, does Browne's yew walk with its double row of yews. There are fine trees and wildflowers on the battlefield itself – and in spring it is enlivened by banks of daffodils.

LEFT The ruined abbey dorter overlooks the battlefield and inspiring sweeps of daffodils in spring.

RIGHT The early nineteenth-century thatched dairy.

Mount Grace Priory

NORTH YORKSHIRE

WITH ITS ruined medieval buildings, Mount Grace Priory, on the edge of the North York Moors, seems typical of the many religious sites in the care of English Heritage, but it has several unique points. Its monks were Carthusians, who lived almost as hermits, seeing fellow brethren only at meetings in chapter, certain church services and a three-hour walk once a week. Each monk had his individual cell (in fact, more like a two-storey house, with a bedroom, living room and workshop); the cells were set around the cloister or the outer court and each had its own little garden, with a latrine at the end. Interestingly, these plots appear to have been exactly the same size as the gardens on the ninth-century scale plan of an idealized monastery found at St Gall in Switzerland.

Although the monks were largely vegetarian (they ate some fish), such small gardens could never have been expected to nourish their individual inhabitants completely and their food was actually cooked by lay brethren in a kitchen near the church, and delivered to each cell through a revolving hatch in the cloister wall. But the monks probably grew vegetables, herbs and flowers for medicinal purposes.

One of the Mount Grace cells was rebuilt in about 1900, and the garden behind was planted up with herbs in 1994 to reflect what the monks might have grown. They include fennel, a carminative which the monks ate during the Lenten fast to suppress the noisy effects of hunger; germander, which alleviated the symptoms of gout and lowered fevers – though it probably destroyed their livers in the process; rue, which was believed to protect against the plague; sweet woodruff and marjoram, for strewing underfoot to mask unpleasant smells; heliotrope, used as a sedative; lovage, which usefully relieved both tiredness and flatulence; pennyroyal for eradicating fleas; and hyssop, a purgative which also gave a bitter note to the famous Chartreuse liqueur, originally produced by Carthusian monks at their monastery near Grenoble.

Archaeologists first worked at Mount Grace as long ago as 1896, and there have been frequent investigations since. Because it is a very wet site, little relating to the gardens has been discovered apart from indications of some paths and tree holes. But where the soil was disturbed during the most recent work in 1991–2, one area, in an archaeologist's words, 'erupted in a forest of weld (*Reseda luteola*)'. This seed was probably not medieval, but as weld is not native to the area, it must have been planted here deliberately, possibly because it produced a yellow dye and was used for setting broken bones.

LEFT Roses and herbaceous plants flourish on the terraces of Mount Grace House.

RIGHT A reconstruction drawing shows how each monk's individual cell was surrounded by a garden.

ABOVE The seventeenth-century house built within the ruins of the abbey guest house was altered in the Arts and Crafts style in c.1900 and gardens were made below it.

OPPOSITE ABOVE One of the fourteenth-century conduit or 'cundy' houses built to protect the springs that supplied the abbey with water.

OPPOSITE BELOW Water from the hillside was later diverted to form a rill, now edged with prunus.

Although the cell and garden at Mount Grace are reconstructions, two conduit houses on the hillside to the east do remain from the fourteenth century. These small buildings protected the springs which supplied the priory with fresh water, efficiently piped through three outlets. One irrigated the fishpond outside the walls, another supplied a water tower in the middle of the Great Cloister, and a third fed into a channel which ran behind the monks' cells, washing out their latrines and allowing them to water their gardens.

Another unusual feature of Mount Grace is that the manor house on the edge of the site was not, as so often, constructed immediately after Henry VIII dissolved the priory in 1539. Rather, it was built within the ruins of the guest house over a century later, in 1654, for Thomas Lascelles, a member of one of the great Yorkshire families. Known as Mount Grace House, it was bought in 1899 by Sir Lowthian Bell, Bart, who had made a fortune in industry and owned several

wide arbour, planted with a quickset hedge, probably of whitethorn. To its south was another arbour, square this time, with another quickset hedge round its edge and a further 'close arbour' inside, which had a light timber frame over it, again planted with quickset. This sequence of arbours was possibly a bit on the prickly side for dalliance but provided privacy for the king, which he may have needed, as Eltham had become one of the largest palaces in the kingdom. Its length considerably exceeded that of Hampton Court; the Great Hall was the third largest in England, after Westminster and Christ Church, and its chapel was no little oratory but a church as large as the hall.

In spite of this magnificence, Henry's successors preferred to spend their time at Greenwich Palace, not that far away but more accessible by river. Elizabeth I, James I and Charles I each came to Eltham only once, and after the latter's

execution in 1649 most of the estate was sold, the trees were cut down and the deer killed. A view published in about 1650 shows that all the buildings were then standing, though they were described as 'out of repair'. The estate's value was estimated at £2,753 plus the 'charge of taking it down'. The new owner was Colonel Nathaniel Rich, a Parliamentary soldier and friend of Oliver Cromwell, who did indeed pull down everything except the Great Hall and chapel, and even they were abandoned. The diarist John Evelyn, visiting on 22 April 1656, commented: 'I went to see his Majesty's house at Eltham, both Palace and Chapell in miserable ruines, the noble woods and park destry'd by Rich the Rebell.'

In the next century, the remains came to be much appreciated by tourists and artists. Some saw them as fine examples of the now more appreciated Gothic architecture, while others admired their Picturesque decay. Paul Sandby

painted several views showing the still-magnificent Great Hall in the 1780s, a very young J.M.W. Turner did a watercolour of it in 1791 and Thomas Girtin showed it full of hay bales in about 1795. Yet the hall was threatened with demolition in 1828 and had to be saved by one of the first ever public preservation campaigns. Even then, it was used as a barn, and later as an indoor tennis court, while the chapel disappeared except for its foundations.

From time to time various houses and villas were built in the grounds. (One of them was the elegant seventeenth-century Eltham Lodge, by Hugh May.) Gardens, including a kitchen garden complete with glasshouses, were made around them and also in the moat, which over the centuries had become dry on three sides. Almost all the land immediately around the Great Hall was eventually filled with houses and other buildings, including a hotel and some pigsties, or was planted as gardens. Although parts of the estate were kept in good order, its kernel continued to deteriorate. In 1894 the lease reverted to Crown ownership and the Great Hall was gradually repaired, but in 1906 it was reported that 'all within is desolate'.

Over the centuries the extensive royal hunting park around the palace was also gradually developed. In the early eighteenth century the apothecary James Sherard, brother of the botanist William Sherard, had a garden in the village which contained enough rare plants to impress the German botanist Johann Dillen who, with input from William, published a catalogue of them, *Hortus Elthamensis*, in 1732.

In spite of this phase of house building, John Roque's 1745 map of the area still shows much of the park as farmland. By the 1930s this had mostly been sold off for housing and the area had become just a London suburb. But suddenly the remaining parkland was saved from development and the palace was brought back to life when Stephen Courtauld and his wife Virginia took up a ninety-nine-year Crown lease on the property in 1933. They pulled down the buildings that had been added to the historic site, cleared away most of the little gardens and refilled parts of the moat. The Great Hall was refurbished, with the addition of a minstrels' gallery at one end, and was used as a sitting room, complete with rather anachronistic 1930s upholstered armchairs.

After much discussion with various bodies, particularly about the three surviving Tudor gables, plans were eventually approved to link the hall to a substantial new house built on one of the 'butterfly' ground plans very fashionable at the time. For the outside, the Courtaulds eschewed 1930s

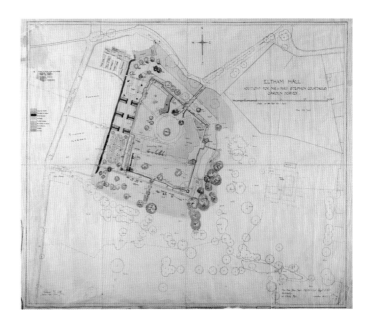

modernism in favour of a politely classical style, with nods, appropriate in the royal context, to Wren's work at Hampton Court; but inside, from the dining room to the bathrooms, the house was decorated in the most exotic Art Deco fashion. (As well as possessing a fortune derived from the Courtauld textile company, founded by his great-uncle, Stephen was a director of Ealing film studios, which may account for the Hollywood atmosphere introduced by the interior designers.) Around the house, gardens were laid out in a charming if rather conventional formal style, which in no way reflected the extraordinary interior.

Stephen Courtauld was a dedicated horticulturalist. He had scenic wallpaper depicting the Royal Botanic Gardens at Kew specially made by Sandersons for his bedroom; he collected orchids on his foreign travels and propagated them in special orchid houses, winning prizes at Royal Horticultural Society shows for his introductions and making cine films about them (some of which can be viewed in one of the rooms of the house).

Andrew Mawson, son of the great Thomas Mawson, was commissioned to design the gardens but the Courtaulds do not seem to have been happy with what he produced.

LEFT The Great Hall can be seen in the centre of this aerial photograph, with the two wings of the Courtaulds' house on the right.
ABOVE Seely and Paget's project for the house and gardens.

Although his plans were exhibited at the Chelsea Flower Show in 1935, the layout was then adapted by John Seely and Paul Paget, the architects of the house; and even after work had started, the Courtaulds themselves introduced further changes to make it all easier to maintain. Luckily, they knew John Gilmour, the Assistant Director of Kew, who advised them; and they may have picked the brains of some other friends connected with serious gardens. These included the McLarens, who owned Bodnant in Wales, the Husseys of Scotney Castle in Kent, and Ruth Hanbury, whose family was connected with both the Royal Horticultural Society's garden at Wisley, in Surrey, and the botanic garden at La Mortola in Italy.

In spite of all the dithering, the project went ahead quickly and by May 1937 things were far enough advanced for a series of three articles on the house and gardens to be published in *Country Life*. The author was their friend Christopher Hussey, a respected authority on country houses and gardens. Some of the illustrations were photographs taken by the architects in July 1936, which can be compared with a set they took in 1933 before work started. The 'before' photographs show the site crammed with buildings, including glasshouses and sheds in varying states of repair. Between and around them, rampant vegetation grew all over, from vegetables in the main courtyard to a formal garden on one area of the ramparts above the moat. They explain the comprehensive clearing of the site which had to be undertaken to make space for the Courtaulds' vision of their house and gardens, shown in the 'after' photographs. Although they kept the best of the mature trees, Hussey admits that the previous year there had been much lamentation in the press about the loss of Eltham's picturesque character.

The Courtaulds and their guests would have approached the house by crossing the medieval bridge over the moat to enter a large turning circle, which they ornamented only with a lawn and a lime tree (which is now quite huge). Instead of entering the house, those who chose to wander off to the right, and over the lawn, came to the remains of the medieval walls, acting as a sort of long parapet, from where the whole of London lay before them, as far as Westminster. Seventy years later, the view is somewhat different but still extraordinary.

Once inside the house, the Courtaulds had numerous ways out into their gardens, which spread right round on every side. Almost all the main ground-floor rooms had French windows leading outside, and the gardens were also

designed to look well from the bedrooms upstairs. At the point of the V made by the two wings of the house, a covered loggia, where Stephen's orchids were sometimes displayed, was designed to link the central entrance hall to the gardens. On its outside are four circular stone medallions, carved by Gilbert Ledward, symbolizing the Courtaulds' interests: the one immediately to the right has a spade and a watering can and represents gardening. The loggia opened on to a terrace with views over the moat and a little *jet d'eau*, and steps led down from it and, through a gate in the bastion, to the edge of the moat, where the Courtaulds would feed their black-necked swans.

The pergola on the edge of the terrace was built using columns salvaged from the eighteenth-century Bank of England in the City of London, which was being remodelled at that time. Smothered in wisteria, this makes a romantic sight in early summer.

Turning left, visitors find the Triangular Garden, where a corner of the terrace was turned into a chequerboard of narrow stone paths and square beds, now planted with herbs such as thyme and purple sage. Although not as dramatic as the triangular garden at the Villa Noailles at Hyères, which the Courtaulds may well have seen, this looks like one of the most innovative areas in their whole garden. A photograph probably taken in the 1950 or '60s shows it planted up with banal bedding plants, which are unlikely to have reflected the Courtaulds' taste.

Turning right, visitors come to the south side of the house, set off by lawns and fine trees, including a catalpa and a tulip tree (*Liriodendron tulipifera*), which create a dignified atmosphere. Little is set against the façade of the house, except a *Magnolia grandiflora*, probably dating from the Courtaulds' time, and also a Banksian rose, a vine, some specimens of ceanothus and a *Fremontodendron californicum*.

As visitors continue round the house to the east, steps lead down into one of the dry parts of the moat. Virginia particularly loved roses and grew them in many areas – here in a formal, sunken rose garden. This was restored in 1999 using Hybrid Musk roses, which were just being introduced in the 1930s, and so were available to the Courtaulds (though the varieties chosen, including 'Felicia' and 'Buff Beauty', are in paler colours than were then considered tasteful). A visitor remembered that Virginia imported her roses from McGredy's in Portadown, Northern Ireland, and that they included 'Glory of Rome' and 'Sunset Rose', which would both have injected some quite vivid tones. The former, a bright fuchsia pink, was only bred in 1937 by Dominico Aicardi (a lawyer and nurseryman who was also the Fascist mayor of San Remo in Italy); the other was probably 'McGredy's Sunset', which is yellow with orange markings, and was introduced by McGredy's in 1936 – so Virginia was right up to date.

On top of the retaining wall which runs all round the Rose Garden is a lavender hedge, newly replanted, while the bronze fountain of a boy with a dolphin, which played at its centre in the Courtaulds' time, is being restored.

The sunken Rose Garden looks very new in the 1936 *Country Life* photographs, but one of these shows on the parapet above, outside the new squash court, a more mature formal garden. Sometimes called the Linear Garden, this

area had box hedges surrounding curving beds planted with tulips and some tall topiary cones, and ornamented by a baluster, bought when London Bridge was sold off, and used as a sundial. The area can also be seen, much overgrown, in the 'before' pictures, so clearly the Courtaulds chose to keep some of the existing gardens. This charming garden disappeared during post-war archaeological excavations, as did a series of beds, complete with topiary bird, the Courtaulds made or restored in the South Moat.

The vista continues in a sequence of garden 'rooms'. Changes in level as you move round the house mean that this area lies within the moat enclosure and below the 'parapet' of medieval remains with their views over London. Consequently it is very sheltered. Although on the Seely and Paget plans these two 'rooms' were divided by clipped hedges, their sides were actually planted informally with

LEFT From the window behind the onyx basin in her bathroom, Virginia could look out on the Rock Garden.

RIGHT Wisteria hangs from the pergola made from columns salvaged from the Bank of England.

shrubs, some of which are still there: a *Poncirus trifoliata*, for instance, and a *Viburnum* x *burkwoodii*. The latter would have been quite rare when chosen by the Courtaulds, so where, over the years, gaps appeared in their plantings, replacements have been chosen in the same adventurous spirit from shrubs that are uncommon today, such as *Edgeworthia chrysantha*, *Daphne bholua* 'Jacqueline Postill' and stachyurus.

Stephen and Virginia Courtauld may have intended the 'rooms' to be a shade feature. There is a spreading beech tree and they went to a great deal of trouble to find and plant three quite rare and remarkably beautiful Chinese privet trees (*Ligustrum lucidum*) – two plain and one variegated – which have matured today and create a delightful diffused light. In spring, there are particularly delicate hellebores in these borders, as well as leucojums and shrubs such as ribes,

Daphne odora 'Aureomarginata', *Lonicera elisae*, corylopsis and camellias.

The sequence of 'rooms' ends in a square formal pool with a simple *jet d'eau* at its centre, beyond which the mood changes. The serpentine moat reappears and begins its meander round the next two sides of the palace, the banks edged by grass and willows. Many people say their favourite part of the whole garden is the simple spot where one of the willows sits on a little island near the medieval stone bridge.

From here, visitors can take a stepped path up to the Rock Garden. This steep bank, with its little cascade, was intended as a Japanese garden but, like so many 'Japanese' gardens, bears little resemblance to what is actually found in Japan. With the eye of faith, a couple of rocks look suitably enigmatic, and a few pine trees and maples cling to the slope. From the top of the bank, Virginia Courtauld would have enjoyed the views across the moat and lawns to the house, and on this spot, where it could be seen from her bedroom window, she placed an obelisk to mark the grave of her pet lemur, Mah-Jongg.

Today, a new path leads back to the car park, passing on its way an area known as the Cutting Garden. The Courtaulds had formal beds in the middle of the lawn here, to provide cut flowers for the house. Although the name has survived, these beds have not been reinstated, but the lawn is softened by mixed borders of shrubs and ornamental ground-covering perennials around the edge of the grass.

Also on the way back to the car park is another small garden created by the Courtaulds. Known as the Quadrant Garden, it was built in the shelter of the original Tilt Yard wall and, with its dark brick paths in a typical 1930s sun-ray pattern outlining a series of beds holding more of Virginia's roses, it is one of the most charming parts of Eltham's elaborate design.

In addition to Stephen's orchid house, in his day there were also glasshouses, a modern kitchen garden, orchards and the by then obligatory swimming pool and tennis courts, all situated a good way from the house.

The Courtaulds opened the grounds once a year to the public and also for one-off events such as a Scout jamboree; but sadly they never saw the gardens grow to maturity. After

LEFT ABOVE The Rose Garden begins a sequence of garden 'rooms'.
LEFT BELOW A beech tree shades another of the 'rooms'.
RIGHT The magnificent trees on the main lawn include a catalpa and a tulip tree (*Liriodendron tulipifera*).

war broke out in 1939 it became impossible to continue their lavish way of life. From fifteen gardeners, they were reduced to two, and Virginia found it difficult to endure the bombing of the area, which came close enough to damage the Great Hall. So in 1944 they went to live in Scotland, taking with them, it is said, many shrubs from the garden and the obelisk that marked Mah-Jongg's grave. From there they moved in 1951 to Southern Rhodesia (now Zimbabwe), where they

made yet another good garden, again with Jongy's memorial at its heart, and Stephen created a red rose which he named 'Virginia Courtauld' in honour of his wife.

The Courtaulds may have been socialites, but there was a strong philanthropic element in the family genes as well. Stephen's brother Samuel gave his own valuable collection of paintings to what became the Courtauld Institute of Art, and Stephen only surrendered the lease on Eltham Palace on

ABOVE Mr Smith, who was head gardener around the turn of the twentieth century.
RIGHT A willow stands on a small island in the moat below the medieval bridge.

condition that an educational use could be found for the house. So from 1945 until 1992 it was used by various army educational bodies, while the Department of the Environment had responsibility for the Great Hall and the other pre-Courtauld areas. From 1975 the Royal Parks kept the grounds in order, using them as the training ground for all their horticultural apprentices. They planted some trees, rebuilt the greenhouses which blew down in the Great Storm of 1987 and maintained the lawns impeccably, while the kitchen garden is said to have been dug and re-dug many times in the pursuit of different student projects. But no one was interested in the history of the gardens, which declined after the folding of the Royal Parks Apprenticeship Scheme. Until English Heritage took over, only the most basic maintenance was undertaken.

When English Heritage was set up it took over all the earthworks, buildings and ruins (generically known as Ancient Monuments) that had been in the care of the Ministry of Works, and so became responsible for Eltham's Great Hall and the ruined areas of the old palace. In 1995 the Ministry of Defence offered English Heritage a 'dowry' to take over the rest of the property and from that date a period of careful research, including archaeological investigation, led to the conservation of both house and gardens.

As well as restoring much of the Courtauld gardens as accurately as possible, or at least in the spirit of their times, English Heritage decided that the border along the wall of the South Moat (known as the Long Border because of its 110-yard/100m length) would be better redesigned in a late twentieth-century style. There had been a border there in the 1930s and old photographs showed a long narrow bed containing standard roses on the other side of the path. This had been grassed over (its outline can still faintly be seen in the lawn) and a decision was taken not to reinstate it, as maintenance would be too high-cost. The border itself had not properly been kept up. The soil had become pure clay, and by the 1990s the only plants to survive were a few euphorbias, two fig trees, a colutea and some wall shrubs – all dominated by huge clumps of *Crambe cordifolia*.

This area of Eltham together with the Walled Garden at Osborne were designated the first two in English Heritage's Contemporary Heritage Gardens Scheme announced in 1999 (see page 200). Five eminent garden designers were invited to compete with each other to produce layouts and planting suggestions for the Long Border which would be 'in the spirit of the 1930s Courtauld garden' and 'reflect the elaborate interiors of the house'. The Shade Garden at the east end of the moat, so called because it was overshadowed by beech, holly and yew trees, also needed attention, and creating a better view of this from the top of the moat wall was another requirement.

The schedule was tight – they were given only just over a month, from 15 April to 24 May 1999, to submit their outline designs; work had to start in the autumn and it was intended that the results would be open to the public in the summer of 2000 – and the design brief did not make an easy read either. Planting was to be 'imaginative and innovative'; the Long Border had to have 'interest from April–October' because it was to be 'a major attraction'. The high maintenance requirements of such a scheme for the Long Border were recognized, though the Shade Garden had to have a low-to-medium maintenance requirement, while still providing 'interest in spring, early summer and autumn'. What would attract visitors had to be balanced against budget restrictions and the need to gain extra income from events such as weddings. For instance, the lawn area may have marquees erected on it in summer.

The estimated cost of the new design and its implementation, including any necessary cultivation and associated hard, decorative or remedial works, was not to exceed £25,000, to which fees would be added. The competition was won by Isabelle Van Groeningen, who was then invited to do a detailed design and planting plan.

Her approach was to accept the dominance of the high irregular wall, a combination of greyish stone and red brick, which backed the border. Feeling that its great length demanded boldness, she planted big clumps of tall plants such as miscanthus, which would show up against the lighter areas, together with a great range of herbaceous plants. Many were repeated in subtle variations to give rhythm: for instance, she chose 12 different delphiniums, 11 hemerocallis, 18 poppies and no fewer than 21 varieties of peony. To entice visitors in spring, she planted bulbs everywhere and to extend the season into autumn, she included plants with good seed heads, such as achillea and veronicastrum, and others, such as sedums, which turn into spectacular colours.

Van Groeningen felt that the boldness and bright colours of this variation on the famous English mixed border were in keeping with 1930s Art Deco gardens, but the constraints of working on a historic site appeared when she had to obtain special permission to put wires in the walls to support the climbers.

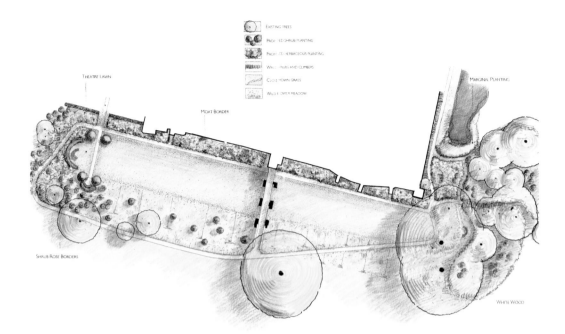

THEATRE LAWN

MOAT BORDER

MARGINAL PLANTING

SHRUB ROSE BORDERS

WHITE WOOD

LEFT Isabelle Van Groeningen's masterplan for the South Moat Garden.
RIGHT ABOVE The Long Border in the Courtaulds' time, when there were beds of standard roses in the lawn.
RIGHT BELOW Autumn colour in the Long Border reflects the brick and stone of the medieval walls.

The new garden was indeed opened in 2000 – on 7 July – but it has been changed a surprising amount since. A large beech (*Fagus sylvatica*), which dominated one end of the lawn, has died – a blessing in disguise, as the loss of a magnificent tree is compensated for by the extra light in that area. In 2003 everything was taken out, the soil was dug over and improved and the plants put back, though in different places and with some additions and certain omissions – only half the number of delphiniums, for instance.

The Shade Garden was renamed the White Wood because of all the white bulbs and white-flowered plants, such as white cyclamen, white foxgloves and *Geranium phaeum* 'Album', which Isabelle Van Groeningen set out in drifts to reflect the light. At the other end of the south lawn, the yew arbours with oak seats were part of the newly designed area, as were three large box balls matching those planted by the Courtaulds. Near this, a collection of Moyesii hybrid roses has been planted to fill an awkward corner. With their wonderful display of hips, these are an attraction in autumn as well as summer. Beyond is the Old Rose Border, filled with shrub roses such as the dark pink 'Rose de Rescht'. Virginia Courtauld's standard rose border may have been lost, but in twenty-first-century terms these less formal shrubs are a more than adequate compensation.

English Heritage owns 19 or so acres (7.7ha) around the house, of which 8 acres (3.2ha) are gardened intensively and the others are left as parkland, and it was necessary to rethink the way visitors would move around the whole site. They would need different paths, steps and bridges, and possibly safer ones, to see the garden compared with the Courtaulds' smaller groups of guests, and would make much more impact on it in terms of wear and tear. There were also legal requirements for disabled access. A car and coach park has recently been made in the old kitchen garden and the varied modern planting around its edge, and along the walk to the house entrance, provide a taste of the horticultural pleasures of the main gardens.

One of the most remarkable things about Eltham is that there are only three paid gardeners, including head gardener Jane Cordingley. Contractors cut the grass and hedges, and much of the rest of the work is done by a team of eight volunteers. They raise as many as possible of the plants they need from seed or cuttings, making good use of the glasshouses. The *Primula japonica* in the Cutting Garden, for instance, are all grown from seed. Some plants are even grown specially for other English Heritage gardens: sweet peas, for example, for Kenwood.

Stephen Courtauld died in 1967 and Virginia five years later. If they came back today they would see strange additions, such as the London Eye, added to their view over London, but surely they would find almost all the rest of their unique house and its gardens quite familiar and looking as beautiful as they could ever have dreamed.

Walmer Castle

KENT

ONE OF THE LAST castles built in England, Walmer Castle in Kent was constructed in 1539–40 on the orders of Henry VIII as part of a chain of defences along the south and east coasts which would provide warning and fire power in the event of invasion by the French. During the Civil War, it was besieged and damaged by Colonel Nathaniel Rich, who was also responsible for the serious depredations at Eltham Palace (see page 174). After times turned more peaceable, the beach built up to separate the fort from the sea and the tides no longer washed into the moat. Walmer turned from fortress into pleasant country house and in 1708 became the official residence of the Lord Warden of the Cinque Ports,

OPPOSITE A shrub garden softens the severity of the moat.

BELOW The fantastical shapes of the yew hedges in the Broad Walk.

a ceremonial post granted to distinguished prime ministers and other worthies. Four of them – William Pitt the Younger, Earl Granville, Earl Beauchamp and the late Queen Elizabeth the Queen Mother – had a major effect on the gardens – and several others also shaped what we see today.

When William Pitt the Younger was appointed Lord Warden in 1792 the only cultivated area at Walmer – clearly marked on a map of 1725 as 'The Governor's Garden' – seems to have been a kitchen garden, probably growing fruit and flowers as well as vegetables. Pitt was related to Lord Cobham, who had made the great landscape park at Stowe, and his own father had also employed 'Capability' Brown at Burton Pynsent in Somerset. With this background, it is perhaps reasonable to credit Pitt with the development of the grounds over the next few years (and Lord Curzon, who was Lord Warden a century later and wrote a book about Walmer, believed this) but there is little direct evidence.

Certainly, Pitt extended the estate by leasing more land to the north and west, and probably planted trees there for shelter against the salt-laden winds, creating the pleasant Woodland Walk which runs round two sides of the gardens. It is also likely to have been Pitt who made a large lawn on the axis from the south-west bastion, which was planted with

trees, including limes, to emphasize its oval shape. The trees flourished and by the middle of the nineteenth century they were over-mature and had to be cut back, and some actually removed. Several commemorative trees were planted here by later holders of the office: a lime by Lord Wellington, a tulip tree (*Liriodendron tulipifera*) by Sir Winston Churchill, purple beeches by Sir Robert Menzies and oaks by the Queen Mother. Today the space retains much of its original character and is used for picnics and concerts.

In 1803 Pitt's niece, Lady Hester Stanhope, came to live at Walmer and act as hostess for her unmarried uncle. Hester, later famous as a traveller in the Near and Middle East, had been brought up at Chevening, in the north of the county, where her father, the 3rd Earl Stanhope, had remade the park in a Brownian style, so it was not surprising that she also set about improving the park and garden. In her Memoir she recounts that once, when Pitt was away, she persuaded the local militia to do some landscaping and planting as a surprise for her uncle when he came back. Luckily, he expressed himself charmed and praised her taste.

In 1805 she made a 'glen' in a former chalk quarry, an early example of a 'natural wilderness' type of garden with winding walks, planted with ferns. She also received numerous trees and shrubs as a present from Lord Guilford, who was broke and stripping his nearby estate of Waldershare; but these may have been planted not in the glen but in a walled garden that was made at this time to the south of the castle.

By the time Pitt died in 1806, a paddock had also been added – oval like the lawn and similarly planted with trees – and the 'Governor's' kitchen garden replanted. Today, this is one of the most attractive parts of the whole estate, with its original paths, white glasshouse, espaliered fruit trees and unusual vegetables and cutting flowers, grown in a new design each year. The glasshouses provide colour, foliage and scents, with permanent plantings and seasonal potted displays. Plants, foliage and flowers grown here are also used to decorate rooms within the castle, particularly when the Lord Warden is in residence.

Lord Liverpool, Pitt's successor as Lord Warden, bought the land Pitt had leased, so that it should never be developed, but he made few changes to the estate.

The Duke of Wellington, who became Lord Warden in 1829, was extremely fond of Walmer. He stayed in the castle very often, living in a simple fashion that belied his high status, and died there in 1852. Much of the inside is dedicated to the Iron Duke's memory, but outside there is little to recall his tenure. In the year of his death, a guidebook referred to a kitchen garden in the moat, which seems strange, as the Governor's Garden, used for that purpose for centuries, had been regenerated by Pitt. Perhaps the moat garden was purely for growing fruit: a fig tree still flourishing there is believed to have been planted by Wellington himself, the espaliered pear trees on its walls are said to be scions of some planted in his time and one of the walls may have been a 'hot wall' against which peaches were cultivated.

A survey made in 1859 shows Pitt's garden still clearly existing: the two ovals – lawn and paddock – the walks through wooded areas round the edge, the glen, again with informal walks, and two areas laid out more geometrically – the Governor's Garden and the walled garden to the south. The main views from the castle continued to be south-west across the oval lawn, as Pitt intended – but that was about to change.

OPPOSITE LEFT AND RIGHT The kitchen garden is the oldest garden at Walmer. Box hedges and espaliered fruit trees edge the vegetable and flower beds.

RIGHT William Masters's ribbon-effect design for the planting in the Broad Walk.

The 2nd Earl Granville, who was appointed in 1865, arrived with a new young bride, upon which Pitt's bachelor residence was turned into a family home. The Earl's cousin, the Duke of Sutherland, owned both Cliveden and Trentham, two stupendous properties where new gardens had been made in the Italianate style, and the changes Lord Granville made to the gardens at Walmer reflect this fashion for formality. After the tidying of the many overgrown trees, one of his first acts was to order the planting in 1866 of an avenue of holm oaks (*Quercus ilex*), planted in clumps of four, to line what was, until the 1950s, the main entrance drive.

Granville employed a well-known landscape designer, William Masters, who owned the Exotic Nurseries in nearby Canterbury. Masters was in his seventies, but reacted with vigour to the commission. After the avenue, he laid out a wide straight gravelled path, 87 yards (80m) long, known as the Broad Walk, edged on either side by yew hedges and 10

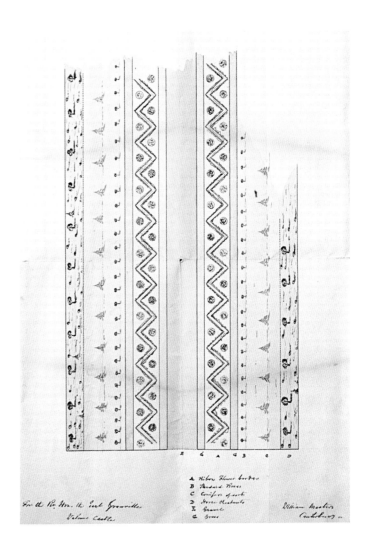

feet (3m) deep borders. The elegance of Pitt's oval lawn was lost, as one side of it had to be straightened, and a good part of the Governor's Garden was taken into the new layout; but the beds Masters created on either side of the walk were a magnificent example of Victorian gardening. They were planted with a mixture of standard roses and annuals which ran in ribbon patterns the length of the borders, their bright colours set off by dark yew hedges behind.

During the First World War these enormous beds were changed to become herbaceous borders and they have retained this slightly less maintenance-heavy style. Nowadays they are planted with sturdy perennials such as day lilies, *Acanthus mollis*, *Verbena bonariensis*, iris and phlox in a colour scheme of pastel shades, starting with blue at each end, moving into white, then pink, then yellow, and finally darker shades in the centre.

By 1959, probably because of post-war neglect compounded by heavy snow lying on them in the severe winter of 1947, the yew hedges at the back of the Broad Walk beds were best described as 'naturalistic' – a tactful way of saying that they had lost their formal shape and become charmingly blowsy. This effervescence has been allowed to develop so that a virtue has been made of it and now, 10 feet (3m) tall and nearly 7 feet (2m) wide, they are seen as one of the great attractions of the gardens.

In the mid-nineteenth century, the axis of the Broad Walk had been further extended by William Masters across two shallow grassed terraces. The lower one was intended as a croquet lawn (and visitors are encouraged to play on it), although its trapezoidal shape was later squared off to create a tennis court. The upper one is still semicircular and in spring its beds are vivid with polyanthus in tones of yellow and orange. In summer the pretty low-growing pink Floribunda rose 'Queen Mother' comes into flower, and a sundial at its centre has been replaced by an armillary sphere, made by David Harber and presented by English Heritage to

Queen Elizabeth the Queen Mother as a 100th birthday present in 2000, when she was Lord Warden.

Lord Granville enjoyed a long period of office which lasted to 1891, and at some point during his tenure, Wellington's kitchen garden in the moat was turned into an ornamental garden, emphasizing that the castle no longer served a defensive purpose. Offering a subtle romantic contrast to the more formal areas elsewhere, the moat's sides and walls are filled with shrubs including lilacs, fuchsias, hydrangeas and a *Magnolia grandiflora* – a mass of blooms in spring – as well as the cordon pear trees originally planted by the duke. Along the middle, running right round the castle, is a wide grass path and, because this needs mowing, the moat garden is accessed by a long slope, rather than steps, so that the lawn-mower (in the past, drawn by a pony) can be brought in.

The next Lord Warden to put his mark on the gardens was the 7th Earl Beauchamp, who was appointed in 1913. A rich but not very successful politician, he and his second son were said to be the models for Lord Marchmain and Sebastian Flyte in Evelyn Waugh's *Brideshead Revisited*. Like William Pitt, Lord Beauchamp had family connections with Chevening, and he copied one of the landscape features there, the famous 'keyhole' cut in the trees to lead the eye to and beyond the horizon, by extending the axis of Lord Granville's Broad Walk and terraces with a path through Pitt's paddock. The keyhole is no longer apparent, but the path is still there, as is the flight of steps he had made in the terraces to lead up to it. Today this informal area is full of daffodils in spring and becomes a wildflower meadow in summer, and also contains groups of orchids such as the pyramid orchid (*Anacampsis pyramidalis*).

Lord Beauchamp also reflected early twentieth-century taste by making a rose garden and two tennis courts in Pitt's walled garden and this area was subsequently changed again when Lord Willingdon became Lord Warden in 1936. He and his wife did much to make the gardens more ornamental by installing seats and statuary, including a small pool with a polar bear fountain. This has been lost but was probably a copy of François Pompon's then very popular sculpture L'Ours Blanc. Indeed, most of what the Willingdons added

has been removed except for the statue of Mercury Lady Willingdon set halfway along the path through the paddock.

Another world war and changing social conditions led to staff cutbacks, and by the time Queen Elizabeth the Queen Mother became Lord Warden in 1978 only the herbaceous borders and parts of the moat garden were maintained. Although it had been state owned and open to the public since the beginning of the century, the castle was run, until 1984 when English Heritage took over its management, by the district council in nearby Dover and received few visitors apart from local people.

English Heritage, although not aware that Walmer's landscape had any great historic interest, commissioned a restoration and management plan from landscape architects Land Use Consultants. Though it is now standard practice, the idea that the past should be researched and all possibilities considered before any work on a landscape started was then a fairly new concept. LUC discovered that there were

LEFT The deep borders of the Broad Walk are planted more informally today.

RIGHT The armillary sphere on the terraces was a present to Queen Elizabeth the Queen Mother.

submit plans and (cravenly rejecting one featuring reclining mermaids) English Heritage chose a formal design by Penelope Hobhouse which blended many historic references, including touches of the Islamic gardens so dear to that author-designer's heart. The pavilion at the castle end, its loggia and Doric columns designed by Sir Anthony Denny, is clearly classical, as is the rectangular pool in which it is reflected. The pool, which has Islamic echoes as well, was made 95 feet (29m) long to mark the connection with the queen's ninety-fifth birthday, and is speckled with water lilies, which came from Osborne House, another royal garden.

Clipped yews in the lawns recall the Queen Mother's childhood home at St Paul's Walden Bury, in Hertfordshire, whose garden is, with Wrest Park, one of the very few early eighteenth-century formal landscapes to survive in England. At the opposite end to the castle is a viewing platform – an idea that harks back to Tudor or Stuart gardens. It was made from the spoil when the pool was created and is topped by a clump of yews clipped into a castellated castle. At its base, in compliment to Her Majesty's name, lie two E-shaped beds – a very Elizabethan conceit. Even the seats had a historic background, as they were copies of eighteenth-century benches.

The queen was a knowledgeable gardener herself (and a practical one, too, until very late in her life) and she took a personal interest in the planning of her garden. The deep borders around the edge were planted with her favourite highly scented flowers, including roses and lilies, and with shrubs such as rosemary, philadelphus, abutilon, hoheria, choisya and melianthus, which thrive in a maritime setting, while the formality was further softened by rows of terracotta pots from Crete, filled in late spring with tulips.

The Queen Mother officially opened her garden on 21 July 1997, and since then, and in spite of several dry summers (this part of Kent can be as parched as Morocco), the half acre (2,023m²) has matured well. The first new garden created by English Heritage, it was both the spectacular culmination of three centuries of gardening at Walmer and the unexpected impetus for an innovative step forward for the organization: the Contemporary Heritage Gardens Scheme (see page 200).

surprisingly few records of this important estate. Although an espaliered pear in the moat and the avenue of holm oaks showed up on the historic radar, there were, for instance, no details of what had been planted in the herbaceous borders – in spite of the fact that a gardener wonderfully called Paramor had been at Walmer for over thirty years, starting as a boy in Lord Granville's time and working his way up to be head gardener in the early twentieth century.

Like the rest of Kent, the woodland areas at Walmer suffered horribly in the Great Storm of 1987. All the seaward shelter belt was lost and had to be replanted.

The most recent major change at Walmer came when English Heritage decided to mark the ninety-fifth birthday of the Queen Mother in 1995 by presenting her with a new garden. 'I have been given many presents before,' she said, 'but never a garden.' A suitable site was located in Pitt's walled garden: the roses planted by Lord Beauchamp had never been successful, and it was still walled on three sides, making it well sheltered from winds. Several designers were invited to

LEFT Cherry blossom sets off the statue of Mercury in the paddock.
RIGHT Two E-shaped beds affirm that this new garden was made for Queen Elizabeth the Queen Mother.

Carisbrooke Castle

ISLE OF WIGHT

ENGLISH HERITAGE'S NEWEST GARDEN is at Carisbrooke Castle – the only medieval castle on the Isle of Wight and a place where, as so often in this book, the weight of history lies heavy. It was the residence of the governors of the island and its fortifications were improved, when he held that post in the 1530s, by Richard Worsley, one of the family who owned Appuldurcombe (see page 50). Then towards the end of the sixteenth century massive earthworks were erected as a defence against likely attack by Spain; and, in the mid-seventeenth century, a bowling green was laid out in the middle of them for the pleasure of Charles I when he was confined at Carisbrooke for fourteen months before his trial. (Ironically, just a few years later, Nathaniel Rich, responsible for damaging both Eltham Palace and Walmer Castle in the Parliamentary cause, was imprisoned here, accused of not being anti-Royalist enough.)

Carisbrooke had a 'herber next the chapel' in the late thirteenth century, though the record fails to make clear which of the two chapels this probably medicinal garden was near. St Nicholas, the chapel by the entrance, probably had a cemetery and by the eighteenth century this space had been planted with trees and may have been an orchard. By the middle of the nineteenth it had become a classic kitchen garden, with a perimeter path and further paths crossing in the middle. Postcards from later in the Victorian period show intensively planted beds with, eventually, two rustic arches to support climbing plants.

At the very end of the nineteenth century the castle came to be associated with Princess Beatrice, the youngest daughter of Queen Victoria. She fell in love with Prince Henry of Battenburg and married him in the church at Whippingham, near Osborne, which had been built by Prince Albert, her father. Prince Henry was later appointed

LEFT The bowling green offered the imprisoned Charles I a space for recreation.

RIGHT On this eighteenth-century map point O is described in the key as 'now a garden'.

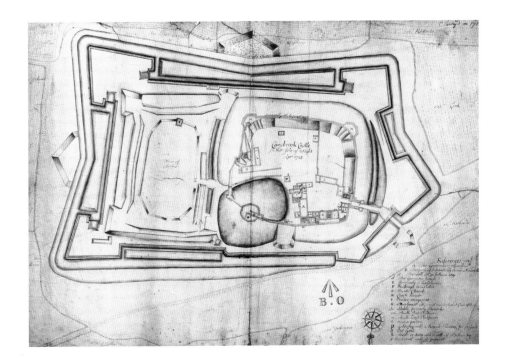

governor of the Isle of Wight, and when he died in 1896 Beatrice took over the role, spending several months each summer in the governor's apartments at Carisbrooke.

The kitchen garden was turned into a flower garden for her use and, in theory if not in practice, the public could enjoy it when she was not in residence. Apart from a wooden summerhouse on wheels which could be moved around, and a few pieces of old carved stone used as decoration, the garden seems to have been quite simple. The cross paths of the kitchen garden had been suppressed, creating a central lawned space in which five rectangular flower beds were placed, and there was a shrub border against a wall.

The princess lived on until 1944 but, even in her lifetime, and well before the Second World War posed inevitable problems with regard to manpower, many of the flower beds in what was now called the Privy Garden had been laid to grass. Some roses and herbaceous plants could be seen as late as the 1970s, but by the early years of the present century, although red and white valerian flourished – and more clung self-sown to the castle walls – there was little evidence of horticultural effort other than a pleasant border filled with old roses, lavender and a few medlar trees. English Heritage had long wanted to revitalize the spot with a new garden (indeed, it was a serious contender for becoming a Contemporary Heritage Garden), and in 2004 a bequest of £100,000 by a local resident, Mrs Dorothy Frazer, enabled the dream to be turned into reality.

But before the garden could be planned, what lay underneath the site had to be investigated. Work was carried out in 2006 by English Heritage's in-house team of archaeologists, who confirmed most of what they expected to find – what was visible in old plans, for instance. Sadly, they found nothing new or exciting that might have suggested a theme for the new design.

LEFT ABOVE Princess Beatrice, photographed in her Privy Garden towards the end of her life.
LEFT BELOW One of the carved stone fragments used as decoration in her day.
OPPOSITE ABOVE A blocked-up gateway has been reinstated as the entrance to the new garden.
OPPOSITE BELOW FROM LEFT TO RIGHT Edwardian-style plants in the new garden include *Agastache* 'Black Adder', *Geranium pratense* 'Black Beauty' and *Digitalis ferruginea*.

A further dig was undertaken in February 2009 while a blocked-up nineteenth-century gateway was being reinstated as the main garden entrance, mid-way along the wall separating the bailey from the Privy Garden. A twelfth-century building, probably demolished in the seventeenth century, came to light, and its age and the fact that it was previously unknown emphasized the importance of English Heritage's pledge when improving its sites – that nothing should ever be done to damage them. So in some areas of the new garden digging could be no deeper than 6 inches (15cm) and nor could any worn-out soil be taken off the site.

Various designers were asked to submit draft plans that would reflect the spirit – loosely Edwardian – of the time when Princess Beatrice lived in the castle, and provide a relaxing space for visitors. TV gardener Chris Beardshaw was given the commission. Describing the princess as 'a big personality, even in the shadow of her mother', he decided to make the garden both formal and fun. He saw it as typical of the Edwardian garden – having beds with softer plantings than the rigid Victorian ones at Osborne – and of the English garden as it is pictured by people all over the world.

Filling the rather dull enclosure with a multitude of compartments hedged with tall hornbeam or yew, he laid out two main axes which meet by a low square fountain, which has seating around its rim. In the beds he planted a mix of herbaceous plants that could have been grown in Edwardian times – alchemilla and asphodel, the striking

oriental poppy 'Patty's Plum', eremus, euphorbia and *Eryngium bourgatii* (sea holly), campanula and delphiniums, thalictrum and cardoons – all chosen to offer the widest range of height, shape and colour. Further variety is added by trees, such as cercis and loquats, some conical yews, and a pair of Chusan palms (*Trachycarpus fortunei*) by the entrance. There are, too, rows of standard fruit trees – white mulberries, walnuts and figs. Because of the restrictions on digging deep holes imposed by the archaeologists, these had to be planted in large Versailles tubs specially made of English oak, and for the same reason, the roots of the hedges were restricted by landscape fabric.

The historical element was interpreted quite loosely. Hedged compartments are indeed a device often found in Edwardian gardens, and here they also protect against the eddying winds. The red, blue and gold colours that predominate in the plantings were chosen to reflect those in the stained glass of the nearby chapel as well as in Princess Beatrice's coat of arms. Nods to earlier periods can be found at various points, for instance in the way the main paths cross in the centre, as they did in the nineteenth-century kitchen garden. The virtual circular 'bastions' at the ends of the paths reflect the castle's medieval fortifications and, more importantly, the three trees planted in the centre of each and the wooden seats make them a pleasant place to sit. The 'grotto' to one side is another reference to the past which provides an extra quiet space within this tranquil area. All this can be appreciated from the many benches set around the garden and from the ramparts above.

At present the whole garden can be seen at once, but when the hedges dividing the compartments have had time to grow and are clipped to their intended 5-foot (1.5m) height, it will take on a different atmosphere, with each compartment not only separate but almost invisible from the others. Because the plants, including spring bulbs and fruit trees, offer colour throughout the year, Princess Beatrice's garden, as it comes to maturity, will offer an incentive to visitors to make repeat visits to this well-loved and now reinvigorated site.

LEFT The new Princess Beatrice's garden soon after it was planted in the spring of 2009. When mature, the hedges will divide it into compartments.
RIGHT Tubs were specially made of English oak because trees planted in the ground might damage the historic subsoil.

Contemporary Heritage Gardens

THE CONTEMPORARY HERITAGE GARDEN SCHEME was born out of the success of the new garden at Walmer Castle (see page 186). When this was opened in 1997, English Heritage suddenly began to be seen as an organization that owned gardens and as one that was involved in the modern world and not just with ruined buildings from the distant past. Comments from public and press were approving, and visitor numbers to this far corner of Kent shot up by 47 per cent in the first two years.

Sir Jocelyn Stevens, then Chairman of English Heritage, was also aware of the statistic that more people visit 'stately homes' to see their gardens than to see the house or its contents, and he saw a chance to draw to English Heritage properties visitors who might not be attracted by the medieval monasteries and Tudor castles that form so much of its portfolio. So in 1999 the Contemporary Heritage Gardens scheme was launched with English Heritage announcing that it would commit £1.5 million to the creation of ten new gardens – two each year for the next five years – with the cream of England's garden designers being invited to enter a series of competitions.

All of English Heritage's sites – over four hundred – were looked at to see whether they might be enhanced by a new garden, a list of possibles was drawn up, new archaeology and other research was done at some of them and finally six definite locations were chosen, to which four more would be added. Some were adjuncts to an existing garden, others were in places where there was currently no garden at all. Kirsty McLeod, then chair of English Heritage's Historic Parks and Gardens Panel, said she was 'keen to mix the venerable with the contemporary'. The idea was 'to respect the past, but not copy it' and to give some of today's designers the opportunity to create new gardens.

It was decided that the first two Contemporary Heritage Gardens would be made at Eltham Palace and Osborne House. Both were places where there was a historic garden already, not to mention an important house that attracted a good number of visitors. English Heritage risked an extremely tight schedule: work was to start in the autumn of that same year, 1999, and it was intended that the gardens would open the following summer. Surprisingly, both were finished on time – and both were much admired. (For a fuller description of these gardens, see pages 174 and 98.)

After this successful start, the second pair, the Medieval Bishops' Palace in the cathedral city of Lincoln and Richmond Castle in the middle of a Yorkshire country town, were tougher situations. Both were medieval ruins and chosen as places where new gardens would enhance surroundings that seemed of greater interest to historians than to the average member of the public. Both sites elicited a more cerebral and a more obviously modern response from the chosen designers.

The cathedral at Lincoln is set high on one of the rare hills in an extremely flat part of eastern England and its medieval bishops built their splendid palace just below it on the southern slope, sheltered from the winds that drive in across the North Sea out of Siberia. In the 1320s, Bishop Henry Burghersh obtained land for a garden, and in 1647, although the palace had been damaged in the Civil War, there were still 'high mounted longe walks on one side, set with fruit trees, and . . . a green courte, bowling greene, orchard, a garden'. But by the end of the twentieth century, the palace was a ruin and no trace of any garden remained.

In March 2000 four landscape architects were invited to submit designs for a Contemporary Heritage Garden to be made on the upper of two terraces to the south of the palace, quite possibly where the medieval garden had been. Their brief was to bridge the historic and contemporary, while maximizing the small rectangular space – only 33 by 20 yards (30 by 18m) – which had a high Roman wall at its back and the lower medieval wall of the palace to one side. On its third side was a vertiginous drop, offering views over the city which the design was expected to enhance; and on the fourth lay a vineyard, one of the most northerly in Europe, which had been presented in 1972 by Lincoln's twin town in Germany, Neustadt-an-der-Weinstrasse, recalling the fact that vines were recorded growing as far north as this in the past.

The design competition was won by Mark Anthony Walker, whose practice was in nearby Ely, so he knew the area well. His plan was inspired by both the vineyard and the

cathedral, and contains many references to both. Visitors see the garden first from above, as they come down a flight of ancient steps and through an opening in a medieval wall. Entering the garden, they find themselves not at ground level but just over 3 feet (1m) above it on a viewing platform, which Walker describes as 'resolutely not medieval', although it is made in solid English oak. From there they look down on a lawn intersected by a lattice of brick paths, a visual reference to the ribs supporting the cathedral's roof, and at the nine points where the paths bisect each other they can discern a single tree, a hornbeam (*Carpinus betulus*) clipped into a tall pointed shape recalling the towers and spires.

Each tree is set in a circle of polished stainless steel – the circles being visual links to the bosses where the ribs meet, and echoing, too, the silver communion plates in the cathedral's treasury. Two more of these shining disks, decorated rather than plain, are placed at opposite corners of the garden. One is etched with a labyrinth, an early symbol

ABOVE LEFT An aerial view of the Medieval Bishops' Palace in Lincoln shows how the geometry of the new garden complements that of the adjacent vineyard.

ABOVE RIGHT An oak platform provides the best view of the garden.

RIGHT Central to the design are clipped hornbeams, brick paths and stainless-steel disks.

of the Christian life, while the other has a pattern of vine leaves, which echoes both the vines below and a carving in the cathedral's cloister.

This elegant, architectural garden is softened by its plantings – yew hedges, hydrangeas, hellebores, acanthus. Purple-blue lavender is subtly placed in the purple-blue slate 'beds' which extend the lawns, and the dark red rose 'Guinée' climbs the metal fence that protects against the deep drop. The red dahlia 'Bishop of Llandaff' was planted as a gentle ecclesiastical pleasantry, while the valerian growing wild on the Roman wall offers a romantic touch for those who glance up – and an appropriate one, too, as it gets is name from one of the oldest Roman families, the Valerii.

Paradoxically, although he made so many references to the garden's religious context, and in spite of all the stone in the cathedral and the palace, Walker saw his use of brick, steel and slate – what he called 'a palette of new materials' – as a very conscious way of going against the grain of what lay around the garden. It is a further paradox that the Lincoln Medieval Bishops' Palace garden, in contradicting English Heritage's

core subject matter (ruined religious and secular buildings built in stone), is perhaps the most successful in aesthetic terms of all the organization's new gardens.

It was opened on 6 September 2001 by the Duke of Gloucester, an English Heritage Commissioner and the first member of the royal family to become a professional architect. An exceptionally good video describing the garden's making can be watched in the visitor centre, and nor should visitors miss the view down over the garden from the turf roof that has been made on top of the palace's East Hall.

The new garden at Richmond Castle also incorporated references to the site's past, but this time with more modern and political associations. It could perhaps be seen as continuing in the tradition of those great eighteenth-century landscape parks, such as Wrest Park or Stowe, that were laid out to convey a hidden message, their aristocratic owners using follies and sculpture to express sympathy for the Whigs or the Tories or, in France, for the Rights of Man.

Richmond Castle was begun in 1071 by one of William the Conqueror's followers on a site that towers above the River

Swale and it is the most complete eleventh-century castle to survive in England. It has a much more recent resonance as well, being where the Richmond Sixteen – early conscientious objectors who, in the First World War, refused to fight or to be involved with the military in any way – were imprisoned. Their moving story is told inside the castle, and sixteen topiary yew trees, planted to symbolize the sixteen men, are almost the first thing visitors see on entering the garden.

A walled enclave about 1 acre (4,000m²) in size, the site slopes steeply eastwards from a flat terrace down towards the river. As at Lincoln, it offers fine outward views – though this time over countryside, with the cascading waters of the River Swale, rather than a townscape. Another similarity with Lincoln is that the garden was intended to be viewed from above as well as from within. This space always lay outside the main fortifications of the castle, and a remarkable feature of the solar at one end of Richmond's baronial hall is a door in its external wall, which once opened on to a wooden gallery running along the outside of the curtain wall. As this gave the family and privileged friends somewhere to relax and look towards the river, it is fair to assume that the space underneath was planted in a way that made it agreeable to look at.

Unfortunately, neither archaeology nor archive research yielded information about what was there, whether paths, arbours or plants; and although it was called the Cockpit, neither is there any evidence that cockfighting ever took place here. Probably it was a kitchen garden, and certainly by the late nineteenth century a small glasshouse stood there and six trees, which were likely to have been fruit trees, as one old specimen of the cooking apple 'Catshead' survived and was incorporated in the new garden.

By March 2000, when the design competition was launched, the area had become little more than a rough field, and one requirement of the design brief was that it should continue to provide an open space in which people could gather for summer parties and firework events and where outside lessons for schoolchildren could be held. So it was not surprising that the competition was won by Neil Swanson of Landscape Projects in Manchester, a practice that specialized

LEFT Sixteen symbolic topiary yews surround an old apple tree at Richmond Castle.

RIGHT Colourful Prairie-style plantings enhance the grandeur of Richmond's medieval walls.

in creating the sort of urban green space where people in large numbers, as well as plants, have to be factored in.

Swanson decided to devote the centre of the site to a generous grass amphitheatre, with a circular declivity at its heart which could serve as a performance area. This was one of four distinct spaces within the new garden, each defined by yew hedges and linked by the original cobbled paths. Above it, at the top of the slope, an existing flatter area was regraded to create a terrace into which a rectangular panel of light-coloured pebbles was set. Within this, the sixteen yew trees were planted in groups inside box hedges in a circular bed which was mulched with slate. Alongside them stands the old apple tree, and by an arch in one of the hedges is a cork oak (*Quercus suber*) which was also there before work started.

Below this terrace, and also along the right-hand side of the site, Swanson designed a walk that would give different views out through *claires voies* in the walls and hedges. On the other side, a series of seats was set in hedged enclosures against the south-facing, late twelfth-century wall, and climbers, such as *Schizophragma hydrangeoides*, *Lonicera* x *tellmanniana*, *Solanum crispum* 'Glasnevin', *Clematis armandii* and the delicate yellow Banksian rose, were planted against it.

From the seats there are fine views back to the castle and in front of them a path runs down the slope, edged on the lawn side by a herbaceous border, planned by Rachel Devine. She devised a modern scheme in the Prairie planting style, using mostly grasses and similar tough subjects and fewer of the high-maintenance perennials found in classic herbaceous borders. Grasses such as *Miscanthus sinensis* 'Silberturm' and *Pennisetum orientale* were mixed with sturdy perennials such as *Achillea filipendulina* 'Cloth of Gold', *Crocosmia* 'Lucifer',

Echinacea purpurea, *Euphorbia characias* subsp. *wulfenii* and *Helianthus* 'Loddon Gold', and the whole was further enlivened with poppies, which carry through the First World War allusions.

One of the intentions of adopting the Prairie style was that the chosen plants would self-seed and allow the space to evolve and develop over time. Since the Cockpit Garden was opened on the 28 May 2002 (the fourth Contemporary Heritage Garden to be completed) the plantings have indeed changed subtly, but it remains a garden that manages to be both innovative and in sympathy with its ancient setting.

Another place where the historic context imposed its references on the designer of a Contemporary Heritage Garden was the Governor's Garden at Portland Castle on the Dorset coast. The fifth of the series, Portland, as a site, had more in common with Walmer than with the ruinous medieval Lincoln or Richmond, being one of the Device Forts built from Kent to Cornwall by Henry VIII in the

BELOW Portland harbour can be glimpsed beyond the stone seats and waving grasses of the Governor's Garden at Portland Castle.

1540s to defend England's south coast. Portland is still complete and, unlike most of the others, retained its importance to the armed services into the late twentieth century. (Because the harbour was a naval base, English Heritage did not get control of the whole site until 1999, although it owned the castle from 1984.) After the departure of the Royal Navy, the district became run down and one of the purposes of the new garden was to attract tourists to aid its regeneration.

The competition was won by Christopher Bradley-Hole, a noted proponent of the minimalist school of design. The Contemporary Heritage Gardens scheme had moved a long way from the opulent plant-based designs at Eltham and Osborne.

Known as the Captain's as well as the Governor's Garden, the rectangular site was tiny – only about a quarter of an acre (1,000m²) – and surrounded by rubble walls on three sides and, on the fourth, a dry moat which allowed views over Portland harbour. In the early nineteenth century, when for a time the governor's house was the private residence of the local rector, this area was used for growing fruit and vegetables, and an 1816 plan shows a neat walled garden, with fruit trees. A later (1848) plan shows a less formal landscape with what was probably a small greenhouse.

After the Second World War the kitchen garden was abandoned and what Bradley-Hole found there were beds edged with metal railway lines, filled with an uninteresting mix of flowers, roses, trees and shrubs, some self-sown, linked by concrete paths to a variety of derelict sheds and greenhouses. He was allowed to sweep all this away (prisoners from a local jail came in to do the work) but not to touch the historic walls or moat, and could only thin or replant the trees on the harbour side, not remove them completely.

Basing the design on his signature circular shapes, which also echo the circular shape of the castle, Bradley-Hole placed a round lawn in the centre of the space, surrounded by a wide circular path. Most of the path's perimeter was edged with a wall of beautifully cut Portland stone, famous since the Middle Ages. Low enough to be used as a seat, this wall enables the lawn to become a performance area and it is backed by a higher wall of the same stone, providing another row of seats. These concentric circles are entered by a walkway recalling a gangplank and edged on the harbour side with metal rails like those on a ship. Beyond lies the bulk of the castle, and the white sails of small boats are visible through the trunks of the mature sycamore and Corsican pine trees (*Pinus nigra* subsp. *laricio*).

This austerity is tempered by rectangular beds in the lawn, set at the main compass points to recall Portland's maritime history, and filled with tall grasses such as *Miscanthus sinensis* 'Flamingo', *M.s.* 'Gracillimus' and *Stipa arundinacea*. These sway and rustle in the sea breezes and catch the light, while sedums lend autumn colour and geraniums cover the ground on the higher levels. The plants were chosen for their resistance to the salt-laden air, and as far as possible are native to the area – though Bradley-Hole resisted the temptation to make a local allusion by planting Portland roses, perhaps because their origin is so vague and they seem to have no connection with this part of the Dorset coast.

Being a fortification, the castle has little obvious space for gardening, but its staff do horticultural wonders. Outside the walls lies a mixed border rich with roses, hebes, *Brachyglottis Dunedin Group* 'Sunshine' (formerly *Senecio greyi*) and montbretia, while inside the main enclave outside the ticket office is a small bed, designed by Kim Auston, containing grasses and box balls in a happy mixture of formality and informality. Day lilies enliven the courtyard, while the car park outside is softened by catmint and a row of old roses, perhaps 'Roseraie de la Haÿ', which are said to have been here a long time. The dry moat has been planted with more ornamental grasses, such as *Deschampsia cespitosa,* euphorbias and hardy white geraniums, with bulbs to provide interest in spring. Even the tea room is horticultural rather than military, being decorated with photographs of other English Heritage gardens.

Completed in July 2003, the great achievement of the Governor's Garden was to make a very small space seem several times larger than it really is. As many as two hundred people can be seated in its amphitheatre. It turned out to be the last of English Heritage's true Contemporary Heritage Gardens. Although a sixth was made, it was different in spirit.

This was at Witley Court, near Worcester (see page 134), and by January 2001, when the competition for a Contemporary Heritage Garden was launched, much of the nineteenth-century garden there was in the course of restoration. English Heritage had also taken the opportunity in 1996 to buy a further area, known as the North Park, to add to the ornamental gardens and burnt-out house it already owned. This was the remains of that part of Witley's late eighteenth-century park called the Wilderness, a romantic and naturalistic landscape with paths and rides surrounding the large lake known as the Front Pool. The Wilderness area purchased was less than half what it had once been, the mature trees – oak, beech, sweet chestnut and American exotics – had been felled for timber and the space they left had deteriorated through lack of management. But this fragment was the first place visitors would now pass through after they bought their tickets, and so it was important to turn the overgrown woodland into an inspirational route to the lake and then on to the more formal gardens.

English Heritage had set up a partnership with the Jerwood Foundation, which offered sculpture by artists such as Anthony Gormley for permanent display at Witley. Although there had been statuary in the nineteenth-century parterres (sold off by the salvage dealer who bought the property in 1954), when the modern works were displayed

there it was felt that this was no longer appropriate and they were moved to a part of the new wooded area. This made a better backdrop, so it was decided to divide the space and make a woodland garden, based on a collection of rhododendrons that had been added in the nineteenth century, while the rest would be a Contemporary Heritage Garden. The idea was to restore the historic path network and adapt the spaces between to provide a sequence of atmospheric settings. It was hoped that the form and colour of these spaces would enhance the permanent pieces of contemporary sculpture – abstract as well as figurative – and that temporary exhibitions would also be organized there, the first to be of work by Elizabeth Frink.

Again five designers were invited, and the winners were Michael Ibbotson and Mark Darwent from the long-established Gloucestershire partnership of Colvin and Moggridge. Their plan removed most of the self-sown sycamores and encouraged regeneration of the surviving box edging to some of the rides. They envisaged the gradual replanting of the broadleaved trees, whose canopy would shelter shrubs and bulbs and some herbaceous plants. A small pool was to be made, and a series of glades and wildflower meadows among the trees, one of which would provide a visual link to the Flora Fountain in Nesfield's east parterre.

The garden has now matured into a pleasing leafy atrium en route to the formal rooms of the parterres, and it is a space that will surely be more appreciated as it becomes more established; but the partnership with the Jerwood Foundation proved less successful and in 2004 Jerwood decided to move the sculpture collection elsewhere. The only sculpture there today is a wicker snake made by a group of people with learning difficulties as part of a project with Wyre Forest District Council.

A change of emphasis at English Heritage meant that the Contemporary Heritage Gardens Scheme was quietly abandoned. The two new gardens English Heritage made next, at Kenilworth Castle in Warwickshire and Carisbrooke Castle on the Isle of Wight, were to lay more emphasis on the historic context than on a modern perspective.

LEFT ABOVE Sunshine filters through the canopy of the glade at Witley Court.
LEFT BELOW A wicker snake slithers through the meadow.

Some Other Gardens

Acton Burnell Castle, Shropshire

Acton Burnell Castle was built in the thirteenth century as a fortified manor house for Robert Burnell, Chancellor of England, who also made himself a deer park on the hillside beyond. By the seventeenth century, though, it had passed to the Smythe family, who in the 1750s built a new hall and created a landscape park, within which the old castle became a garden feature.

Today, even the Smythes' landscape is largely obscured, as a college occupies much of it, with the remainder being used for farmland. However, the castle is open to visitors, who can still see it against the backdrop of the deer park.

Auckland Castle Deer House, County Durham

The bishops of Durham have, since the twelfth century, been fortunate to enjoy a country residence at Auckland Castle, in Bishop Auckland. In 1754 Joseph Spence was made a canon of Durham Cathedral and soon made suggestions as to how the grounds at Auckland Castle could be 'improved'. It is not, however, clear how many of these were carried out.

Today, the castle and gardens are still occupied by the Church and so public access is limited. However, the medieval walled deer park is let to the local council, and so is open to the public as a magical place in which dogs are walked under ancient trees. Auckland Castle's designed landscape is an extensive one, decorated with buildings of Gothick design, including the park gatehouse and the walls of the palace gardens. One such building is a Gothick crenellated deer house which was built in 1760, possibly to a design by the multi-talented Thomas Wright, who was an astronomer, architect and garden designer but also a local boy – being born at nearby Byers Green. More like a miniature palace than animal accommodation, the curious deer house would have been used as an eye-catcher for human enjoyment as well as shelter for beasts. It is now managed by English Heritage.

Castle Acre Priory, Norfolk

When they were founded in the eleventh century, the castle and priory at Castle Acre formed the basis of an important and bustling Norman settlement, the priory housing a Cluniac order. Today the priory (and castle) is in ruins, but we can still see the outline of the cloisters, where monks would have enjoyed writing, studying and contemplation in covered walkways surrounding an open garden area. The spirit of monastic gardening has been brought alive by a herb garden, next to the visitor centre, showing the kind of plants that the monks would have grown for food and medicine.

Denny Abbey, Cambridgeshire

While the ruined twelfth-century abbey at Denny is in the custody of English Heritage, its grounds are run by the Farmland Museum, which documents rural life. This reflects the abbey's use as a farmhouse for many years, post-Dissolution. Within Denny's grounds is Walnut Tree Cottage, which is furnished as though it were still occupied by a 1940s farmworker and his family. The small domestic garden attached to this cottage is well worth a visit, as it is planted and gardened according to wartime methods.

LEFT Auckland Castle Deer House.

Finchale Priory, County Durham

Ruined and picturesque, in the eighteenth century Finchale Priory (or rather the adjacent farmhouse) became a well-used rural retreat for the landscape commentator Joseph Spence at the time when he was also a canon of Durham Cathedral. Spence followed a naturalistic style of design, rejecting artifice, so he no doubt gained inspiration from the spot's considerable Picturesque beauty on the banks of the River Wear.

Spence was not the only admirer of Finchale and when his neighbour, Ralph Carr, decided to make a landscape park for Cocken Hall, a property built on land once part of the same estate as the priory, he incorporated views of the nearby ruin, making it into a striking garden feature. In 1768 Count Karl von Zinzendorf described walking to Finchale from Cocken Hall:

> The garden [at Cocken] has a circuit of more than 5 miles, consisting of a wood including a number of different trees and shrubs, where countless gravel paths are cared for, and open grassland. But the most beautiful of all is when one descends to the river, where one is led between the murmurings of the water obscured by the woodland, and the threatening rocks, covered here and there by honeysuckle, ivy, apricot trees and wallflowers. There one discovers on the other bank the venerable ruins, many Gothic arches surviving of the ancient abbey of Thinkley [Finchale], which was built on the banks of the river where it forms a headland.

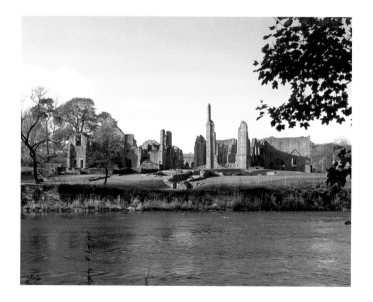

Please note: the priory is owned by English Heritage and open on summer weekends, with river walks similar to those enjoyed by Count von Zinzendorf. However, Cocken Hall is in private ownership and not open to the public.

Old Gorhambury House, Hertfordshire

In 1625 Francis Bacon published a collection of influential essays of which 'Of Gardens' was one, beginning: 'God Almighty first planted a garden. And indeed it is the purest of human pleasures. It is the greatest refreshment to the spirits of man, without which, buildings and palaces are but gross handyworks.' In it he set out his strong views on garden design, writing of scented flowers, mounts, alleys, fountains, aviaries, hedges and fruit trees, and consequently set the creative tone for centuries to come.

Bacon's view of the ideal garden was based closely on the gardens that his father Sir Nicholas had created at the family home at Gorhambury, Hertfordshire. When Bacon inherited the house, he improved his father's gardens, and created a fashionable garden at the edge of the large estate with a moat, islands, a banqueting house, lines of beech and lime and geometric walks. Today these are all lost (the gardens were already in decay only a few decades after Bacon's death) but the porch and some remains of the Bacon family home are maintained by English Heritage and are the focus of a pilgrimage to be made by garden lovers.

Please note: in the eighteenth century a 'New' Gorhambury house and gardens were created near by, using the Bacon porch as an eye-catcher for the park. These are privately owned but nevertheless open to the public.

Great Yarmouth Row Houses, Middlegate Gardens, Norfolk

English Heritage owns two seventeenth-century Row Houses in Great Yarmouth, originally built as merchants' houses and then converted into tenement homes. The space between these houses and the neighbouring Nelson Museum was derelict and uninspiring, so in 2005 English Heritage worked with local groups to create a modern new garden with reference to the area's connections with the sea.

Hill Hall, Essex

In 1791 Humphry Repton produced one of his famous Red Books of design ideas for Hill Hall, originally created in the sixteenth century, but it is not known how much of his advice was actually implemented. The greatest interest of

Hill Hall, then, is in the early twentieth-century involvement of Reginald Blomfield and Philip Tilden.

Hill Hall had been owned by the Smyth or Smijth family since the sixteenth century but in 1908 it was let to Charles and Mary Hunter, who commissioned architect Reginald Blomfield to tweak and extend the house and also carry out some work on the gardens, setting out terraces and a courtyard. In 1925 it was sold to Sir Robert Hudson and he employed Philip Tilden to create a rockery and sunken Italianate pool.

Hill Hall was gutted by a fire in 1969 and acquired in 1980 by English Heritage, who restored the frontage and then passed it on to a developer, who converted it into apartments. The gardens are open by appointment, with a striking view across the Essex countryside (and the M25) to London and Canary Wharf.

Lyddington Bede House, Rutland

Like the Bishops' Palace at Lincoln (see page 200), this atmospheric place was once home to Bishop Henry Burghersh. Over the centuries he and other bishops of Lincoln came to Lyddington to hunt deer in the park. The property was sequestered by Henry VIII and later converted by Sir Thomas Cecil into an almshouse, a home for twelve poor old men (known as bedesmen) and two women. Then the picturesque veranda was added in 1745 to give them shelter. These ancient buildings, which remained an almshouse until about 1930, had been only part of a large medieval palace. Beyond it lay elaborate fishponds and the bishops' deer park, whose traces were first researched by the composer Stanford Robinson, whiling away his time in the Home Guard here during the Second World War.

The Bede House is a fine example of how an old building can be enhanced by a modern garden. The one here was created in about 1990 by Peter Clarke, who was then Regional Horticultural Officer for English Heritage. Divided up by a picket fence and a diagonal path leading to the house, the garden is dominated by its surrounding stone walls. Simple straight beds run along three sides; in the south-west part these are edged with box and contain crescent-shaped compartments of box, while those in the north-eastern half are plain. The plants with which they are filled were chosen for their links to medieval gardens, where almost everything had a culinary or therapeutic use – or both. They include rhubarb, lavender, rosemary, lemon balm, *Salvia officinalis* (the species name indicating its use in medicine), honesty,

alchemilla, phlomis, acanthus, *Liatris spicata* and golden rod, with *Rosa gallica* var. *officinalis* and other old roses to lend height. The beds surround well-kept lawns in which flourish three mature trees: a sycamore, an old eating apple and a horse chestnut, which in fact spreads over the wall from the adjoining churchyard.

The bishops had an orchard here, whose profits were of interest to Henry VIII, and an echo of this can be seen in the recently planted fruit trees in a walled area reached through a stone arch. At the far corner of this is a small medieval turret, which may have been a gazebo overlooking a garden – or, more likely, a watchtower for ensuring the bishops' safety.

OPPOSITE A view of Finchale Priory across the River Wear.
ABOVE AND TOP Lyddington Bede House.

Northington Grange, Hampshire

From far off, the shell of this important country house looms like a storm-tossed Greek temple that has floated across the Aegean and come aground in the Hampshire countryside.

It was built from 1804 for the banker, Henry Drummond, around the core of a seventeenth-century house. Designed by William Wilkins, later the architect of London's National Gallery, it was in the Greek Revival style, which was then relatively new. The property was soon sold to another banker, Alexander Baring, who became Lord Ashburton. Baring, who belonged to the Royal Horticultural Society, decided that the eighteenth-century park, with its serpentine lake made from the dammed Candover stream, needed modernizing. So he commissioned C.R. Cockerell to design an iron and glass orangery, also in classical style, and to create formal terraced gardens in front of both buildings, which were completed by 1826. Photographs taken in *c*.1870 (in Winchester Museum) show that the gardens had all the elaborate plantings, balustrades, clipped trees and fountains typical of the mid-Victorian period.

From the seventeenth-century garden, only the original gate piers survive, moved to flank a curving stone bench. The orangery became a ballroom, then a picture gallery, and since 2003 has found a fresh lease of life as a summer opera venue. William Wilkins, who, as well as being a distinguished architect, was the owner and designer of several theatres, would surely have been delighted. When not peopled by opera-goers in evening dress, Northington is usually agreeably empty and visitors can enjoy the recently restored terrace and unspoilt views over the lake and eighteenth-century parkland.

Roche Abbey, South Yorkshire

'Capability' Brown is frequently criticized for destroying earlier formal gardens to make way for his flowing parks to spread from the house to the horizon. When laying out Sandbeck Park for the 4th Earl of Scarborough, from 1774, he went a stage further and altered a major historic structure because it did not fit his vision. Brown had already completed one phase of work at Sandbeck in the early 1760s. Now, for the first time, he was asked by a patron to incorporate an existing medieval ruin as a picturesque element in a landscape. Roche Abbey, the twelfth-century Cistercian foundation that found itself in his line of sight, had been pillaged at the Dissolution and then neglected well into the eighteenth century. But the remains were still substantial – and not ruined enough for his eye. He demolished the buildings of the cloister and inner court, and lowered many walls. Using the spoil from other changes made in the countryside, the level of the ground around the abbey ruins was raised by as much as 6 feet (1.8m), so that from a distance, with the foundations invisible, the ruins of the transept walls (and they alone) rose up from a greensward. In the words of William Gilpin, they appeared to stand on 'a neat bowling green'. Much of Brown's work at Sandbeck, except for a cascade and two lakes, was later removed. The ruins were separated from the main estate in 1921 and eventually came into the care of English Heritage;

but, together with Sandbeck Hall and the rest of the park (which is rarely open to the public), they still actually belong to the Earls of Scarborough.

Rufford Abbey, Nottinghamshire

Gardens have been made at Rufford in every century from the seventeenth to twenty-first – and possibly earlier, though there is little evidence. Only traces survive of the highly innovative layout, comprising a triple ride, four wilderness areas, a formal garden and a water garden with a cascade, designed in the 1690s by the otherwise unknown William Thonous. Changes made in the eighteenth century included the building in 1728–30 of an elegant bath house, later turned into a conservatory, and the damming of a stream in c.1750 to create a large lake. All these formal gardens were swept away later in the eighteenth century, when an informal landscape park was developed. There was much new work in Edwardian times: a circular lily pond and an Italian garden were added and the old orchard was turned into a fashionable Japanese garden. In the 1980s a herb garden was made, as was a replacement rose garden, and both have recently been revitalized. These are not recreations of past gardens but made in a spirit described as a 'harking back'. The rose garden reflects the history of the rose through time and was also designed with the great rosarian Dean Hole, who lived in a nearby village, in mind. At its heart is a rare heliochronometer, made by sundial expert John Gunning to replace an Edwardian one that was sold off. Rufford's latest garden project is a timber maze laid out by the doyen of maze designers, Adrian Fisher.

Although much of this historic site has been lost, there is still a great deal to enjoy: the eighteenth-century lake and woodland walks, the later gardens – and the two ice houses that remain out of the five it once boasted.

Rushton Triangular Lodge, Northamptonshire

At first glance, this strange building seems to have nothing to do with a garden, standing as it does, isolated in a small field. In fact, it was originally set on a far corner of an extensive late Elizabethan estate belonging to Sir Thomas Tresham. Built in 1594–7, ostensibly to house his warrener (rabbits, like fish, were an important part of the diet and rich men had rabbit warrens as well as fishponds), it was more of a statement about Tresham himself. Although knighted by Elizabeth I at Kenilworth during her 1575 visit (see page 14), Sir Thomas lost favour when he became a devout Catholic at a time when Catholicism was illegal in England. He spent his considerable fortune on fines for being a recusant and in creating buildings which, strangely to modern minds, managed both to be in the latest fashion and also to express his faith emblematically.

The Triangular Lodge's very shape evokes the Trinity and it is covered with other Christian symbols, as is the vast unfinished cruciform house, known as Lyveden New Bield, which he set on the other side of his estate. There an orchard with apples, pears, damsons, plums, cherries and walnuts was linked to a complex garden that had spiral mounts, canals, a maze, raised walks, terraces and flowers beds mixed with soft fruit such as raspberries. Twenty years before starting work at Lyveden, Tresham had seen Robert Dudley's garden at Kenilworth and may have been influenced by it. But his was intended to impress his friends for longer than three weeks.

Ironically, the garden at Lyveden was almost completely lost, not only on the ground but in memory too. By the late twentieth century it was covered in scrub and the canals were silted up. But much of it has now been restored, thanks to a team, mostly volunteers, working under the direction of the National Trust, which has owned Lyveden New Bield since 1922.

OPPOSITE LEFT The restored parterre at Northington Grange.
OPPOSITE ABOVE 'Capability' Brown would have appreciated this 1950s view of Roche Abbey.
LEFT The memory of the lost Japanese Garden at Rufford Abbey survives in an early twentieth-century photograph by Alfred Newton.

his good taste but without making claims to an authority that would have threatened powerful neighbours.

The castle stayed with the Ludlows until the end of the fifteenth century, when it passed to the Vernons. In 1620 it was bought by the Cravens, who built the charming gatehouse and also added a wooded deer park on the slopes facing the castle, through which stunning walks can be enjoyed today. Over the following centuries Stokesay became used primarily as a base for farming activities and gradually slipped into dereliction until 1850 when a local lady, Mrs Stackhouse Acton, headed an initiative to restore and preserve it. In 1869 it was bought by J.D. Allcroft, who financed a major programme of restoration, one continued by his son. Eventually, in 1992, the Allcroft family passed Stokesay to English Heritage. Today it is still a beautiful spot, standing next to a medieval church amidst a wildflower meadow and surrounded by a moat planted with spring bulbs. There is a delightful cottage garden within the castle's green courtyard, from which to admire the beautiful views.

Wenlock Priory, Shropshire

When, at the turn of the nineteenth century, Lady Catherine Milnes Gaskell decided to start a garden around her home, Wenlock Abbey (never actually an abbey, but rather the prior's lodgings attached to the Cluniac Wenlock Priory), it was almost inevitable that she would make the most of the adjacent ruined priory as a feature.

The result was a striking and romantic garden, described rather beautifully in *Country Life* magazine on 20 April 1907:

The Triangular Lodge should be visited and 'read' together with Lyveden New Bield – and perhaps tea could be taken afterwards at nearby Rushton Hall, now a hotel but once the home of the Tresham family, and the heart of Sir Thomas's estate. Here he made another garden, which had a mount, but this has been overlaid by later designs, including an early twentieth-century garden by Thomas Mawson. The Triangular Lodge acts as a kind of eye-catcher to what remains of this palimpsest of landscapes.

Stokesay Castle, Shropshire

Essentially a fortified manor house, built in the thirteenth century for Laurence of Ludlow, a wealthy wool merchant, Stokesay Castle became a hub of medieval Shropshire life. The architectural merit of the building is clear but more tantalizing is the belief of garden historians that the woods, fields and ponds around Stokesay are actually a designed landscape carefully composed by Laurence to create a beautiful and impressive setting for his new house. The castle's positioning and design were intended to demonstrate

Here we have the old cloister garth, with the grey and lichened ruins rising out of velvet turf. There is a walled rose garden profuse with bloom on bush, on standard and on pillar. Over its walls peeps the varied roofage of the dwelling, or, between the trees, rises the great perpendicular west window and the tall spire of the parish church, while one gap in the more immediate surroundings allows the eye to travel afar on to the hill country behind. On the side of the bowling green where the town huddles close up to the old monastic precincts, a yew hedge, so high and massive as to rival the solidity of the mediaeval ruins around, ensures privacy, while on the other side it is kept low and offers a smiling prospect over the rich meadow-lands of the vale.

Although the 'abbey' and thus much of Lady Catherine's gardens are still in private ownership and closed to the public, the priory (and the fabulous topiary animals that she planted among the cloisters) is now run by English Heritage and very much open to visitors.

Whitby Abbey, North Yorkshire

Behind the majestic ruins of the thirteenth-century abbey which dominates the little port of Whitby lies a handsome house, now used as a visitor centre and museum. It was built in about 1672 for the Cholmley family and linked to their older house in the monastic buildings. In front of the New House lay two formal courtyards, of which only the one closer to the house survives. Known as the Inward Court, this is a rare example of a 'stone garden' or 'hard garden', filled with stone cobbles laid in a pattern. Here the pattern is quite simple: the cobbles are laid in line and divided from the others by thin lines of stone laid on the opposite axis. Sir Hugh Cholmley the younger had been acting governor of Tangier (which was English at the time as part of Queen Catherine of Braganza's dowry) and the courtyard may have been inspired by his travels through France and Spain to get to Morocco. Certainly, this sort of decoration is more common on the Continent.

OPPOSITE LEFT Tresham's Triangular Lodge at Rushton.
OPPOSITE RIGHT Edwardian topiary nestles among the ruins of Wenlock Priory.
RIGHT A reconstruction drawing of the New House and 'stone garden' at Whitby Abbey as they would have looked in 1700.

Around the edge of the courtyard was a raised walkway, accessed either by steps on each side of the gate between the two courtyards or from the pedimented front door of the house, which allowed the cobbled pattern to be appreciated from above. The courtyard had been turfed over but was rediscovered by archaeologists in 1998 and restored.

The archaeologists left, however, one puzzle. A rectangular, lobed area in the middle was free of cobbles, and that this was deliberate and not due to later damage is proved by a rough square marked on a plan of the property made at about the same time as the garden. What ornamental feature did it represent? It may have been a pond or fountain, but it is more likely to have been the base of a statue. Just ten years after the New House was finished, the Yorkshire antiquarian Ralph Thoresby described the mansion as having 'large courts and walks with iron grates [railings], and a curious statue in solid brass as large as life in the midst of the square'. The 'curious statue' would have softened the courtyard's somewhat stark appearance, as would the specimen plants and shrubs that were once displayed in pots or tubs around the edge. It was probably a copy (in bronze, rather than brass) of the famous first-century BC statue known as the Borghese Gladiator, and so quite a rarity. Copies of the Gladiator in lead were popular features in eighteenth-century gardens (there was one at Chiswick House, for instance), but only two other bronze copies are known, both dating from the 1630s and made by Charles I's Huguenot sculptor Hubert Le Sueur. Later, the Whitby version seems to have been moved to the east side of the courtyard, where its plinth can still be seen set into a later wall. A copy was recently replaced in the original central position – but what happened to the original is a mystery.

Index

Acknowledgments

The authors would like to thank: the two Richards for their help and patience; Rob Richardson and Adele Campbell of English Heritage's Publishing Department for their advice in the early stages of this book, and René Rodgers for her efforts in seeing it through to the end; Frances Lincoln's Anne Askwith and Anne Wilson for helping the book to read and look as it does; James Davies and Peter Williams for taking most of the modern photographs; Javis Gurr and Jonathan Butler in the Photo Library; Nigel Wilkins and Graham Deacon at the NMR for help tracking down archive illustrations; members of the English Heritage Gardens and Landscape Team, past and present – John Watkins, Jenifer White, Christopher Weddell, Annabel Brown, Ari Georghiou; the English Heritage historians for their eagle-eyed and ruthless fact checking – Andrew Hann, Paul Pattison, Susan Westlake, Nicola Stacey, David Robinson, Richard Hewlings (also for material on Belsay), Richard Lea, Jeremy Ashbee, Susie West, Mark Douglas, Shelley Garland, Jenny Cousins, Steven Brindle; all the many enthusiastic people, English Heritage staff or otherwise, who provided us with information and tours of the gardens in this book – Brian Dix for information and support with the chapters on Kirby, Kenilworth and Ashby de la Zouch; Juliet and Jeff West for their generous provision of information on Audley End; Kathy McVittie at Denny Farmland Museum Trust; James Collett-White for help with Wrest Park at the Bedfordshire and Luton Archives and Records Service; Sarah Jo Hindhaugh, Adam Stenhouse and Anthony Scholl for help and delightful tours at Belsay; the excellent staff at the Northumberland Collections Service for their efficiency while researching Belsay; Henry Summerson for his insights into Stokesay; Twigs Way for hand-holding through Wrest; Lorna McRobie for Wrest, Mount Grace Priory and Audley End; Dominic Cole for Walmer Castle, Wrest Park, Old Wardour Castle and Audley End; Andrew Widd for Audley End; Richard Squires for Witley Court and more; Adrian Cook for Chiswick; Drew Bennellick for Marble Hill and Kensal Green Cemetery (or removal of!); Louisa Sherman for Castle Acre; Martin Roberts, Nick Owen and Mrs Watson for Finchale; Anne Padfield for Hill Hall; Paul Jackson, Andrew Ginner and the charming Arthur Oxford for Kenwood; Paul Stamper for Boscobel and others; Chloe Cova for Witley Court; Beryl Spearman for Kirby Hall and Lyddington Bede House; Joe Prentice and Tamsin Rosewell for Kenilworth; Vicky Basford, the Hampshire Gardens Trust and Philip Masters at ACTA for Appuldurcombe; Fiona Cowell for allowing access to her thesis on Richard Woods for Old Wardour Castle and her generous guidance on Audley End; Jane Cordingley at Eltham Palace and Toby Beasley for Down House and Osborne House (who both also helped with illustrations); Debs Goodenough and Alan Hickey for Osborne House; Philip Savins at Bayham Old Abbey; Lorraine Cooper at Richmond Castle; and Charles Rogers at Lincoln Medieval Bishops' Palace; Michael Turner for information and advice on Osborne and Eltham; Percy Flaxman for comments on Osborne and information about Kenilworth; the volunteer research team at Brodsworth and the curator, Caroline Carr-Whitworth, as well as the head gardener, Dan Booth, and Michael Klemperer for his unpublished thesis of 2003; Randal Keynes for advice on Down House and for allowing access to his essay on the Sandwalk; Robin Watson Picarle for Kirby Hall, Peter Clarke for Lyddington and Kirby; Linda Hardy and Sue Blaxland for Rufford; Rupert Golby, Isabelle Van Groeningen, Mark Anthony Walker and Neil Swanson for talking about their designs for the Contemporary Heritage Gardens Scheme, and Susie Brigg and Fergus Alexander of Landscape Projects for providing information about the Cockpit Garden at Richmond Castle; other English Heritage staff – Peter Smith, Nick Hill, Roy Porter, Sarah Lunt, Robin Bain, and particularly Will Holborow; Ellie Hughes in the Press Office; and Sue Harris at Richborough Castle, who let us see her delightful private garden, with its heritage greenhouse; Robert Peel for Bute expertise and kindly checking that our boxes were packed correctly; Charles Quest-Ritson for help tracing roses and Maggie Campbell-Culver for help with John Evelyn.

Our apologies to anyone we have missed out, and a special bouquet to Management Research Ltd of London SW8, who provided the Recycling Report on Osborne, by far the most poetic of all the reports we read!

There is no bibliography for this book because it was largely based on unpublished internal English Heritage research reports, for which we thank the various authors.